Enclosures in Neolithic Europe

Essays on Causewayed and Non-Caueswayed Sites

Edited by

Gillian Varndell and Peter Topping

Oxbow Books

Published by
Oxbow Books, Park End Place, Oxford OX1 1HN

ISBN 1 84217 068 6

A CIP record for this book is available from the British Library

This book is available direct from

Oxbow Books, Park End Place, Oxford OX1 1HN
(Phone: 01865-241249; Fax: 01865-794449

and

The David Brown Book Company
PO Box 511, Oakville, CT 06779
(Phone: 860-9459329; Fax: 860-945-9468)

or

from our website
www.oxbowbooks.com

Cover: Overlooking a bend of the Charente, this site comprises a series of ditch-systems delimiting the promontory. BAPC no. 1928-A. Balzac (France), Les Coteaux de Coursac. Neolithic éperon barré. Aerial survey and copyright of Jacques Dassié.

Printed in Great Britain by
Short Run Press Ltd.
Exeter

Contents

Introduction

The papers presented here represent the proceedings of a conference held on the 23rd October 1999 in London entitled *'Neolithic Causewayed Enclosures in Europe'*. The conference was organised jointly by the Royal Commission on the Historical Monuments of England (RCHME; a part of English Heritage since April 1999) and the Prehistoric Society, with assistance from the Neolithic Studies Group.

The conference was designed to present an overview of recent work on causewayed enclosures in continental Europe (probably the first British review since the conference held in Newcastle in 1984[1]) to complement an RCHME project which had systematically recorded all known Neolithic enclosures in England by both analytical topographic survey techniques and aerial transcription. The overall aim of the RCHME project was to produce a new national corpus of surveys to both assist management needs and inform the academic debate. This approach allowed the sites to not only be accurately recorded and interpreted but also considered in their individual, regional and national landscape contexts at a more detailed level than has previously been possible. The resulting data from this project has allowed a radical reinterpretation of themes such as the recognition of regional groups of enclosures, for example. During the course of the project a secondary focus developed which studied a representative sample of more unusual upland stone-built enclosures: the sites were chosen where morphology or other evidence suggested the possibility of a Neolithic context. This latter element of the project was intended to broaden the discussion about the structure and form of Neolithic enclosures beyond lowland England, and review the geographical range of causewayed monuments and what may have been their non-causewayed counterparts. Collaboration with sister organisations and individuals in Scotland (Strat Halliday and RCAHMS), Wales (Toby Driver and RCAHMW) and Ireland (Jim Mallory) provided complementary information from these countries.

During the preliminary organisation for the conference, it became clear from those who responded to the 'Call for Papers' that the subjects being offered mirrored the evolution of the RCHME project. Not only were studies of causewayed enclosures sent for consideration, but also others that did not conform to the traditional site typologies but had been proven by excavation to have a Neolithic context. The conference programme included papers on the Tavoliere Plain in South-Eastern Italy from Skeates, La Hersonnais in Ille-et-Vilaine from Tinevez, West-Central France by Burnez and Louboutin, Scandinavia by Andersen, Central Europe from Braasch, Ireland by Cooney, and an overview of the RCHME project from Oswald (not included in these proceedings, see Oswald et al. 2001[2]). One further paper from Saville broadened the debate by reviewing the lithic assemblages from causewayed enclosures in the UK. A number of complementary papers have been included in the proceedings which either increase the range of the volume or present evidence of newly discovered enclosures (contributions by Barfield, Brown, Butler, Darvill, Horne, MacLeod & Oswald, Pearson & Topping, and Vaquer).

Overall this volume of papers has a primarily European focus to complement the RCHME project volume and although sadly together they cannot claim to provide a comprehensive overview

---

[1] See Burgess, C., Topping, P., Mordant, C. & Maddison, M. 1988. *Enclosures and Defences in the Neolithic of Western Europe*. Oxford. British Archaeological Reports, International Series, 403.

[2] Oswald, A., Dyer, C. & Barber, M. 2001. *The Creation of Monuments: Neolithic Causewayed Enclosures in the British Isles*. Swindon. English Heritage.

of the European evidence in its entirety, they do produce a series of snapshots of some of the sites and regions at the forefront of current research. It is to be hoped that the European archaeological community does not have to wait another 15 years before we see a further conference reviewing these enigmatic sites, particularly as new discoveries continue to increase their distribution into some of the previously '*blank*' areas of the continent such as the Netherlands and Eastern Europe (cf. Braasch this volume). It is clear that as a 'community' within Europe we archaeologists need more such fora in which to discuss our research and progress our studies of common themes or site-types.

This volume has deliberately been edited with a light hand; where papers by contributors whose first language is not English are concerned the editors have tried to ensure clarity without sacrificing the individual voices of the authors.

Gillian Varndell and Peter Topping
London and Cambridge
November 2000

Acknowledgements

The organisers would like to thank the former RCHME and English Heritage and the Prehistoric Society for generously supporting the conference. The Neolithic Studies Group through their co-ordinators Tim Darvill and Gordon Barclay helped to promote the event and also deserve thanks.

The conference organisers would like to thank the venue, the Scientific Societies Lecture Theatre, New Burlington Place, London, and specifically the manager Mr Colin Powell, for their assistance during the planning of the event and helping to ensure that the conference proceeded smoothly. In addition, the assistance of anonymous referees from the Prehistoric Society was greatly appreciated during the preparation of these proceedings. To everyone involved go our sincere thanks.

List of Contributors

Dr N. H. Andersen
Forhistorisk Museum, Moesgård
DK-8270 Højbjerg
Denmark

Dr L. Barfield
Department of Ancient History and Archaeology,
University of Birmingham
Birmingham B15 2TT

O. Braasch
Matthias-Hoesl-Straße 6
D-84034 Landshut
Germany

M. Brown
Archaeological Investigation
English Heritage
24 Brooklands Avenue
Cambridge, CB2 2BU, UK

C. Burnez
Le Moulin Haut Laubaret
16130 Gensac-la-Pallue
France

A. J. Butler
Archaeological Geophysics
University of Leicester Archaeological Services,
University Road
Leicester, LE1 7RH, UK

P. Clay
Archaeological Geophysics
University of Leicester Archaeological Services
University Road
Leicester, LE1 7RH, UK

Prof. G. Cooney
Department of Archaeology
University College Dublin
Belfield
Dublin 4, Ireland

Prof. T. Darvill
School of Conservation Sciences
Bournemouth University
Dorset House, Talbot Campus
Fern Barrow, Poole
Dorset, BH12 5BB, UK

J. Dassié
28 Avenue de la Victoire
17260 Gémozac, France

P. Horne
Aerial Survey
English Heritage, 37 Tanner Row
York, YO1 6WP, UK

Dr C. Louboutin
Musée des Antiquités Nationales, BP3030,
78103 Saint-Germain-en Laye, France

D. MacLeod
Aerial Survey
English Heritage, 37 Tanner Row
York, YO1 6WP, UK

A. Oswald
Archaeological Investigation
English Heritage, 37 Tanner Row
York, YO1 6WP, UK

T. Pearson
Archaeological Investigation
English Heritage, 37 Tanner Row
York, YO1 6WP, UK

Dr A. Saville
Archaeology Department
National Museums of Scotland
Chambers Street
Edinburgh, EH1 1JF, UK

Dr R. Skeates
Department of Archaeology
South Road
Durham, DH1 3LE, UK

J. Thomas
Archaeological Geophysics
University of Leicester Archaeological Services
University Road
Leicester, LE1 7RH, UK

Dr J-Y. Tinevez
Service Régional de l'Archéologie de Bretagne
UMR 6566,
Civilisations atlantiques et Archéosciences, FRANCE.

P. Topping
Archaeological Investigation
English Heritage
24 Brooklands Avenue
Cambridge, CB2 2BU, UK

G. Varndell
Department of Prehistory & Early Europe
The British Museum
Great Russell Street
London, WC1B 3DG, UK

Dr J. Vaquer
Centre d'Anthropologie
UMR 8555
Toulouse, France

1   Neolithic Enclosures of Scandinavia

Niels H. Andersen

The first Neolithic enclosure to be found in Scandinavia was *Büdelsdorf* near Rendsburg in the northern part of Germany in 1968 (Hingst 1975, 33), but was quickly followed by the discovery of the *Sarup* site on the island of Fyn in Denmark. The *Sarup* enclosure was first recorded in 1971 and to date we know of a further 30 sites in Scandinavia (Fig. 1.1). All these sites belong to the northern group of the Funnel Beaker Culture (TRB Culture – North) and are dated to a very short period between 3400 and 3200 cal BC: i.e. about 500 years after the introduction of the Neolithic economy to the area (Andersen 1997, 267).

At the beginning of the Neolithic in Scandinavia the wooded landscape characteristic of the Mesolithic Ertebølle Culture had changed only a little towards a more open landscape. Amongst contemporary finds assemblages are the bones of domesticated animals such as cattle, pigs and goats, and also grains of wheat. The first great funerary monuments – the unchambered long barrows – were now to be seen in the landscape, containing the remains of one or more persons. Some of these were structurally very complex. In certain wetland areas, sites have been located where sacrifices of ceramics, animals and, on rare occasions, humans took place.

Fig. 1.1: Sarup-type enclosures in Scandinavia.

Some 500 years after the introduction of a farming economy, about 3500 to 3400 cal BC, we see distinctive changes. Studies of pollen grain from bogs and from megalithic graves reveal the influence of man on nature. This is represented by a smaller quantity of pollen pertaining to oak and lime forest and a higher proportion from birch and later from hazel: the pollen characteristic of an open landscape – grasses and herbs – also increased. These changes in the pollen spectrum are known as Iversen's Landnam [ie landtaking / colonization] (Iversen 1941; Aaby 1985, 70) which undoubtedly represents the deliberate creation of open areas for both cereal cultivation and grazing (Andersen, S. T. 1993).

The buried soils beneath some megalithic barrows have preserved traces of the primitive plough: the ard. Ploughing with an ard drawn by bullocks required large fields cleared of big stones, trees and stumps. These Neolithic people no longer had the type of field characteristic of the first period, where corn was grown in small areas cleared in the woodland. Excavations have revealed that the fields were ploughed only about three times; in other words people moved quickly on to new areas following a shifting pattern of land use, thus the demand for new areas would have been great. This less demanding method of cultivation allowed cereal production to be increased (Hedeager & Kristiansen 1988, 47–8) and previously 'unprofitable' areas could be brought into cultivation. The introduction of the ard may have brought with it a series of changes in social relations, for example men undertaking cultivation and women carrying out tasks at the settlements. Land rights and inheritance would now have become important, as a great deal of time had been invested in clearing the cultivable plots and one had to be able to return to previously cultivated areas. Rights to the land could thus easily lead to conflicts between different groups (Sherratt 1981, 298–9). Sherratt (ibid.) has characterised the introduction of these innovations as the '*Secondary Products Revolution*'.

In this second period we also see the first megalithic monuments: dolmens and passage graves. Some of these monuments were built with boulders weighing more than 20 tons. Recent studies of the rate of destruction of these sites suggest that the original number of such structures in Denmark could have been around 25,000 (Andersen 1985, 16; Skaarup 1993, 104).

Since the Second World War two new monument types have come to light in the northern group of the Funnel Beaker Culture: the cult house of the Tustrup type (Becker 1993), and enclosures.

Antiquarian rescue excavations had previously revealed some of the Neolithic enclosures, but others were found during the re-assessment of earlier excavations; as in the case of *Trelleborg* and *Troldebjerg*, for instance (Andersen 1982; Skaarup 1985, 46–9 and 362–3). Both Madsen (1988) and the author (1993; 1997) have published synopses of some of the definite Neolithic sites.

Only a few of the Danish structures have been extensively excavated, but the two sites at Sarup are well investigated – and published (Andersen 1997; 1999). Only *Sarup II* has been totally excavated, i.e. 30,000 m². Of *Sarup I* some two-thirds, i.e. 60,000 m² has been uncovered. Other sites have mostly been examined by means of the thorough excavation of several ditch segments. All of these sites have so far only been published in short, interim articles, so it is not possible to analyse and interpret the sites and their finds individually.

The earliest available dating for the construction of these sites relates to two contemporary phases, the Fuchsberg phase on Fyn and in Jutland and the Virum phase on Sjælland and in Skåne (Andersen & Madsen 1978; Ebbesen & Mahler 1980), dated to about 3400 cal BC, although *Store Brokhøj* was constructed in phase MN A IA and *Sarup II* in the slightly later phase MN A IB. The latest construction date is that from *Sigersted III* (Nielsen, P. O. 1985) of MN A II (the Blandebjerg phase, contemporary with *Sarup III*, about 3150 cal BC).

The enclosed sites consisted of interrupted ditches (up to 5 concentric circuits), palisades (on the inner side of the ditches), entrance areas, fenced enclosures, and an interior area. The sites were placed in conspicuous locations (Fig. 1.2) such as hilltops (e.g. *Bjerggård, Markildegård, Liselund* and *Store Brokhøj*) or on promontories (e.g. *Büdelsdorf, Lokes Hede, Lønt, Sarup* and *Stävie*). The enclosing structures may encircle the site, as at *Bjerggård, Büdelsdorf, Store Brokhøj* and *Toftum*, or have a semicircular plan laid out between two slopes as at *Mølbjerg* (Andersen 1997, Fig. 285), *Lønt, Sarup* and *Stävie*. The sites seem to have adapted their form to the topography. Several of them, for instance, were located on promontories of virtually triangular shape, e.g. *Sarup II* and *Stävie*, while *Sarup I*, by contrast, is of a more oblong plan. At other sites, however, the enclosures paid no attention to the terrain, particularly those with circular ditch systems. *Büdelsdorf*, for instance, had a height difference of 11 m (over a distance of 140 m) between the highest placed ditch and the lowest, an 8% (or 5°) slope (Hingst 1975, 33). At *Toftum* there was a height difference of about 7 m over 150 m and at *Sarup I* the difference is 3 to 4 m over 150 m. The enclosing structures were thus located with regard to factors other than just the easiest and most economical way of defining an area. From a distance, *Büdelsdorf* and *Toftum* must have looked like a crown sitting askew upon a head: both sites would have been quite visible from the low-lying areas they faced.

In terms of area, there was considerable variation between sites, ranging from 1.6 ha at *Bjerggård* (Madsen 1988, 309) to more than 20 ha at *Lokes Hede* (Birkedahl 1988, 158; 1994). The question of how closely spaced the sites were is currently difficult to assess, although *Bjerggård* and *Toftum* were only 3.5 km apart (Madsen 1988, 327, Fig. 17.10) and *Sarup* and *Sarup Gamle Skole* only 500 m apart. Even though these sites were not constructed at exactly the same time, we must assume that the Neolithic populations of the area knew of their existence. This is illustrated by the persistent recutting of

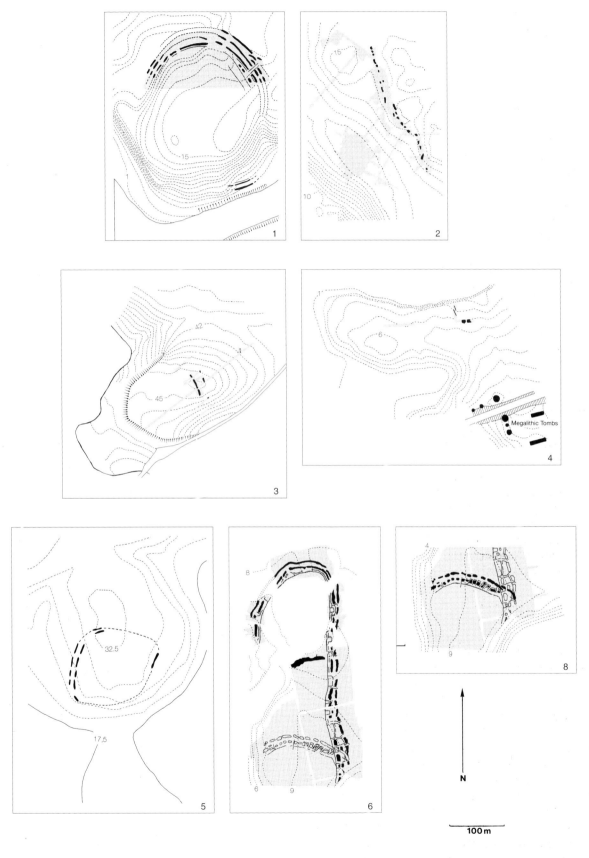

Fig. 1.2: Plans of enclosed sites from the northern group of the Funnel Beaker Culture (TRB-North) in Scandinavia:(1) Büdelsdorf, Kreis Rendsburg (Hingst 1975, 33 Abb, 1). (2) Markildegård, by Vordingborg (Sørensen 1994, 32). (3) Vasagård, Bornholm (P. O. Nielsen & F. O. Nielsen 1989, 112, Fig. 93) (4) Lønt, by Haderslev (E. Jørgensen 1983b, 45, Fig. 12). (5) Toftum, by Horsens (T. Madsen 1988, 304, Fig. 17.2). (6) Sarup I. (7) Sarup II.

the ditch segments, clearly showing that the existence and location of the sites was known of for several generations.

Most of the enclosures lay close to wetlands, and indeed were often surrounded by them. A proximity to a 'necropolis' of megalithic graves seems to have been typical of the enclosed sites. This is the case at *Büdelsdorf*, for instance, with 13 megalithic graves, the nearest 400m from the site (Bauch 1988, 43 Abb. 1); *Lønt*, with 7 graves, the closest 100m (Jørgensen 1983 b, 45, Fig. 12); *Toftum*, with 9 graves, the nearest no more than 300m from the site (Madsen & Petersen 1984, 61); and *Sarup*, with many clusters of megalithic graves, the nearest 150m from the site (Andersen 1997, 97, Fig. 126).

The sites were enclosed by between one and five circuits of segmented ditches. The original number of ditches can only be determined by excavation since many were subject to recutting, as a result of which several

originally separate ditches could be joined together. At *Sarup I*, for instance, forty three ditch segments have been recorded, but the original number is thought to have been at least seventy eight (Andersen 1997, Fig. 46). In the case of both *Sarup I* and *Sarup II* both the inner and outer circuits of ditches are thought to have been contemporary since various lines of fencing linked them together (Fig. 1.3; and Andersen 1997, Figs 29, 33–4, 37 g and 40 g). The two concentric circuits of segmented ditches at *Toftum*, by contrast, are not considered to have been dug at the same time (Madsen 1988, 315).

The ditches also vary greatly in size, but their width was around 4m, their depth between 0.3m and 2.5m, and their bases about 2m wide (Fig. 1.4). The base was usually level although at *Büdelsdorf* several were found to be rounded (Andersen 1997, 286 b).

The bases of the ditches were often covered with a

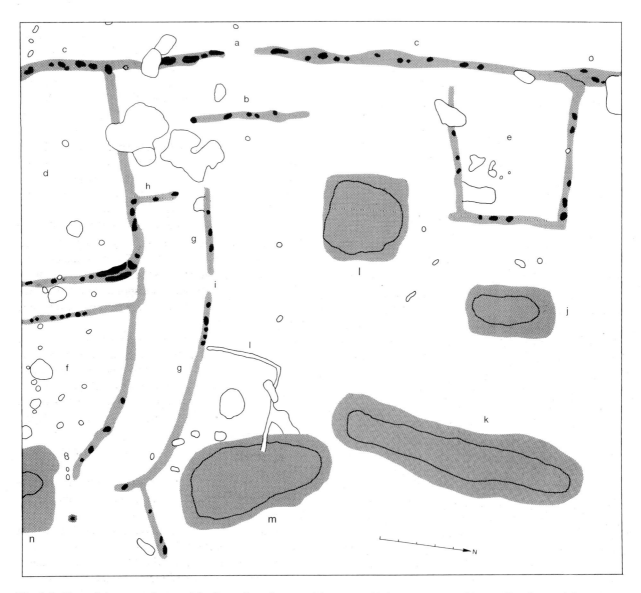

Fig. 1.3: Plan of the central part of the Sarup I *enclosure with traces of (a) an entrance; (b) a wall in front of the entrance; (c) the palisade; (d) an oblong fenced enclosure; (e) a square fenced enclosure (see also Fig. 5); (f) an outer fenced enclosure; (g) an extra fence, perhaps forming a gateway; (h) a fence crossing the gateway; (i) a break in the northern side of the gateway; (j–n) ditch segment; (o) a semicircular trench, probably of Iron Age date.*

Fig. 1.4: Photograph of the section wall in a ditch segment at Sarup I . *The fill consists of fine water or wind-deposited sand at the bottom, overlain by a redeposited layer containing stone and gravel. In the upper part are cultural layers from a later part of the TRB Culture. View looking south.*

layer of virtually sterile soil about 10cm thick, which is interpreted as a natural deposit of silt and sand from the side walls of the ditch. On top of this layer, or on the base of the ditch itself, there may be special finds and layers. Such layers could include decomposed organic deposits of limited extent, as found at *Bjerggård* and *Toftum* (Madsen 1988), or clear and well-defined layers containing charcoal as at *Büdeldsdorf* (Hingst 1975, 34), *Stävie* (Larsson 1982, 69, Fig. 5 structure 367) and *Bjerggård* (Madsen 1988, 310). At *Toftum, Ellerødgård, Sarup I* and *Store Brokhøj* (Madsen 1978a, 166, Fig. 3; Nielsen 1994, 28; Andersen 1997, Fig. 51; Fiedel & Sterum 1988, 161, Fig. 315) these layers were covered by a spread of stones. At *Skævinge Boldbaner* the stones are reported to have been sandstone slabs of the kind used in dry-stone walling in megalithic graves (Andersen, A. H. 1987, 56). No layers of cultural material with large quantities of waste have ever been found at the bottom of the segmented ditches, only apparently specially selected items. Of interest is the presence of human skulls, or skull fragments, at, for instance, *Bundsø* (Asmus, in Hoika 1987, 265–6; Nielsen 1981, 105), *Hygind* (Andersen 1997, Fig. 287) and *Sarup I*. Other human bones have been discovered, such as a jaw at *Sarup I* (Andersen 1997, Fig. 59), a burnt tooth and a thigh bone at *Åsum Enggård* (Jensen & Nikolajsen 1989, 123), and other human bones at *Ballegård* (Wincentz 1994, 176) and *Troldebjerg* (Nyegaard 1985, 449). Whole pots deposited singly have been found on the base of some ditches (Andersen 1999, Figs 52–3), while *Ellerødgård* produced a notable group of several vessels (Nielsen 1988; 1994). At *Markildegård* it was noted that several vessels had been placed on mats of birch bark (Sørensen 1995, 19). In a ditch segment at *Store Brokhøj* there was a layer measuring 0.7m² containing burnt daub and potsherds from at least 70 vessels (Sterum 1986, 110; Madsen & Fidel 1988, 84–6).

Practically no flint has been found on the ditch floors, although at *Bjerggård* flint was found in one concentrated deposit which contained a lot of waste flakes (Madsen 1988, 310). Greenstone or flint axes (often fragmentary, sometimes burnt) have been found at, amongst other sites, *Lønt* (Jørgensen 1983b, 47, Fig. 16) and *Sarup II*. Fragments of battle-axes have been found at *Toftum* (Madsen 1978 a, 176, Fig. 12) and *Büdelsdorf* (Hingst 1971 c, 219). Cattle and sheep skulls have been found at *Hygind* (Andersen 1997, Fig. 287) and *Sarup II*, pig skulls at *Sarup II*, and dog skulls at *Bjerggård* (Madsen 1988, 310).

Of special interest is the new 1998 discovery of a miniature dolmen placed at the bottom of a ditch segment in the enclosure at *Sarup Gamle Skole*. This dolmen measures only 72cm by 36cm internally. In its interior we found only a few sherds of a Funnel Beaker, but at the south-west side of the dolmen a further 146 sherds of this Beaker were recovered. It is of interest to see that all sherds are of approximately the same size – the vessel must have been deliberately destroyed and placed at this spot (Andersen 2000, 27, Fig. 7).

After their primary use, the majority of the ditches appear to have been deliberately backfilled with the soil that was originally dug out of them. Many of them were then subjected to recutting. Traces of these secondary cuttings can be seen by studying the plan of the ditches or their cross-sections, e.g. at *Büdelsdorf*, with up to 5 recuttings (Andersen 1997, Fig. 286b; Bauch 1993, 6 and 8), *Bjerggård* (Madsen 1988, 307, Fig. 17.5), *Lønt* (Jørgensen 1988, 205–6, Figs 15–17), *Sarup I* (Andersen 1997, Fig. 46 and 84–5), *Store Brokhøj* (Madsen & Fidel 1988, 79, Fig. 2) and *Toftum* (Madsen 1988, 313, Fig. 17.8). Limited recutting has been found at one end of a ditch at *Toftum* (Madsen 1988, 315). The finds from the bottom of the recuts usually correspond to those from the base of the ditches themselves, being limited and selective in their range.

Other recuttings from later phases often had deposits richer in finds and of a more comprehensive nature that can be interpreted simply as cultural layers. Such layers at *Sarup* belong to the phases MN A II – MN A V and are referred to as *Sarup III–V* (see Andersen 1997, Chapter 4). The site of *Ballegård*, for instance, had cultural layers dating to the Single Grave Culture, the Late Neolithic, and the Early and Late Bronze Age (Wincentz 1994, 176). No traces of banks have been found at these sites. The ditch fills show that the soil was thrown back in from both sides and thus must have lain there while the ditches were open.

Traces of palisades characterised by trenches or rows of postholes have been found at some sites, including *Büdelsdorf* (Andersen 1997, Fig. 286 a) where a foundation trench and two rows of double posts were discovered (Hingst 1971 a, 191); *Lønt*, with several foundation trenches (Jørgensen, E. 1988, 205, Fig. 15); *Markildegård*, where a foundation trench was replaced a couple of times by rows of posts (Sørensen; 1995, 26–7);

Troldebjerg, with a foundation trench and a single row of postholes (Skaarup 1985, 46–7, Fig. 17); *Sarup I* had a foundation trench (Fig. 1.3 a; Andersen 1997, Figs 18–23); and *Sarup II* had several rows of small postholes (Andersen 1997, Figs 77–80).

In and by the palisade trench at *Sarup I* there was a lot of pottery, burnt bone (including human), scorched stone and charcoal from hearths (Andersen 1997, 32). Fences, other than those which are thought to be palisades, were also found at *Sarup I* (Fig. 1.3 g; Andersen 1997, Fig. 37 g) and *Hygind* (Andersen 1989, 121).

The many causeways between the ditch segments might have served as entrances, although their highly variable width and the presence of regular post-built passages show that there was access to these sites at special locations. One causeway ran through four ditch circuits and associated palisades on the eastern side of the *Büdelsdorf* site (Fig. 1.2, 1; Andersen 1997, Fig. 286 b). This 4–5m wide causeway was flanked by substantial postholes which reached a depth of 1.4m (Hingst 1975, 34–5). *Sarup I* (Fig. 1.3 g and h; Andersen 1997, Figs 40 g and h) had a passage 27–28m long leading to the only entrance into the site. This entrance was just 1.6m wide (Fig. 1.3 a) and its outer side was screened in a way that suggests that one should not be able to see into the site (Fig. 1.3 b), or indeed to look out from the interior.

Characteristic of the two *Sarup* sites were a series of fenced enclosures, which at *Sarup I* were attached to the palisade fence or to other structures outside the ditch system (Figs 1.3 d, e and f; 1.5; Andersen 1997, Figs 28–40). At *Sarup II*, too, there were fenced enclosures on the outer side of the palisade but these now encompassed the inner row of segmented ditches (Andersen 1997, Figs

Fig. 1.5: Traces of a square fenced enclosure abutting the palisade seen in the cleaned surface (see also Fig. 1.3e). View looking west.

80–2). The placing of the segmented ditches inside the fenced enclosures suggests a close connection between the activities carried out in both the fenced enclosures and those in the ditches. Fenced enclosures like those at *Sarup II* were also found at *Büdelsdorf* (Andersen 1997, Fig. 286 c; Hingst 1975, 33–4; Bauch 1993, 7).

The inner areas have been examined at some sites, although only at *Sarup II* has the entire interior been uncovered. At *Sarup I* two-thirds of this area was excavated, as were large parts of the inner area at *Büdelsdorf*, where pits, cooking pits and traces of structures dating apparently from the Iron Age were found (Hingst 1971 a, Abb. 1). The excavations in the interior at *Sarup* produced 87 features from *Sarup I* (one feature per 600 m²) and 144 from *Sarup II* (one per 205m²). Primary and secondary functions could be attributed to some of these, giving primary functions as follows: ritual features (11 at site *I* and 26 at site *II* (Figs 1.6 and 1.7)); storage features (3 at *I* and 13 at *II*); and postholes (28 at *I* and 61 at *II*, although none formed part of buildings). The secondary functions were waste disposal (25 at site *I* and 86 at site *II*); deposition of tools (3 at *I* and 10 at *II*); and deposition of human bones (0 at *I* and 2 at *II*). Analyses have shown the human bones to be burnt and to belong to a young girl. The body had been defleshed before being burnt (Andersen 1999a, 250, Fig. 5.86).

In respect of the wealth of finds in the pits, it should be noted that at *Sarup I* and *II* 9% and 18% of these pits respectively contained more than 1,000 finds per cubic metre of soil. The average for *Sarup* is 380 finds per cubic metre. 40% of the pits at site *I* and 48% of the pits at site *II* were above average. At *Sarup I* and *Sarup II* some pits contained concentrations of waste far greater than one would anticipate, and this is all the more obvious when the lower layers of the segmented ditches are compared, where there were at most 9 finds per cubic metre of excavated soil.

The hinterlands of the sites have usually only been investigated to a minor extent, although several hectares to the north of *Sarup II* were stripped (Andersen 1997, Fig. 12) in connection with the excavation of *Sarup I*. No features contemporary with *Sarup II* were found outside the site.

In all circumstances the finds from the sites seem to have consisted of specially selected material such as fragments of human bone, whole or deliberately crushed pots, axes and so on. Smashing (the pottery) or burning (flint axes, grain, clay and human bones) had deliberately broken up some of this material. Other artefacts occurred in unusually dense concentrations, such as layers of sherds (*Store Brokhøj*; Madsen & Fidel 1987) and waste in some of the pits. The difference in the numbers of quernstones discovered at *Sarup* is remarkable, with 2 found at *Sarup I* and 21 at *Sarup II*. In respect of the finds, however, we do not yet have comparable assemblages from 'ordinary' settlements to enable us to study the variation within the material record. An approach to such studies is, however, being made in the area around

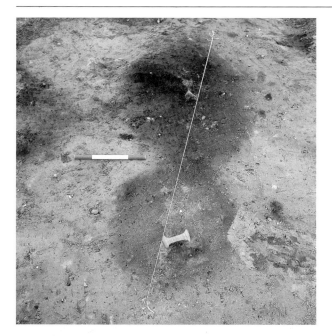

Fig 1.6: Pit (A1978) in Sarup II *with a well-preserved, complete battle axe of striated sandstone (see also Fig 1.7).*

Fig. 1.7: Battle axe (x20.000) from pit (A1978) at Sarup II *(see also Fig. 1.6). Photo: Preben Delholm.*

Lønt (Jørgensen 1988), *Toftum* (Madsen 1988) and *Sarup* (see Andersen 1997, Chapter 3).

The Neolithic enclosed sites of Scandinavia are a relatively recent discovery. Excavations at a number of these has thrown light on many aspects, and the finds show that they shared many characteristics with other European sites, not least those of the Michelsberg, Chasséen, Windmill Hill and Wartberg Cultures. Although these cultures are not entirely contemporary, they do have features in common such as the structure of their settlements (although these are rare), the use of megalithic graves (not, however, within the Michelsberg Culture), and essentially the same type of pottery. One

must assume that the enclosed sites could also have served similar functions for these different cultures.

It is not only important to know a lot about all similar enclosures; it is also important to know something about the local landscape around the site: to know all of the contemporary finds such as megalithic tombs, settlements etc. Since 1988 we have carried out intensive surveys of the fields around the *Sarup* site in order to learn more about the landscape in the Neolithic. Within about 20 km² approximately 800 prehistoric sites have been located. Only a small proportion of the finds recorded from this area are diagnostic of either *Sarup I* or *Sarup II*, so this material has not been treated separately (Andersen 1997, 89). Up to 2000, 158 sites from this area – with associated finds – have been confirmed from the period of *Sarup I* and *Sarup II*.

At a more detailed level, in the environs of Sarup 57 sites are currently regarded as settlements of the Funnel Beaker Culture, and 22 of these can be dated to the same period as *Sarup I* or *Sarup II* (Andersen 1997, Fig. 121). These settlements were of limited size, about 500m², and were most frequently situated on flat, sandy (i.e. well drained) terraces on the boundary between the wet meadowlands and the more hilly hinterland. Some settlements lay on the points of sandy promontories or on small islands in the wetter area beside the Hårby River, while a few sites were in a higher landscape zone more than 10m above sea level. The location of sites in different zones must mean that the Stone-age farmers at Sarup made use of a variety of topographical situations so that there were sites for hunting and fishing, for cattle herding, for pig farming, and for cereal cultivation.

The partly analysed finds assemblages from the settlement sites suggest that the Neolithic population around Sarup lived in small units. The settlements that have been excavated probably served only one or two families living in a single house. Comparative analysis of the finds from the settlements and the *Sarup I* and *II* enclosures show that the settlements had a more varied range of finds than *Sarup I* and *II*. The settlements had many different tool types and clear evidence of toolmaking, plus variety in the livestock and cultivated cereals. The analyses of the settlements thus reveal significant differences from the enclosures in respect of size, location and finds.

The number of recognised megalithic graves, however, probably bears little resemblance to the original number, which must have been greater. Recent intensive survey work in the Sarup area alone has revealed the presence of 119 megalithic graves to add to the four that were previously known (Andersen 1997, Fig. 121). These megalithic graves are now preserved only as plough-damaged sites. The graves survive as spreads of head-sized stones, patches of raw clay, sandstone flags, and fire-crazed flint, while irregularities in ploughing indicate the presence of large stones beneath the surface. In recent years I have conducted excavations at 22 of these megalithic graves.

The megalithic graves are the clearest mark this period

has left upon the landscape. They developed from small dolmen chambers that are slightly reminiscent of the body-length earthen graves of the preceding period (albeit built of stone) to large dolmen chambers, dolmens with a passage, and passage graves (in the period of *Sarup II*). These stone chambers were most often placed within a barrow, although they can also be surrounded by stone circles (round dolmens), oblong stone enclosures (long dolmens) or by a palisade enclosure. The megaliths were either scattered individually over the landscape or grouped in clusters (Andersen 1981, 81; Andersen 1997, Figs 120–21).

In the period around the time of the construction of *Sarup II* there was a fundamental change in the building of megalithic graves. Megalithic graves with a regular stone and earth-covered corridor were now built: passage graves or large dolmens with a passage (*jættestuer* in Danish). This change seems to have been more than just a change in building technique, as the graves with a covered passage must have been created with some symbolic purpose. The presence of a covered passage suggests that entrance into the chamber was some form of rite of passage in which one had to crawl through a small entranceway in order to stand in a high, dark and damp megalithic vault. In this connection it is noteworthy that the largest numbers, and the most profuse votive deposits of pottery, are found in front of megalithic graves with a passage.

It is also of interest that no complete primary burials are found in these megalithic graves, only body parts. A similar situation exists at the causewayed enclosures too, where parts of buried individuals have been found, a detail that can be suggested to form a link between the megalithic graves and the causewayed enclosures such as *Sarup* (Andersen 1997, 343, n. 290).

The distribution of the megalithic graves in the area of south-western Fyn and eastern Jutland indicates that the graves were often concentrated in clusters which, in terms of Thiessen polygons, can divide areas into equal sized units that are treated here as territories. Such a division or segmentation of the area into land units of equal size, taken together with the many small settlements of relatively uniform size, may be signs of the social organisation of a segmented tribal society (Renfrew 1976, 205f; Chapman 1988, 26).

The *Sarup* enclosures were placed in a conspicuous location in the centre of the many territories of south-western Fyn – a site which must have been shared by several territories from the evidence of the labour expenditure necessary for construction alone. It is possible to see the enclosures at *Sarup* with its division/segmentation into many fenced enclosures and segmented ditches as a picture – a microcosm – correlating with the settlement pattern of the surrounding area (Dillehay 1991, 228). Thus the individual ditch segments may have symbolised or have been associated with a family, a settlement, a clan or a land unit (Chapman 1988, 37).

In a segmented tribal society the *Sarup* sites served as a unifying symbol that embraced a large number of equally-sized territories or settlement areas. When the

Fig. 1.8: Reconstruction of the entrance area at Sarup I *(see also Fig 1.3). View looking south-west. Drawing: Louise Hilmar.*

deceased were temporarily buried at *Sarup*, the dead (and their souls) were brought into the wider community. The site may thus have been the place where the deceased, during a dangerous transitional phase, were transformed from individuals into members of the realm of the dead. The rituals performed here could well have occassioned gatherings of people.

Through a 'network' of this kind linked to the *Sarup* enclosures, a social forum would have been created, which (through the mediation of the dead) would have been able to facilitate the resolution of conflicts over, for instance, land rights and food distribution in times of shortage; it might also have acted as a force for social reproduction (Chapman 1988, 30), and might have represented an element of stability in a period which saw many innovations.

The *Sarup* sites consolidated the integration of the individual components (ie the ditch segments) within the whole (Edmonds 1993, 132) and legitimised the communal use of the land in a period which saw profound changes in social structures.

Dispersed settlements and a relatively varied economy gave a system which was better able to withstand crop failure, and minimised the risk of strife between the individual groups or families. It was the occupants of these small settlement sites who constructed the *Sarup* enclosures as a major communal enterprise. Common undertakings like this are often just as important for social cohesion as the rituals that may have been performed at such sites (Chapman 1988, 37). Participation in activities at these ceremonial sites would undoubtedly have strengthened social, economic and religious institutions, while a close familiarity with a site would also have made it easy for one to identify oneself with it (Chapman 1988, 22). By taking part in common enterprises one could also come to be part of some distributive system for food, if there were a shortage, while shared projects also tended to enhance the uniformity of society (Chapman 1988, 30). In the Sarup area, the sites were used primarily in Phases *Sarup I* and *II* (ie from the Fuchsberg Phase to Phase MN A I B, or 3400–3200 BC).

In the next Phase, *Sarup III* (MN A II, about 3100 BC), there were further social changes in the Sarup area. The pattern consisting of a major enclosure associated with a large number of small settlement sites comes to an end. We now see a concentration of settlement at fewer sites (Andersen 1997: Fig. 160), one of which – on the promontory of Sarup itself – was about 4 ha in size and thus 80 times larger than the settlements that had formerly been occupied. Burials in the area re-use megalithic graves, in which complete bodies were interred, not just body parts; causewayed enclosures were no longer constructed. In addition to the settlement activities taking plac at *Sarup* itself, however, others of more ritual character continued, represented by pits containing complete artefacts (Andersen 1997, Figs 133–141).

In recent years a new type of palisaded enclosure has been found in Scandinavia, consisting of one or more concentric settings of posts covering an area of 2ha to 4ha. Extensive excavations are currently being carried out at two of these enclosures. Material recovered from the postholes date to the last part of the Funnel Beaker Culture, about 2800 BC. Very little has so far been published about this very new type of enclosure (Karsten et al. 1997, 239–41; Nielsen F. O. 1998).

BIBLIOGRAPHY

Abbrevations:

Aarb   Aarbøger for Nordisk Oldkyndighed og Historie. København.
Acta: Acta Archaeologica. København.
Arbejdsmarken   Nationalmuseets Arbejdsmark. København.
AUD: Arkæologiske udgravninger i Danmark, Rigsantikvarens Arkæologiske Sekretariat. København.
JDA   Journal of Danish Archaeology. Odense.
MLUHM   Meddelanden från Lunds Universitets Historiska Museum. Lund.
PPS   Proceedings of the Prehistoric Society. London.

Aaby, B. 1985. Norddjurslands landskabsudvikling gennem 7000 år. Belyst ved pollenanalyse og bestemmelse af støvindhold i højmosetørv. *Antikvariske Studier,* 7. København.

Andersen, A. H. 1987. Nr. 16. Skævinge Boldbancr. *AUD* (1986), 56.

Andersen, N. H. 1981. Befæstede neolitiske anlæg og deres baggrund. *Kuml* (1980), Århus. 63–97.

Andersen, N. H. 1982. A Neolithic Causewayed Camp at Trelleborg near Slagelse, West Zealand. *JDA,* 1.

Andersen, N. H. 1985. Megalitgrave. *AUD* (1984), 15–18.

Andersen, N. H. 1989. Nr. 126. Hygind. *AUD* (1988), 121.

Andersen, N. H. 1993. Tragtbægerkulturens store samlingspladser (Causewayed camps of the Funnel Beaker Culture). In Hvass and Storgaard (red), *Da klinger i Muld...* (Digging into the Past). Århus. 100–103.

Andersen, N. H. 1997. *The Sarup Enclosures. The Funnel Beaker Culture of the Sarup site including two causewayed camps compared to the contemporary settlements in the area and other European enclosures.* Århus. Jutland Archaeological Society Publications XXXIII: 1.

Andersen, N. H. 1999a. *Saruppladsen. Tekst. Sarup vol. 2.* Århus. Jutland Archaeological Society Publications XXXIII: 2.

Andersen, N. H. 1999b. *Saruppladsen. Katalog. Sarup vol. 3.* Århus. Jutland Archaeological Society Publications XXXIII: 3.

Andersen, N. H. 2000. Kult og ritualer i den ældre bondestenalder (Cult and Rituals in the TRB-Culture). *Kuml* (2000), Århus. 13–57.

Andersen, N. H. & Madsen, T. 1978. Skåle og bægre med storvinkelbånd fra Yngre Stenalder. *Kuml* (1977), Århus. 161–84.

Andersen, S. T. 1993. Jættestuernes landskab. In S Hansen (red), *Jættestuer i Danmark. Konstruktion og restaurering.* København. 68–75.

Bauch, W. 1988. Eine Nachbestattung der Einzelgrabkultur mit Pferdeschädel in einem Megalitgrab von Borgstedt, Kreis

Rendsburg-Echernförde. *Offa*, Band 45 (1988), Neum"unster. 43–73.

Bauch, W. 1993. Ein neolithisches Erdwerk in Schleswig-Holstein. *Archäologie in Deutschland*, Heft. 2 (1993), Stuttgart. 6–9.

Becker, C. J. 1993. Tragtbægerkulturens kulthuse (Cult houses of the Funnel Beaker Culture). In Hvass and Storgaard (red), *Da klinger i Muld... (Digging into the Past).* Århus. 110–111.

Birkedahl, P. 1988. Nr. 299. Lokes Hede. *AUD* (1987), 158.

Chapman, J. 1988. From "Space" to "Place": A Model of Dispersed Settlement and Neolithic Society. In C. Burgess, P. Topping, C. Mordant & M. Maddison (eds), *Enclosures and Defences in the Neolithic of Western Europe.* Oxford. British Archaeological Reports, International Series, 403. 21–46.

Dillehay, T. D. 1991. Mapuche ceremonial landscape, social recruitment and resource right. *World Archaeology*, 22, 221–241.

Ebbesen, K. & Mahler, D. 1980. Virum. Et tidligneolitisk bopladsfund. *Aarb* (1979), 11–61.

Edmonds, M. 1993. Interpreting Causewayed Enclosures in the Past and the Present. In C. Tilley (ed.), *Interpretative Archaeology*. Oxford. Berg. 99–142.

Fiedel, R. & Sterum, N. 1988. Nr. 315. St. Brokhøj. *AUD* (1987), 160–161, nr 315.

Hedeager, L. & Kristiansen, K. 1988. Oldtid o. 4000 f.Kr. – 1.000 e.Kr. In Bjørn et al. (red), *Det danske landbrugs historie I.* København. 11–107.

Hingst, H. 1975. Die Sicherung des Geländes der jungsteinzeitlichen Siedlung in Büdelsdorf, Kreis Rendsburg – Eckernförde. Ein Beitrag sum Denkmalschutzjahr 1975. *Hammaburg NF 2* (1975), 33–36.

Hoika, J. 1987. Das Mittelneolithikum zur Zeit der Trichterbecherkultur in Nordostholstein. Untersuchungen zu Archäologie und Landschaftgeschichte. *Offa-Bücher. Band 61,* Neum"nster.

Iversen, J, 1941. Landnam i Danmarks Stenalder. *Danmarks Geologiske Undersøgelse. II. Række, Nr. 66.* København.

Jensen, N. M. & Nikolajsen, E. 1989. Nr. 136. Åsum Enggård. *AUD* (1988), 123.

Jørgensen, E. 1983a. Høje og hegnet næs. *Skalk* (1983), 5. Højbjerg.

Jørgensen, E. 1983b. Lønt. En gammelkendt stenalderlokalitet. *Nordslesviske Museer,* 10, Haderslev. 29–52.

Karsten, P., Svensson, M., Andersson, M. & Lund, K. 1997 Plats 8B:6/Väg 1178/1179 syd – Centralplats från trattbägerkultur, boplats från järnålder samt våtmarksfynd från senneolitikum och järnålder. In M. Svensson & P. Karsten,

Skåne, Malmöhus Län, Järnvägen västkustbanan. *1996–1997.* Lund. Riksantikvarieämbetet Lund, Rapport UV Syd, 1997: 3. 229–247.

Larsson, L. 1982. A causewayed enclosure and a site with Valby pottery at Stävie, Western Scania. *MLUHM*, 4, 65–114.

Madsen, T. 1978. Toftum ved Horsens, et befæstet anlæg tilhørende tragtbægerkulturen. *Kuml* (1977), Århus. 161–184.

Madsen, T. 1988. Causewayed Enclosures in South Scandinavia. In C. Burgess, P. Topping, C. Mordant & M. Maddison (eds), *Enclosures and Defences in the Neolithic of Western Europe.* Oxford. British Archaeological Reports, International Series, 403. 301–336.

Madsen, T. & Petersen, J. E. 1984. Tidlig-neolitiske anlæg ved Mosegården. Regionale og kronologiske forskelle i tidligneolitikum. *Kuml* (1982–83), Århus. 56–120.

Nielsen, F. O. 1998. Nyt fra Ringborgen på Rispebjerg. *Bornholms Museum og Bornholms Kunstmuseum* (1996–1997), 77–96. Rønne.

Nielsen, H. H. 1994. Efter festen – lerkar fra yngre stenalder ved Ellerødgård. Vejdirektoratet og Rigsantivarens Arkæologiske Sekretariat. *5000 år under motorvejen.* København. 28–29.

Nielsen, P. O. 1981a. *Bondestenalderen. Danmarkshistorien.* København. Sesam.

Nielsen, P. O. 1985. 4.02.14. Sigersted III. *AUD* (1984), 51. København.

Nyegaard, G. 1985. Faunalevn fra yngre stenalder på øerne syd for Fyn. In *Skaarup: Yngre stenalder på øerne syd for Fyn.* Rudkøbing. 426–466.

Renfrew, C. 1976. Megaliths, Territories and Populations. In S. de Laet (ed.), *Acculturation and Continuity in Atlantic Europe.* Bruges. 198–220.

Sherratt, A. 1981. Plough and pastoralism: aspects of the secondary revolution. In I. Hodder et al. (eds), *Pattern of the Past.* Cambridge. Cambridge University Press. 261–305.

Skaarup, J. 1985. *Yngre Stenalder på øerne syd for Fyn.* Rudkøbing. Langelands Museum.

Skaarup, J. 1993. Megalitgrave (Megalithic graves). In Hvass and Storgaard (eds), *Da klinger i Muld... (Digging into the Past).* Århus. 104–109.

Sterum, N. 1986. 261. Store Brokhøj. *AUD* (1985), 110. København.

Sørensen, P. Ø. 1995. Markildegård. En tidligneolitisk samlingsplads. *Kulturhistoriske studier.* Vordingborg. Sydsjællands Museum. 13–45.

Wincentz, L. 1994. Nr. 341, Ballegaard. *AUD* (1993), 176. København.

2   The Causewayed Enclosures of Western-Central France from the Beginning of the Fourth to the End of the Third Millennium

Claude Burnez and Catherine Louboutin

1 INTRODUCTION

The area identified as Western-Central France is mostly coastal, stretching from the Loire in the north to the Gironde in the south, including along the coastal zone, part of Poitou, Aunis and, further south, Saintonge. Inland, the territory which is studied here extends no more than 100 kilometers eastward. We will essentially deal with ditched enclosures of Saintonge and, especially, of the lower and middle Basin of the Charente river with opportune reference to major sites outside the considered area.

In Western-Central France, causewayed enclosures are extremely numerous. They are not evenly present over the whole territory and, while there are two or three hundred in the Marais poitevin and Saintonge, they are more thinly distributed between these extremes (Cassen, 1987). Causewayed enclosures are not unknown eastward, but they are definitely scarcer and belong to the perimeter influenced by the Paris Basin type, i.e. a ditch emphasised on its inner side by a palisade.

We are dealing mostly with apparently very complex plans; this historically accepted complexity derived from the subjective aerial approach, which is being contradicted by recent excavations. It has been clearly demonstrated that this visual complexity resulted from regular and systematic re-occupations of the same sites over many centuries and did not belong to one structural phase as had been suggested (Joussaume, 1988; Burnez and Louboutin, 1999).

From the chronological point of view, the earlier causewayed enclosures belong to the beginning of the fourth millennium and seem not to survive after the end of the third millennium when they are superseded by the general adoption of marked ramparts. The phenomenon of causewayed enclosures seems to appear, strangely enough, late in Western-Central France as, so far, none has been attributed with certainty to the Middle Neolithic even if some ^{14}C dates could indicate a chronological proximity. Over this long time-span, we shall see that the Matignons culture reached its final phase with an evolved ceramic style: the Peu-Richard, both cultures belonging to the Late Neolithic (Burnez and Case, 1966). This sequence is ultimately replaced by the Final Neo-

lithic Artenac culture which is argued by the present authors to last into the Early Bronze Age.

We have addressed the architectural and functional problems of the Neolithic enclosures of the Charente Basin in a recent article and consequently will not labour the points already developed (Burnez and Louboutin, 1999).

2 GEOGRAPHICAL AND GEOLOGICAL FRAMEWORK

In stating that the distribution of the sites analysed here is coastal, we have to admit that the emphasis is skewed by the obvious vicinity of the Atlantic but in fact the map (Fig. 2.1) shows the overall important role played by the hydrographic network, principally the river Charente and its southern tributaries in the central part of the area. The Marais poitevin, which at that time was a gulf gradually invaded by alluvial deposits, is another dense zone of enclosures extending over the hinterland along the river Sèvre Niortaise. Between these two areas there is an undoubted scarcity of causewayed sites in spite of extensive aerial surveys. Only the Boutonne river offers a scattering of sites. Further north the recognised enclosures appear to be more restricted to the coastal zone, where geology is favourable. They are present rather sporadically in spite of the recent thorough aerial surveys by P. Péridy (Péridy, 1999).

This general distribution pattern demonstrates that the calcareous Cretaceous zones were preferentially selected without, however, excluding valley terraces. It seems that the high density of water resources in the area favoured the setting of sites as reflected by the map. Even if the majority of enclosures are localised on gentle hills, some of them were in fact established in a very marshy environment being flooded if not continuously at least temporarily. Water molluscs (*planorbis* and *lymnea*) have been found in the ditches of the sites of La Grande Prairie at Vibrac (Burnez *et al.* 1994) and La Mercière at Jarnac-Champagne (Burnez *et al.* 1999) in Charente-Maritime, not only in the primary levels but at higher levels too.

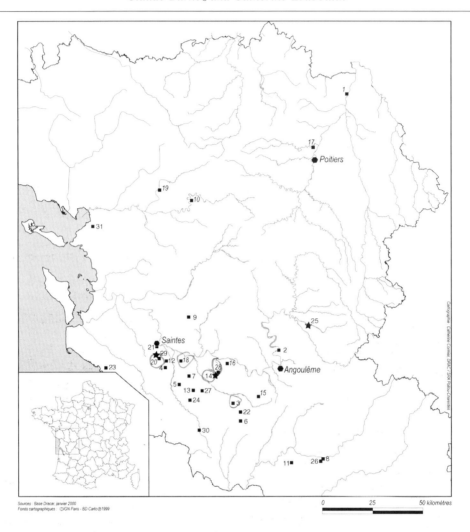

Antran	La Croix Blanche	(Vienne)	1
Balzac	Les Coteaux de Coursac	(Charente)	2
Barbezieux	Font-Rase	(Charente)	3
Berneuil	Le Mourez	(Charente-Maritime)	4
Biron	Réjolles	(Charente-Maritime)	5
Challignac	Le Camp	(Charente)	6
Coulonges	Chasseuil	(Charente-Maritime)	7
Douchapt	Beauclair	(Dordogne)	8
Ébéon	Le Chemin-Saint-Jean	(Charente-Maritime)	9
Echiré	Les Loups	(Deux-Sèvres)	10
Festalemps	Bois du Fau	(Dordogne)	11
Jard (La)	Le Chaillot	(Charente-Maritime)	12
Jarnac-Champagne	La Mercière	(Charente-Maritime)	13
Juillac-le-Coq	Les Matignons	(Charente)	14
Mainfonds	Le Tertre	(Charente)	15
Mainxe	Montagant	(Charente)	16
Migné-Auxance	Temps Perdu	(Vienne)	17
Montils	Moulin de Vent	(Charente-Maritime)	18
Nieul-sur-l'Autize	Champ-Durand	(Vendée)	19
Préguillac	Le Taillis	(Charente-Maritime)	20
Saintes	Diconche	(Charente-Maritime)	21
Saint Bonnet	Chez Got	(Charente)	22
Saint-Georges-de-Didonne	Boube	(Charente-Maritime)	23
Saint-Germain-de-Lusignan	La Coterelle	(Charente-Maritime)	24
Saint-Mary	Artenac	(Charente)	25
Saint-Méard-de-Dronne	Le Gros Bost	(Dordogne)	26
Sainte-L'Heurine	Le Cruchaud	(Charente-Maritime)	27
Segonzac	Font-Belle	(Charente)	28
Thénac	Peu-Richard	(Charente-Maritime)	29
Vibrac	La Grande Prairie	(Charente-Maritime)	30
Villedoux	Le Rocher	(Charente-Maritime)	31

Fig. 2.1: Causewayed enclosures of West-Central France

Fig. 2.2A: *Font-Belle at Segonzac (Charente): aerial photograph (J. Dassié) and plan showing the complex plan and positioning on a steep hill.*

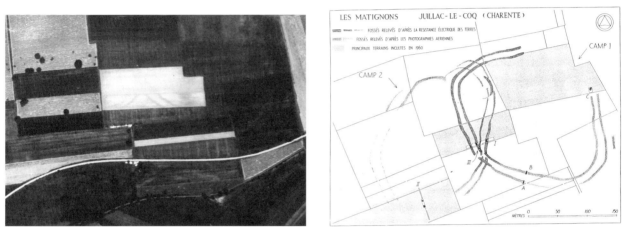

Fig. 2.2B: *Les Matignons at Juillac-le Coq (Charente): aerial photograph and plan showing the double ditches and the stratigraphical relationship between the two enclosures.*

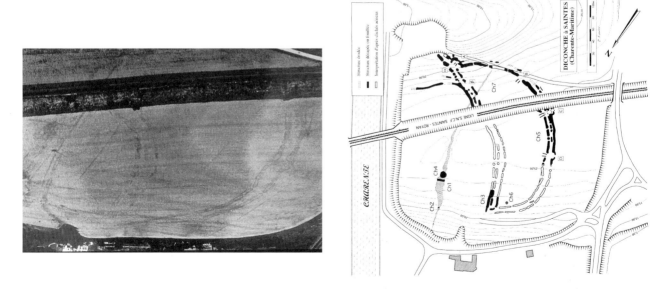

Fig. 2.2C   *Diconche at Saintes (Charente-Maritime): aerial photograph (J. Dassié) and plan with the ditch segments clearly visible and the ditches scrupulously following the previous ones.*

Fig. 2.3A: Chasseuil at Coulonges (Charente-Maritime): aerial photograph (J. Dassié) of a single enclosure.

Fig. 2.3D: Le Chemin-Saint-Jean at Ebéon (Charente-Maritime): aerial photograph (J. Dassié).

Fig. 2.3B: Les Loups at Echiré (Deux-Sèvres): aerial photograph of the smaller enclosure (M. Marsac).

Fig. 2.3E: La Coterelle at Saint-Germain-de Lusignan (Charente-Maritime): aerial photograph (J. Dassié).

Fig. 2.3C: Boube at Saint-Georges-de-Didonne (Charente-Maritime): aerial photograph (J. Dassié) showing multiple enclosures.

Fig. 2.3F: Le Mourez at Berneuil (Charente-Maritime): aerial photograph (J. Dassié).

3 PROLEGOMENA

Within this contribution certain points may appear incomplete, for example overall understanding of the structures, the approximate information given by the aerial photographs, the difficulty of distinguishing different occupation phases and consequently the reconstruction of the history of each site.

Gaps in information are due to the fact that no site has been totally explored. The interiors have never been thoroughly excavated and the ditches only partially dug. Unfortunately no experimental ditch has been dug and studied as in England or Germany. Champ-Durand at Nieul-sur-l'Autize in Vendée is the only site which remained open, thus allowing, over many years, observation of natural infilling (Joussaume 1999). No structures above the ground have remained visible for the periods prior to the Late Neolithic, due to natural and/or human erosion.

Multiple re-occupations on sites confuse the interpretation of information yielded by excavation. The artefacts can only be classified by typological analysis or rare stratigraphical structural relationships.

In spite of these difficulties of interpretation, the astonishing abundance of artefacts and sites and the geographical and temporal closeness of the latter allow a thorough comparison between different occupations whereas generally, in other areas than Western-Central France, comparisons are not easy, due to the presence of only single and/or isolated sites.

4 ARCHITECTURAL FEATURES

4.1 Plans and structures

Severely eroded, the palimpsest plans reflect multiple occupations. We have attempted (Burnez and Louboutin, 1999, 2001) to sort them out according to the space bound modalities, either an adaptation to landscape availability as at Font-Belle at Segonzac in Charente (Fig. 2.2A) or apparently a random choice as at Les Matignons at Juillac-le-Coq in Charente (Fig. 2.2B). With a typological approach, we distinguish single enclosures, for example Chasseuil at Coulonges in Charente-Maritime (Fig. 2.3A); enclosures divided into two zones, sometimes imbricated, such as Les Loups at Echiré in Deux-Sèvres (Fig. 2.3B), not only taking advantage of the sometimes relatively steep hills but also of the confluence of two minor streams whose defensive character appears to be completely valueless such as La Mercière at Jarnac-

Fig. 2.4A: Diconche at Saintes (Charente-Maritime): elaborated 'D' entrance with 'crab's claws' and palisades.

Fig. 2.4B: Font-Belle at Segonzac (Charente): dry stone walling preventing the fill of an earlier ditch from slumping into the new one.

Champagne in Charente-Maritime; and multiple enclosures like Boube at Saint-Georges-de-Didonne in Charente-Maritime (Fig. 2.3C) or Chez Got at Saint Bonnet in Charente.

The perimeter of the enclosures can be delimited by a single ditch but often double ditches have been perceived as playing this role (Fig. 2.2B). In fact, from recent data it is clearly impossible to prove that the two features have been dug contemporaneously. In particular, the evidence of multiple re-cuttings specifically and often scrupulously following the initial lay-out renders this interpretation rather doubtful. This replication applies not only to boundaries but also to the various specific entrances or interruptions, though the latter are often casually distributed. But in almost all instances, the primary plan has been redrawn with an amazing accuracy as for example at Le Chemin-Saint-Jean at Ébéon, La Coterelle at Saint-Germain-de-Lusignan or Le Mourez at Berneuil, in Charente-Maritime (Fig. 2.3D, 2.3E and 2.3F). This is particularly obvious as the ditches are, in most cases, not a continuous trench but a succession of segments perfectly replicating the previous earthwork (Fig. 2.2C). We shall return to this point later, when discussing the possible uses of the ditches.

The absence of recorded structures inside the enclosures cannot simply be explained by the deficiency of aerial survey nor by the selected and limited extension of the archaeological operations. Aerial photographs should have revealed the presence of buildings or palisades, if they had been numerous and of permanent nature, as they did with the outstanding example of Le Camp at Challignac in Charente (Burnez *et al.* 1995; Louboutin *et al.* 1997). Only the entrances are clearly elaborated in their structures, showing in various instances palisades, as at Le Rocher at Villedoux or Diconche at Saintes in Charente-Maritime, or the well known crab's claws complex variation (Fig. 2.4A).

4.2 The banks

Except in the latest phase of the regional Neolithic to which belong vestiges of ramparts, evidence for banks is represented only by the asymmetrical filling of the ditches (Fig. 2.5A). The inner edge shows a collapse of rubble, and, in a few cases, an absence of rubbish on the surface adjacent to the inner lip, for instance at Champ-Durand at Nieul-sur-l'Autize in Vendée. The drastic effect of human and natural erosion is certainly to blame for the disappearance of these banks which could have been made of calcareous blocks or earth. One must keep in mind that in most cases our calcareous substratum in the Charente basin is very weathered and of poor quality. A recent examination of a long barrow at Le Cruchaud at Sainte-L'Heurine in Charente-Maritime (Burnez and Louboutin 1999) has revealed the use of turf stacks instead of stone to partition its compartments. It is not unlikely that, for the enclosures, this technique was also adopted in identical geological subsoil conditions to erect external walls or banks, both very vulnerable to erosion. However it was probably not the case in the Marais poitevin where Bathonian or Bajocian geological layers supply good quality stone and this accounts for a better survival of the structures. Consequently the lesser need for extra quarrying to effect repairs of the banks might justify the greater frequency of single ditched enclosures in this area compared with the Charente basin.

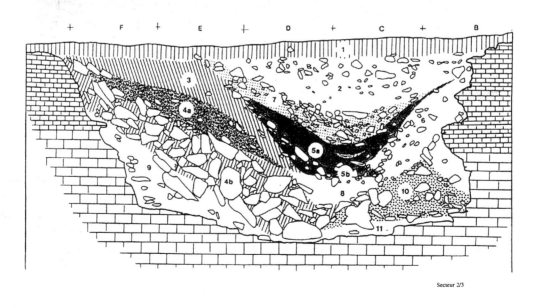

Secteur 2/3

Intérieur de l'enceinte

Fig 2.5A: Les Loups at Echiré (Deux-Sèvres): collapse of rubble from an inner bank into the ditch.

Fig. 2.5B: Font-Belle at Segonzac (Charente): re-use of an old ditch to insert post.

Fig. 2.5C: Le Moulin-de-Vent at Montils (Charente-Maritime): earth infilling of a ditch dug in limestone.

4.3 The ditches

As in other parts of Europe the ditches in our area form not a linear feature but a series of segments (Fig. 2.2C). The organisation of the work with its social implications has so often been discussed that we do not feel obliged to cover old ground.

4.3.1 Infilling phases

The ditches show the funnel like profile which is naturally acquired through erosion from original sub-vertical sides as experimental projects have clearly demonstrated (Overton, Wareham and in Germany – Bell *et al.*1996;

Lüning, 1971–1974; Kuper *et al.*1974). The immediately available sediment for filling depends largely on the size of any berm and then the time-scale and the volume of the possible contribution from the bank. They generally show three phases of silting as suggested by the experimental projects (Overton Down etc.). The first stage of rapid decay is followed by a stabilising period whose span probably varies according to climate, vegetation, faunal action etc., before the last stage of infilling whose origin is not clear. It is undoubtedly clear that in many instances the ditches were very largely filled in with the existing topsoil, if not derived completely from it. It has been assumed that at Font-Belle at Segonzac in Charente, for example, the diggers of the new ditches seem to have been unaware in some instances of the previous structures in the process of re-occupation of the site. The gaps created in the sides of the new ditch were made good using dry stone walling (Fig 2.4B). Taking into account the effect of erosion (at Font-Belle between 80 and 100 cm) attesting an original greater depth of the ditch than at present, and the slowness of the silting observed in the experimental work, one feels entitled to quote M. Bell "The stability of the V-profile Overton Down ditch suggests that some totally sedimented ditches encountered archeologically may have been deliberately back- filled (Bell *et al.*, 1996, p. 236).

The basal layers are normally very poor in artefacts due to the rapid silting. At Font-Belle in the central part there was, in at least two ditches, a thin clayey layer indicating a stochastic climatic event. It is only very rarely, and not indisputably, that thin greyish layers might represent an annual growth of regenerating vegetation. Nevertheless the mollusc study carried out at three enclosures, Les Loups (Burnez dir., 1996), Font-Belle and Diconche, consistently indicates a period of drought.

At some sites, the most representative being Font-Rase at Barbezieux (Charente), the bedrock consists of alternate layers of decayed and hard chalk. In some sections the filling showed a silting process close to that observed at Overton Down and Wareham. In our example the overhanging mats of vegetation were replaced by a cohesive mass of stones which remained more or less stable for a length of time, probably relatively short, but having been strongly undercut, finally collapsed into the ditches. This created stony layers with larger blocks at the centre. It is at this stage that a stabilisation phase usually happened. Organic and even burnt levels have been recorded in some cases which could be interpreted as the beginning of a final and deliberate infilling.

The upper levels are by far the most rich in finds of all sorts (fauna, human bones, pottery, flints) which suggests not only refuse disposal or an old ground surface captured by the sinking of the infilling, but a possible deliberate levelling of the still-visible cavity.

4.3.2 Functions of the ditches

4.3.2.1 The primary function

The specific function of the ditches is not readily and satisfactorily grasped. The obvious explanation is to interpret them as defensive, and/or quarries for banks and other, separate structures: for example, the ditch of Moulin de Vent at Montils in Charente has been dug in limestone and its infilling is just earth (Fig. 2.5C). We have already indicated that banks can be suggested where there is asymmetrical filling, and more precisely, a massive collapse of rubble. We shall return to the general function of the enclosures later on; however, there is fair evidence that the ditches themselves have served different practical purposes. Once re-cut in the loose filling of

a previous ditch, quite clearly their vulnerable sides were not expected to have a long stable life. The retaining partitions which exist at Font-Belle (Fig 2.4B), on the contrary, indicate that the structure was meant to remain open for a certain time. It is consequently rather hard to assume that they were conceived for the same function, even if we are at a loss to provide any rational explanations.

Neither double ditches nor multiple ones appear to have any defensive value, even at Champ-Durand where it was suggested that tower and ramparts had played a defensive role. We prefer to suggest, without having the basic evidence to support it, that the addition of ditches, replicas of the previous ones, was basically devoted to acquiring new material to reinforce or reconstruct ancient banks. The regular interruptions thus offered easy and necessary access to the primary earth or stone structure. The fact that very often segments have a terminal sloping edge could mean that this reduction of depth provided an easy access in and out during the quarrying work. This view tends to interpret the symmetrical layout of the segments as a purely functional organisation providing continuous access for the builders to the structure. This suggests that it might have been kept in a good state of repair during a single occupation or re-appropriated after abandonment of the site or part of the site. The infilled ditches could only provide silts inappropriate to any restoration.

4.3.2.2 The secondary function

In many instances (Diconche, Font-Belle) it seems very likely that the ditches of the first phase have been randomly re-excavated to recover durable materials for a subsequent phase of construction or repair, thus becoming secondary quarries. The clean earthen filling of these ditches cut in chalk can be interpreted as remnant material from this secondary exploitation.

The frequent occurrence of human bones is by no means characteristic of the causewayed enclosures of Western-Central France. It has been assumed that they resulted from the disturbance of burials, and scattered skeletons could be rearticulated in certain instances indicating clearly that layers apparently stratified were in fact disturbed (Debut and Masset, 1991). The excavations of Les Loups, Font-Belle and above all Font-Rase have shown that burials, up to seven in the latter case, have been deposited in half-filled ditches (Fig 2.6). In each occupation this occurred in the outer circuit of the causewayed enclosures and the skeletons were apparently not accompanied by ritual offerings or subjected to special treatment. It is worth mentioning here that one of them bore post mortem cut marks which could not be linked to any ritual (Semelier *in* Burnez, in press). It seems that the discovery of unexpected burials while redigging a ditch provoked in some cases the appropriation of symbolic bones, e.g. the skulls which are often found isolated in the ditch close to an entrance (Diconche, Font-Belle), or the only human bone re-

Fig 2.6: Font-Rase at Barbezieux (Charente): seven burials in a half-filled ditch.

Fig. 2.7: Le Chaillot at La Jard (Charente-Maritime): pot containing a cardium shell overlain by a sheep scapula: a ritual deposit?

covered in the interior (Les Loups). Exposure on banks has often been evoked although it is difficult to offer any sensible argument in favour of this practice.

The use of ditches for ritual deposition has not so far been fully justified. Two bundles of bone tools, one associated with a polished flint axe, at Les Matignons, and a pot containing a cardium shell overlain by a sheep scapula, at Le Chaillot at La Jard, in Charente-Maritime (Fig. 2.7) could however be indications of non-casual deposition. There are two examples of fully horned skulls as isolated deposits in ditch fills. Horn cores are fairly common finds but appear to be distributed haphazardly, not offering any evidence of particularly chosen locations, in contrast to with what has been observed in the Paris Basin (Farruggia *et al.* 1996). Admittedly one should mention in this context finds such as the built

hearth with faunal remains discovered at the bottom of the ditch of Le Taillis at Préguillac in Charente-Maritime, but it seems completely incidental in the process of ditch-digging (Bouchet and Burnez 1992).

4.4 The palisades

Although they had not been much mentioned in the past in the literature of Western-Central France, it has become clear through recent aerial investigations and excavation programmes that the palisades appearing as thin but regular ditches were an important component of enclosure plans. Alternative practices can be shown: the digging of a trench for the sole purpose of erecting a palisade or the re-use of an old ditch to insert posts in its sediments, their packing appearing as a column of stones vertically cutting the primary layers (Fig. 2.5B). This is also the case when a post has been removed for re-use and its packing and the filling of the ditch collapsed into the void thus created. The cavity can also be indicated by a highly organic earth which indicates that the post rotted *in situ*. In this case the width of the original ditch allowed the use of ramps to set the posts, whilst in the slots they must have been inserted vertically. However their frequency on the site of Font-Belle and re-examination of previous sections such as those of Les Matignons or Réjolles at Biron in Charente-Maritime confirm that the palisades were a very important component of the enclosures in our area.

One can add that it is not unlikely that most of the numerous narrow ditches, termed by J. Dassié as "fossés grêles" (Dassié, 1973) belong to the same category of structures. This type of architecture although not frequent is well known in Great Britain. Very different in scale, they are later than ours and their function is not yet clear

Fig 2.8: Le Camp at Challignac (Charente): aerial photograph of the ramparted enclosure (J. Dassié) and the core of the rampart set between two palisades.

too thin to accept this hypothesis without strong reservations.

The setting of palisade enclosures associated with a ditch is a common feature in Northern France, usually reinforcing the inner side. Such enclosures, typical of the Paris Basin, extend southwards around Poitiers (Temps Perdu at Migné-Auxance and La Croix Blanche at Antran in Vienne). Chronological comparisons demonstrate that these are earlier than the enclosures of Western-Central France treated here, and belong to the Middle Neolithic (last quarter of the fifth and first half of the fourth millennium).

4.5 Upstanding structures and ramparts

We have mentioned the complete absence of bank evidence due to erosion but in the final phase of the Neolithic in our area there is an emergence of ramparts which strangely enough have resisted time's natural destructive process albeit ignoring the human one. The fact they have been in most cases overlaid by Iron Age

(Gibson, 1996; Whittle, 1997; Wainwright, 1979). Much earlier, they are present in the Danubian zone having been interpreted as possible ritual or ceremonial structures (Lefranc and Jeunesse, 1998).

It is not possible at this stage functionally to associate or disassociate palisades and ditches. In a recent study of the enclosures of Font-Belle, we have tentatively suggested that the palisade enclosures may have been erected during different and completely independent phases (Burnez, in press). However the evidence is admittedly occupation does not entirely justify invoking this protection to explain their survival. While *éperons barrés* are the most common, two sites locally have demonstrated that circular or sub-circular enclosures were also of this nature, Le Gros Bost at Saint-Méard-de-Dronne in Dordogne (Burnez *et al.* 1991/1997) and Le Camp at Challignac in Charente (Burnez *et al.* 1995; Louboutin *et al.* 1997). We shall return to the chronological implications revealed by this new type of settlement and its relationship to the causewayed enclosures within the same cultural framework. It does not seem that there was a rigid architectural technique but rather as previously an adaptation to the local and geological factors – gravel, chalk etc. There was a large recourse to wood, posts or beams, certainly creating wide deforested areas. This phenomenon has been discussed at length by A Whittle in relation to the West Kennet palisades. In Le Camp (Fig. 2.8) the core of the rampart was set between two palisades over 5 metres apart, each consisting of contiguous posts with a maximum diameter of 30cm. One can extrapolate a figure of over 28.000 posts just for the inner part of the rampart to which should be added the other structures in this enclosed area of between 15 and 18 hectares.

5 THE CULTURAL AND CHRONOLOGICAL PROBLEMS

No type of enclosure, in the present state of research, can be indisputably and exclusively attached to a single regional cultural and chronological group or pattern, in spite of a very large number of sites and abundant artefacts.

Causewayed enclosures appeared in our region at the end of the Middle Neolithic at the earliest, and went on to form a settlement type specific to the Matignons/Peu-Richard sequence. The two phenomena are certainly linked although it is impossible in the present state of research to trace both back to the Middle Neolithic in which they have their natural origin. The dated finds are still too scarce to link them with either the coastal Middle Neolithic or the continental Chasséen. An absolute dating at Font-Rase on the human skeletons indicates the beginning of the fourth millennium and another one on charcoal is very close in terms of the calibrated range. A date on an animal bone from the site of Montagant at Mainxe, Charente, has often been held to date the ditch from which it was recovered but the artefacts associated are in complete disagreement (Boujot *et al.* 1996; Burnez 1996); it can be noted however that with a large standard deviation it partly overlaps the previous ones. If we reasonably accept the beginning of the fourth millennium as the initial development of this type of site, the fall into disuse is rather more difficult to grasp precisely. In fact some ^{14}C dates would tend to place it in the middle of the third millennium. This covers a span of time of about fifteen centuries from the Late Neolithic, overlapping the Bell-Beaker period, to the dawn of the Early Bronze Age.

The obvious approach at this stage is to explore how these dates fit in with the cultural groups of the later Neolithic so far identified in the area. We have primarily the Matignons/Peu-Richard sequence which is followed by Artenac. Let us state straight away that we are following the common path of cultural groups defined by ceramic assemblages. However the researches of the last thirty years have enlarged our knowledge of the other cultural material and have provided invaluable economic data.

5.1 Late Neolithic

5.1.1 Matignons (c.3800– 3500 BC)
This group was brought to light in 1960 following a joint venture between one of the present writers and H. J. Case at the site of Les Matignons (Burnez and Case 1966). Two double ditched enclosures, providing a stratigraphical sequence, were partly explored, each belonging to a different phase. The earlier phase was recognised for the first time and was consequently named after the site. Further cuttings and more extensive excavations on other sites confirmed its cultural identity and its precedence in the sequence. A range of coherent ^{14}C dates gives it a span from the beginning to the middle of the fourth millennium. At settlement sites, Matignons still lays claim to the earliest structures. However at Font-Belle the phase is represented by at least three separate episodes, with an inner enclosure showing a slight increase in size while the outer one showed greater expansion. This probably reflects both demographic and economic growth. It has an extensive geographical distribution from the Marais poitevin southwards into the Périgord (Bois du Fau at Festalemps in Dordogne; Fischer 1999) but eastwards it is still unknown beyond Angoulême (Le Tertre at Mainfonds, Charente). The pottery (Fig 2.9A) is bipartite: a range of small pots with thin walls and burnished surfaces, and larger vessels, flat-based and sometimes carinated. The bases very often show basketry imprints (Fig 2.10), a technique for pottery making which so far seems confined to this cultural phase. They have lugs or handles, often paired, more rarely four. Decoration is very rare, mostly consisting of a medium-sized, vertical single rib or a larger horizontal one underlining the rim or even partly attached to it. Single or double cupules seen in various contexts have been attributed to Matignons but the argument for restricting them here is not beyond dispute. The chronological seriation proposed by some authors is unconvincing in the lack of serious stratigraphical evidence (Boujot *et al.* 1996; Burnez 1996; Cassen 1987).

The lithics, based on blades, show considerably increased poverty both in technique and variety of tools in comparison with the Middle Neolithic assemblage. Transverse arrow heads, very crude, many scrapers, polished axes and awls have been obtained from local flint sources, although some recourse to flint from the Périgord is known (Fouéré 1994).

The economy shows that both agriculture and stock

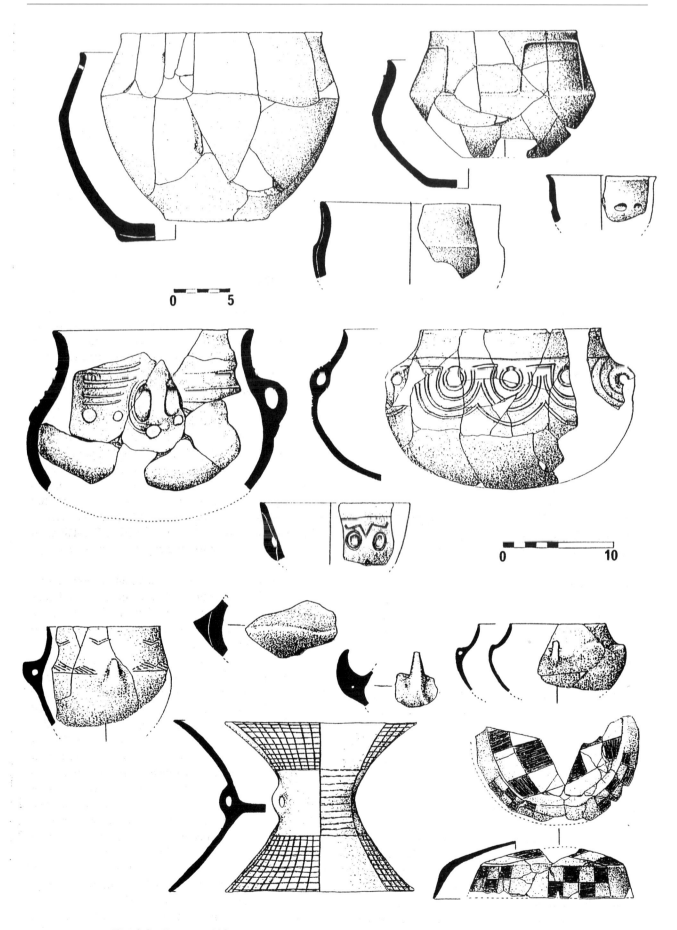

Fig. 2.9: Pottery of Matignons (top), Peu-Richard (middle) and Artenac (bottom) styles.

Fig. 2.10: Le Bois du Fau at Festalemps (Dordogne): basketry imprint on the base of a pot.

breeding were practised with great efficiency; the meat supply from wild animals was very small (Gruet *in* Bouchet and Burnez, 1990; Bartosiewicz and Bökönyi *in* Burnez and Fouéré, 1999; Bartosiewicz, Bökönyi and Braguier *in* Burnez, 1999). However Peu-Richard's recuts of practically all ditches prevented attribution of the faunal remains with certainty to Matignons or to the following phase and therefore had to be analysed in bulk. Best represented were cattle, followed by caprines and pigs. The use of cattle for traction is demonstrated by the pathology of foot- bones, but we cannot ascribe this more to Matignons than to Peu-Richard. The cereals are dominated by barley (*Hordeum vulgare*), and were accompanied by acorns (Rowley-Conwy *in* Burnez et Fouéré 1999).

It should be mentioned here again that Matignons burials were dug into secondary ditch fills.

5.1.2 Peu-Richard (c.3500– 2900 BC)
The development from Matignons to the following phase of Peu-Richard is far from being understood. It is probably masked by the numerous re-uses of sites, mixing new materials with some previously deposited. The pottery (Fig. 2.9B) is generally more uniform in its fabric than that of Matignons, with thin- or thick-walled vessels, having evenly-burnished and well-fired surfaces. The flat-based pots are very numerous, known usually as "flower pots", with four lugs or horizontally perforated lugs often joined by a thick rib parallel to the rim. The carinated wares had disappeared and the vessels show predominantly rounded walls. The chronological change is marked by a decoration which has become exuberant and overpowering although the intermediate stages are not known (see above). Inland it is achieved either by applied plastic decoration, such as (according to size) ribs or thick cordons of the variety formerly known as the Moulin de Vent style, which we prefer now to refer to as Peu-Richard-Continental. The clays of different mineral contents, when fired, produce contrasting colours and a kind of painted effect. On the coastal zone stretching to Saintes it is the channelling technique which is

predominant: the Peu-Richard-Maritime style. Over roughly twenty kilometers between Saintes and Pons, from west to east, the two styles are equally represented. The coexistence of these two contrasting techniques could be produced by a reciprocal "multiplier effect" (Renfrew 1984) with ceramic workshops sharing the same ideological or more simply artistic themes but each having its own technical way of expressing them visually. The differences which some authors seem to have perceived both in the chronological and cultural distribution of these themes are not very consistent, being for the maritime style based on very minor recent excavations or older ones. In the latter case a marked selection of decorated sherds hinders any serious statistical analyses.

The lithic assemblages (we must again emphasise the mixing of chronological and cultural contexts) diverge from Matignons in their finer knapping technique for production of transverse arrow heads, scrapers and a slightly increased number of blades. A specific form of transverse arrow head is the Montplaisir type. A distinctive awl known since the last century as Moulin-de-Vent type has been attributed exclusively to Peu-Richard-Continental (Arnal and Burnez 1957; Burnez 1976): in fact, it appears, sporadically one must admit, in Matignons but is also present in the Peu-Richard-Maritime zone. On some sites many thousands have been picked up on modern ploughsoil. To our knowledge the only use-wear experiment so far conducted suggests bone-working (Scarre, unpublished). The raw materials appear, as with Matignons, to have been exploited regionally, favouring the local supply of Turonian flint for the manufacture of Peu-Richard-Maritime axes. In spite of being close to the same sources Peu-Richard-Continental seems not to have exploited them on a large scale.

Human bones have been recovered in appreciable numbers in the ditches but so far no articulated skeletons can be attributed to the Peu-Richard period, except in the peripheral sites such as Les Loups or Champ-Durand in mixed cultural contexts.

As mentioned above the faunal analyses have not benefited from assemblages which could be securely distinguished as Matignons or Peu-Richard. The cereals at Font-Belle have been sampled extensively from sealed layers of Peu-Richard-Continental and have been studied by P. Rowley-Conwy and his assistants (*in* Burnez Fouéré 1999). The overwhelming majority consists of *Triticum dicoccum*, and *Hordeum vulgare* is only represented by two taxa, along with acorns. At the site of Diconche in the Peu-Richard ditch, the barley *Hordeum vulgare*- with more than 1000 taxa- is accompanied by 12 taxa of *Triticum dicoccum* and acorns. *Prunus spinosa* could have been accidentally included in the sample. At this stage it is not possible to draw conclusions of general value but the contrast between the Font-Belle assemblage and those of Réjolles/Diconche is striking.

We have not yet made any mention of the bone tools of the Matignons/Peu-Richard assemblages but I. Sidéra at Font-Belle tentatively estimates that the techniques offer some similarities with the Middle Neolithic of the Paris Basin (Sidéra *in* Burnez, in press). Working of antlers of roe or red deer is present and amongst the tools special mention must be given to the transverse arrow head shaft and to the axe haft with vertical socket. The latter seems to fall into disuse after the Matignons/Peu-Richard period.

Also, in uncertain stratigraphical contexts (either Matignons or Peu-Richard), there are some stone beads and from Font-Belle a chalk phallus.

5.2 Final Neolithic (c.3100–2000 BC)

The Artenac culture, defined in the early sixties as Early Bronze Age (Bailloud and Burnez 1962), appears in the Final Neolithic (Artenac I) and overlaps with the Bell-Beaker phenomenon (Artenac II). The ^{14}C dates give it a span of over a millennium with very little overlap with the end of Peu-Richard. Instead of having, like the former groups, a limited geographical distribution, Artenac, even if it is still difficult to ascertain the real boundaries of its influence, certainly played an important role in Central France (Krausz and Constantin 1995), less marked towards the south and the north (Burnez and Fouéré 1999). In the present state of research, it appears as an intrusion with very few links with the previous groups. It is in the continued use of the causewayed enclosures that a link can be found (Diconche, La Mercière etc.), and probably also in the funerary aspects. The well known entrances to the enclosures called "crab's claws" seem to belong to this period (Diconche, La Mercière). However, they appear to be a late addition to the previous enclosures, without real practical use, and could be temporary ostentatious features to celebrate special events (Scarre 1998). During a period which cannot be precisely defined, one development led to the building of strong ramparts on open sites as well as *éperons barrés*. The site of Le Camp (still under excavation) has revealed a double-ditched causewayed enclosure within an area later bounded by a rampart which is still in some parts around three metres high. If we are unable to attribute to the Matignons/Peu-Richard and Artenac I groups any trace of buildings, in Artenac II we find huge ones exceeding sixty metres in length such as at Le Camp. There are also sites, such as Beauclair at Douchapt in Dordogne (Fouéré 1998), where buildings have been recognised with only small individual enclosures surrounding them.

The pottery is different not only technically but also in forms and decoration. Two categories of pots are clearly separate: some are rather crude, coarsely built but reasonably well-fired. They are both flat- and round-based and the decoration consists mostly of finger impressions on the rims. This is assumed to have been a domestic unskilled production. However the presence of extremely large storage vessels reflects not only technical competence in their building, but also complete control

of their firing. The other category is on the contrary extremely elaborate from all points of view (Fig. 2.9C). The pots, most of them very well-fired, have thin walls, well-burnished surfaces often with typical lugs or handles which we call nose-like (*nasiforme*). They are mostly round-based, and plates (which were extremely rare in the previous ceramic phases) are very common. The bowls show during the final phase the undulating carination which entails total control of all the processes of highly skilled pottery manufacture. The decoration, occasionally red-washed, is incised, encrusted with white. The motifs are geometric, limited to linear shapes spaced around the body of the pot. In Artenac II the decorated surface is extended up to the rims, and the patterns include chessboard and ladder designs; there are carinated cups where decoration is sometimes arranged axially. This development in the ceramics is attributed to contact with the incoming Bell-Beaker people who seem to have had some difficulty in settling in the hinterland.

This new departure is reflected also in the lithic assemblages. The debitage is based on flakes but beside rough improvised tools appear fine piercing oval arrowheads, and later barbed and tanged ones, daggers and "notched saws".

The bone and antler industry is fairly abundant if not striking. However small antler tools are relatively numerous; beads, bi-perforated plaquettes and axe shafts with transverse perforations show new fashion and probably new practices.

Despite a chronological position well into metal production no irrefutable evidence has yet been met, to our knowledge, for the practice of metallurgy in the Artenac sequence.

The faunal analyses (Bartosiewicz and Bökönyi *in* Burnez and Fouéré 1999) consist of only 4% wild animals, while domestic cattle exceed 50% of the assemblages, followed by caprines and pigs. Cattle were also used for traction and the long-haired sheep recognised by S. Bökönyi as the "chalcolithic" sheep is present at the same time as in the Balkans. The appearance of spindle-whorls first in fired clay and later in stone strengthens this diagnosis.

The site of Les Loups, which is not to be attributed to the Artenac group but is contemporaneous, has produced cereals analysed by F. Gyulai (*in* Burnez 1996). *Hordeum vulgare* is predominant but *Triticum monococcum* and *dicoccum* are present. However during the last stage of Artenac pigs are beginning to take second place in the assemblages, and this could be a sign of a more sedentary way of life.

It is with Artenac that the range of exchange networks becomes wider. The greenstone axes, already present but scarce in the Matignons/Peu-Richard sequence, become less rare. They are mostly of Breton origin, amongst them a few in dolerite A, but supplies from the Massif Central are certainly to be considered. The importation of flint daggers and even rough blades from

Le Grand-Pressigny is attested and in parallel this skilled blade technique was developed by the local miners (Les Martins at Mouthiers-sur-Boëme in Charente and La Léotardie at Lamonzie-Montastruc in Dordogne etc.). An indication of extra-regional exchanges is provided by the few copper objects found not only associated with burials (Artenac cave) but on sites such as Le Camp.

6 CONCLUSION : THE MEANING OF THE ENCLOSURES

We do not claim, given our limited experience of a very localised manifestation of enclosures- very local indeed considering the European Neolithic phenomenon to which they belong- to provide the answers to multiple questions which have been fully treated by many authors. We hope only to supply "the systematic information base which would allow full potential to be realised" following a wish expressed very rightly by I. Kinnes (Kinnes, 1992). This does not preclude proposing some lines of reflection.

Nor do we feel like innovators, as the evidence we can offer has, without exception, been already met somewhere in Europe as Niels H. Andersen in his recent work fully demonstrates (Andersen, 1997). But when archaeological facts become so common and so widespread spatially and temporally, they coalesce into regional phenomena and appear to be the stochastic results of the ways in which fairly basic and general problems are solved in the types of societies with which we are dealing. The fragmentary documents in our possession also tend to question their fundamental and statistical representativeness.

Given this pessimistic view, and considering that the potential scope of research covers hundreds of regional causewayed enclosures, each with multiple occupations and ditches which can develop over hundreds, indeed thousands of metres, we feel that some guidelines appear. The re-use of the enclosures, well demonstrated in other places, seems to be more frequent in Western-Central France and more particularly along the river Charente. The regular spacing (between three and four kilometres) around certain areas such as the Cognac plain suggest that a common territory could have been under the control of the Matignons/Peu-Richard people. The ^{14}C dates tend also to demonstrate that the sites explored here are in calendar years close to the beginning of the Artenac sequence. Does their closeness reflect an attitude not only conservative but rejecting towards evident drastic cultural and economic changes, perhaps even politico-social?

Are all sites meant to meet the same needs? It is possible to classify them broadly, avoiding the intermediate, into two categories: those which consist of a single area bounded by one or many ditches; and the others which possess a double area within the same boundaries. The analysis of the artefacts and their position in the ditches, especially the faunal assemblages, have suggested that both types were reflecting the refuse of settlements. It is tempting to assign to the small area the dwellings and to the larger one activities related to agriculture or husbandry. However no consistent proof

Fig 2.11: Les Côteaux de Coursac at Balzac (Charente): aerial photograph of an éperon barré *with a number of diachronic enclosures (J. Dassié).*

can be offered and in fact the refuse in the entrances is equally abundant in both. It is becoming very clear that during the Matignons/Peu-Richard sequence, settlement type was a hundred per cent ditched enclosures. The sites detected by surface collection are always, when the opportunity of aerial photographs arises, causewayed enclosures. The information for any ritual, corral, or assembly places is meagre not to say nil. The defensive argument is not really very convincing as the defence or just the guarding of such large enclosures -not mentioning the building time which is inestimable- seem to imply unsurpassable temporal and spatial difficulties.

Why not therefore suggest the centuries-old human mania for appropriating a space at all costs and for marking its limits, not for practical purposes, but for ostentatious display of power or cultural identity (Fig. 2.11)?

BIBLIOGRAPHY

Andersen, N. H. 1997. *The Sarup Enclosures*, Sarup vol. 1, 2 et 3, Jutland Archaeological Society Publications XXXIII: 1, 1997; 2 et 3, 1999, Aarhus University press 404 p., 290 fig.

Arnal, J. et Burnez, C. 1957. Die Struktur des franzözischen Neolithikum auf Grund stratigraphischer Beobachtungen, *Bericht der Römisch-Germanischen Kommission 1956*.

Bailloud, G. et Burnez, C. 1962. Le Bronze ancien dans le Centre-Ouest de la France. *Bulletin de la Société Préhistorique Française*, 1962, p. 515.

Bamford, H. M. 1985. *Briar Hill – Excavation 1974–1978*. Northampton Development Corporation.

Bell, M. Fowler, P.-J. and Hillson, S.-W, 1996, *The Experimental Earthwork Project 1996–1982*, Council for British Archaeology, Research report 100, London.

Bouchet, J.-M. et Burnez, C. 1990. Le camp néolithique de Réjolles à Biron (Charente-Maritime). *Bulletin de la Société Préhistorique Française*, t. 87, p. 368–378.

Bouchet, J.-M. et Burnez, C. 1992. La Civilisation des Matignons. Révision des données. *Recherches Archéologiques en Saintonge*, Société d'Archéologie et d'Histoire de la Charente-Maritime, p. 3–34.

Boujot, C. et Cassen, S. 1996. Matignons et Moulin-de-Vent à Montagant/Le Brandart (Mainxe, Charente). *Bulletin de la Société Préhistorique Française*, t. 93, n° 1, p. 63–83, fig. 20.

Burnez, C. 1996. Au sujet de l'article Boujot C. et Cassen S. avec la collaboration de Philippe Chambon et Yves Gruet: Matignons et Moulin-de-Vent à Montagant/Le Brandart (Mainxe, Charente), *Bulletin de la Société Préhistorique Française*, t. 93, n° 3, p. 268–275.

Burnez, C. in press. *Les enceintes du Néolithique récent de Font-Rase à Barbezieux et Font-Belle à Segonzac (Charente)*.

Burnez, C. [dir] 1996. *Le site des Loups à Échiré – Deux-Sèvres*, Musée des Tumulus de Bougon – Conseil Général des Deux-Sèvres, 225 p. 159 fig., 19 ph.

Burnez, C. et Case, H. J. 1966. Les camps néolithiques des Matignons à Juillac-le-Coq (Charente), *Gallia Préhistoire*, t. 9 fasc. 1, p. 131 245.

Burnez, C. et Fouéré, P. [dir], 1999. *Les enceintes néolithiques de Diconche à Saintes (Charente-Maritime), une périodisation de l'Artenac*, Mémoire XXV de la Société Préhistorique Française / Mémoire XV de l'Association des Publications Chauvinoises, 2 vol., 829 p., 99 fig., 58 ph, 277 pl.

Burnez, C. et Louboutin, C, 1999. Le long tumulus du Cruchaud à Sainte-L'Heurine (Charente-Maritime), *Bulletin de la Société Préhistorique Française*, t. 96, n° 3, p. 442–443.

Burnez, C. et Louboutin, C. 1999. Les enceintes fossoyées néolithiques: architecture et fonction. L'exemple du Bassin inférieur et moyen de la Charente, *Bulletin de la Société Préhistorique Française*, t. 96, n° 3, p. 329–352.

Burnez, C., Braguier, S., Sicaud, F. et Tutard, J. 1999. Les enceintes du Néolithique récent et final de la Mercière à Jarnac-Champagne (Charente), *Bulletin de la Société Préhistorique Française*, t. 96, n° 3, p. 295–328.

Burnez, C., Dassié, J. et Sicaud, F. 1995. L'enceinte artenacienne du "Camp" à Challignac (Charente), *Bulletin de la Société Préhistorique Française*, t. 92, n° 4, p. 463–478.

Burnez, C., Fischer, F. et Fouéré, P. 1991/1997. Le Gros-Bost à Saint-Méard-de-Drône (Dordogne). *Bulletin de la Société Préhistorique Française*, t. 88 (1991 publié en 1997), n° 10–12, p. 291–340.

Burnez, C., Fouéré, P. et Tutard, J. 1994. *Enceintes néolithiques – La Grande Prairie, Vibrac (Charente Maritime)*, Association Archéologique et Historique Jonzacaise.

Burnez, C., Louboutin, C. et Braguier, S. 2001. "Les habitats néolithiques ceinturés du Centre-Ouest de la France" in Guilaine, J. (dir.). *Communautés villageoises du Proche-Orient à l'Atlantique (8000–2000 avant notre ère)*, Séminaire du Collège de France, Errance, p. 205–220.

Cassen, S. 1987. – *Le Centre-Ouest de la France au IVème millénaire av.J.C.* BAR International Series 342, 390 p., 112 fig., 7 ph.

Cassen, S. et Scarre, C. 1997, *Les enceintes néolithiques de La Mastine et Pied Lizet (Charente-Maritime)*, Mémoire XIII, Association des Publications Chauvinoises, 196 p., 89 fig.

Dassié, J. 1973. Archéologie aérienne et protohistoire saintongeaise, *Recueil de la Société Archéologique et Historique de la Charente-Maritime et Groupe de Recherches Archéologiques de Saintes* – 1ère livraison t. XXV, p. 59–64.

Debut, A. et Masset, C. 1991. Restes humains épars en milieu chasséen septentrional, Recherches en cours in: *Identité du Chasséen*, Actes du Colloque International de Nemours, Mémoires du Musée de Préhistoire d'Ile de France n° 4, p. 409–412.

Delage, J.-P. 1993. *Les ateliers de taille du silex en Bergeracois durant le Néolithique*. Mémoire de Diplome d'Etudes Approfondies, Toulouse, 103 p., 38 fig. (dactylographié).

Eschasseriaux, E. 1884. Le camp néolithique de Peu-Richard, *Bulletin de la Société des Archives Historiques de la Saintonge et de l'Aunis*, p. 191–215.

Farruggia, J.-P., Guichard, Y. et Hachem, L. 1996. Les ensembles funéraires rubanés de Menneville "Derrière le Village" (Aisne), in: Duhamel P. (dir) – *La Bourgogne entre les bassins rhénan, rhodanien et parisien : carrefour ou frontière*, Actes du XVIIIe Colloque Interrégional sur le Néolithique, Dijon 1991, Revue Archéologique de l'Est, 14e supplément, p. 119–174.

Fischer, F. 1999. Le Bois du Fau à Festalemps: un site Matignons en Dordogne, *Bulletin de la Société Préhistorique Française*, t. 96. p. 444.

Fouéré, P. 1994. *Les industries en silex entre Néolithique*

Moyen et Campaniforme dans le Nord du Bassin Aquitain. Thèse de Doctorat en Préhistoire et Géologie, Institut du Quaternaire, Université de Bordeaux I (dactylographié).

Fouéré, P. 1998. Deux grands bâtiments du Néolithique final artenacien à Douchapt (Dordogne), *in: Production et indentité culturelle, Actualité de la recherche,* Actes de la deuxième session, Arles (Bouches-du-Rhône) 1996, Éditions APDCA – Antibes, p. 311–328.

Gibson, A. 1996. A neolithic enclosure at Hindwell, Radnorshire, Powys, *Oxford Journal of Archaeology* 15 (3), p. 341–348.

Joussaume, R. 1999. A propos de l'enceinte fossoyée de Champ-Durand à Nieul-sur-l'Autize (Vendée). *Bulletin de la Société Préhistorique Française,* t. 96, n° 3, p. 401–408.

Joussaume, R. 1981. *Le Néolithique de l'Aunis et du Poitou Occidental dans son cadre atlantique,* Travaux du Laboratoire d'Anthropologie–Préhistoire–Protohistoire et Quaternaire Armoricains, Université de Rennes I, 625 p., 243 fig.

Joussaume, R. 1988. Analyse Structurale de la Triple Enceinte de Fossés Interrompus à Champ-Durand, Nieul-Sur-L'Autise, Vendée. *in* Burgess, C., Topping, P., Mordant, C. et Maddison. M. *Enclosures and Defences in the Neolithic of Western Europe,* p. 275–299.

Joussaume, R. Pautreau, J.-P. 1990. *La Préhistoire du Poitou,* Éditions Ouest-France Université, 598 p.

Kinnes, I. 1992. *Non-megalithic Long Barrows and Allied Structures in the British Neolithic,* British Museum, Occasional Paper 52, 250 p.

Krausz, S. et Constantin, C. 1995. Un site d'habitat de la culture d'Artenac à Moulins-sur-Céphons (Indre), *Bulletin de la Société Préhistorique Française,* t. 92, n° 3, p. 346–352.

Kuper, R., Löhr, H., Lüning, J. et Stehli, P. 1974. Das Versuchsgelände in Kinzweiler. *In:* Untersuchungen zur neolithischen Besiedlung der Aldenhovener Platte 4. *Bonner Jahrbücher,* 174, p. 482–494.

Lefranc P. et Jeunesse C. 1998. Wittenheim (Haut-Rhin, France). Un enclos palissadé de type "Kreispalisadeanlage" dans le Roessen III du sud de la Plaine du Rhin supérieur ? Actes du XXIII^c *Colloque interrégional sur le Néoloithique (Bruxelles, 24–26 octobre 1997), Anthropologie et Préhistoire,* t. 109, p. 63–70.

Louboutin, C., Burnez, C. Constantin, C. et Sidéra, I. 1997. Beaumont-La Tricherie (Vienne) et Challignac (Charente): deux sites d'habitat de la fin du Néolithique, *Antiquités Nationales,* 29, p. 49–64.

Lüning, J. 1971, 1972, 1974. Das Experiment im Michelsberger Erdwerk Mayen, *Archäologisches Korrespondenzblatt,* 1, 1971, p. 95–96; 2, 1972, p. 251–252; 4, 1974, p. 125–131.

Lüning, J. 1981. Das Versuchsgelände in Kinzweiler, *in:* Untersuchungen zur neolithischen Besiedlung der Aldenhovener Platte 11, *Bonner Jahrbücher,* p. 264–284.

Ollivier, A., Leduc, M. et Diot, M.-F. 1997. L'enceinte néolithique de Temps Perdu, commune de Migné-Auxances (Vienne), *Bulletin de la Société Préhistorique Française,* t. 94, n° 2, p. 217–229.

Péridy, P. 1999. Les enceintes néolithiques à fossés interrompus entre Loire et Marais poitevin, *Bulletin de la Société Préhistorique Française,* t. 96, n° 3, p. 421–426.

Renfrew, C, 1984. *Approaches to Social Archaeology,* Edinburgh University Press, Megaw and Simpson.

Scarre, C. 1998. Arenas of Action? Enclosure Entrances in Neolithic Western France *c.*3500–2500 BC, *Proceedings of the Prehistoric Society,* 64, p. 115–137.

Wainwright, G. J. 1979. *Mount Pleasant, Dorset: Excavations 1970–1971,* Society of Antiquaries, Thames and Hudson.

Whittle, A. 1997. *Sacred Mound, Holy Rings, Silbury Hill and the West Kennet palisade enclosures: a Later Neolithic complex in north Wiltshire,* Oxbow Monograph, 74, 176 p., 87 fig., 49 tabl.

3   Le Mourral, Trèbes (Aude) and the final Neolithic circular enclosures of the Languedoc

Jean Vaquer

A combination of aerial photography and rescue excavation carried out in western Languedoc over the last twenty years has revealed a new type of wide-ditched circular enclosure, attested at six locations. They may be single or double, having at least one entrance where the ditch is interrupted. Trial excavations at Villeneuve-Tolosane (Haute-Garonne), Roc d'en Gabit, Carcassonne (Aude) and Carsac-Mayrevieille, Carcassonne (Aude) have demonstrated a final Neolithic date for these structures (beginning of the third millennium BC). However, the excavations were limited in nature (all being on building sites or vineyards), and so the precise nature of the sites could not be defined (Vaquer 1995). The presence of a substantial bank next to the ditch at Villeneuve- Tolosane suggested a defended settlement, while other factors (double, concentric ditches at Carsac, traces of disturbed burials at Carsac and Roc d'en Gabit, absence of visible settlement structures within the enclosures) may suggest possible morphological similarities to British henge monuments, which are interpreted as ceremonial monuments or as sites occupied by an elite exercising priestly authority (Wainwright 1989). In 1993 came the chance to clear totally and excavate substantially the enclosure at Mourral-Millegrand, Trèbes (Aude). This site was much better preserved than the others, promising a fuller understanding of these monuments and of the cultural, social and economic context in which they were built and used.

1 THE FINAL NEOLITHIC CIRCULAR ENCLOSURES OF THE LANGUEDOC

More than twenty ditched enclosures with evidence for final Neolithic use (Saint-Pons and Véraza cultures) or Chalcolithic (late Véraza and Beaker) have been recorded in western Languedoc between the rivers Hérault and Garonne and the Pyrénées (Fig. 3.1). These were discovered as a result of aerial survey and a series of rescue excavations carried out ahead of public works or cultivation.

Unlike the middle Neolithic enclosures, which have interrupted ditches, these have a continuous ditch with a restricted number of entrances. Several types can be defined according to their siting and morphology: enclosures cutting off a spur or plateau edge, elliptical or rectangular enclosures on level terrain, possession of single or double ditches, the presence of a supplementary palisade or remains of a stone bank. Among these different structures one can single out a group of circular enclosures with substantial single or double ditches having at least one wide entrance where the ditches are interrupted. Their diameter ranges between 47m and 115m and they are mainly found in elevated situations commanding a view over, or controlling, the surrounding land and the main axes of communication.

La Terrasse, Villeneuve-Tolosane (Haute-Garonne)

This enclosure was discovered in 1983 during road and building works. Some trial trenching only was possible, revealing two sections of a circular ditch and traces of two concentric palisades with an east-facing entrance (Fig. 3.2).

The reconstructed plan suggests that the circular ditch may be about 114m in diameter. The entrance, where the ditch is interrupted, is about twenty metres across. The two palisades are concentric and must have framed a bank. The outer palisade is joined to the other at the point at which the entrance occurs and this is flanked by two large posts (0.50m in diameter). This gateway, 2.60m wide, is approached by a kind of passage formed where the outer palisade curves in towards the inner one. Material found in the ditch consists of artefacts characteristic of the final Neolithic or Chalcolithic: flint tools, antler sleeves and round-based pottery. Charcoal from the base of the ditch gave determinations confirming a final Neolithic date: Gif 6314: 4200±90BP (3013–2473BC).

Rivoire, Pennautier (Aude)

In 1991, following a winter flight over a plot recently planted with vines to the east of the Rivoire estate, a circular enclosure was spotted at the top of a remnant of an old terrace of the Fresquel. Sampling showed that the

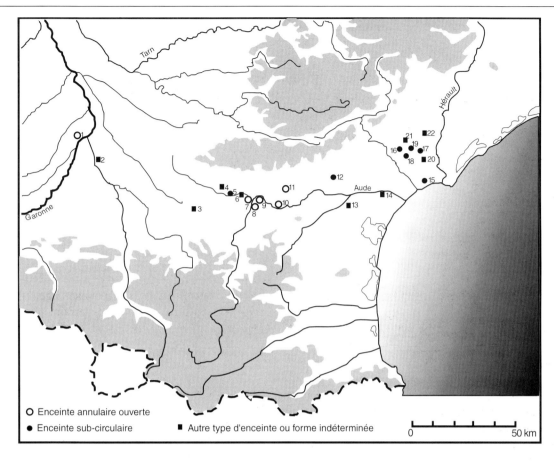

Fig. 3.1: Map of final Neolithic and Chalcolithic enclosures in western Languedoc.

1: La Terrasse, Villeneuve-Tolosane (Haute-Garonne), 2: Tuilerie de Grépiac (Haute-Garonne), 3: L'Agréable à Villasavary (Aude), 5: Poste-Vieille, Pezens (Aude), 6: Saint-Antoine, Caux-et-Sauzens (Aude), 7: Rivoire, Pennautier (Aude), 8: Carsac-Mayrevieille, Carcassonne (Aude), 9: Roc d'en Gabit, Carcassonne (Aude), 10: Le Mourral, Trèbes (Aude), 11: La Serre, Laure-Minervois (Aude), 12: La Carreirasse, Mailhac (Aude), 13: Médor, Ornaisons (Aude), 14: La Moulinasse, Salles-d'Aude (Aude), 15: Les Mourguettes, Portiragnes (Hérault), 16: Le Grand Bosc, Lieuran (Hérault), 17: Le Pierras de l'Hermitage, Servian (Hérault), 18: La Grande Prèpre, Servian (Hérault), 19: La Croix de Fer, Espondeilhan (Hérault), 20: La Croix Vieille, Montblanc (Hérault), 21: Campagne, Abeilhan (Hérault), 22: Fontarèche, Caux (Hérault).

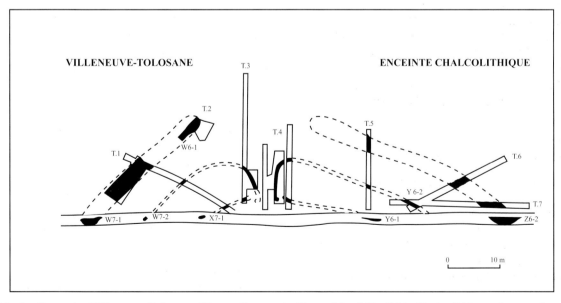

Fig. 3.2: La Terrasse, Villeneuve-Tolosane (Haute-Garonne). Plan of final Neolithic-Chalcolithic enclosure. Structures observed in the embankment of the CD15 (at base of plan) and in the trial trenches are shown in solid black, the theoretical projection of these as dotted lines. (Plan: J. Vaquer).

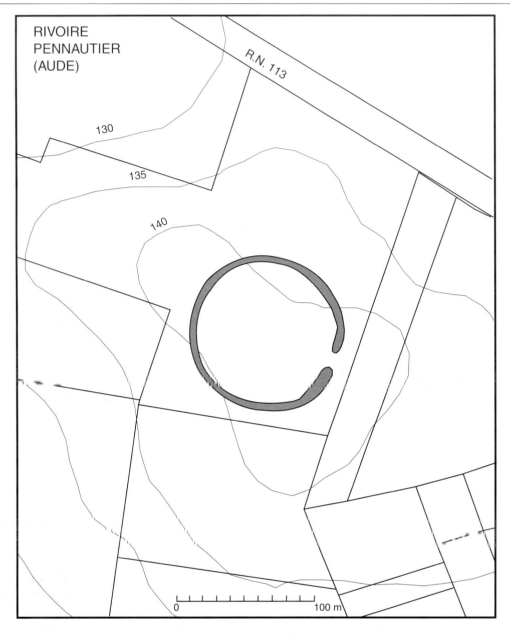

RIVOIRE
PENNAUTIER
(AUDE)

Fig. 3.3: Enclosure at Rivoire, Pennautier (Aude). Ground plan of soil anomalies discovered from the air. (Plan: J. Vaquer).

ditch, filled with black soil, was 4 to 6m wide, forming a circle about 100m across with a gap of about 12m towards the east (Fig. 3.3). No finds were picked up during the survey (just as none were found at Carsac and La Serre, Laure-Minervois following their discovery), but the soil anomaly cannot be of natural origin since the soil at Rivoire consists of ancient alluvia.

Carsac-Mayrevieille, Carcassonne (Aude)

A double-ditched circular enclosure was found in 1987 on the Carsac promontory during an aerial survey of the important protohistoric site extending over 25 hectares to the south of Carcassonne (Fig. 3.4). It first appeared as a soil-mark on ploughed land, a double concentric circle of dark earth standing out quite clearly against the

pale loess covering the site. It reappeared several times, whether after ploughing or under the various annual crops which succeeded the vines. During the winter of 1990–91 the marks were particularly clear as colours were enhanced by moisture or by superficial thawing. Good photographs showed that the concentric ditches were interrupted at the same point, and it was even possible to see traces of pits (Iron Age storage pits). It was decided to carry out a ground survey and to sample the ditches, which had yielded no cultural remains on the surface. It was established that the outer sub-circular ditch measured between 106 and 98m in diameter and that the ditch itself was four to five metres wide, with a gap of five metres at 21°(north-east). The inner ditch, six to eight metres wide, enclosed an oval space 67m long and 55m wide; it had a corresponding gap.

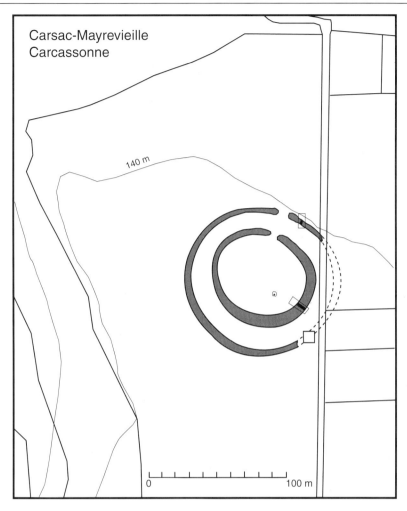

Fig. 3.4: Carsac-Mayrevieille, Carcassonne (Aude). Plan of final Neolithic double enclosure. (Survey: J. Vaquer and J. Coularou).

Trial trenching confirmed the large size of the ditches: the internal ditch proved to be more than eight metres wide and three deep, the external one 4.5m wide and 1.6m deep. The fill of both indicated deposition of material from the interior (a double bank). Cultural remains from the fills are relatively homogeneous and include carinated bowls, and jars with horizontal cordons and bosses typical of the local final Neolithic. [14]C dating of charcoal from within the fill of the inner ditch was consistent with this: Ly. 5581: 4010±60 BP (2858–2471 BC).

A disturbed burial was found in the fill of the inner ditch, suggesting that this type of site- which is radically different from the numerous settlements of the same period known in the area- might have had some special monumental or ceremonial function.

Roc d'en Gabit (hamlet of Montredon), Carcassonne (Aude)

The same systematic aerial survey programme revealed a circular enclosure at this Neolithic and Chalcolithic site, which overlooks the ancient confluence of the Aude and the Fresquel. The enclosure, marked by a ring of black earth with an opening to the west, showed very clearly, if partially, during the winter of 1992 after deep ploughing to remove vines (Fig. 3.5). It was then cleared and sampled. The ditch was filled with dark soil and was dug into yellow loess, so was easily traceable on the ground. It was 8–10m wide where it was cut into the terrace, narrowing to the north in an eroded part of the site. The diameter is about 100m, with a gap of about 15m to the west. A trial trench was put in at a point where the ditch was 8m wide. The ditch was u- shaped in section and more than three metres deep, filled with brown clayey soil with some sand and traces of alluvium and standing water. Little cultural material was found throughout: some animal remains, one human bone, a leaf-shaped flint arrowhead, sherds with cordons and bosses and quern fragments dating to the local final Neolithic (Saint-Ponien or early Vérazien). [14]C dating of layer 4 proved consistent with this attribution: Ly. 6294: 4380±95BP (3330–2784 BC). Amongst the artefacts there were a number of white marble pebbles with opposed cupules, which appear to be blanks for small bracelets which must have been produced in some number at the site. It should be noted that not one Beaker

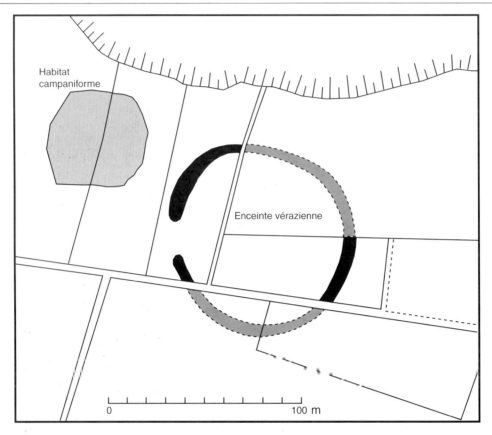

Fig. 3.5: Roc d'en Gabit, Montredon, Carcassonne (Aude). Ground plan of soil anomalies discovered from the air. (Plan: J. Vaquer).

sherd was found in the ditch fill, although there is an important site of the Pyrenean facies about 15 metres to the west of the entrance of the enclosure.

La Serre, Laure-Minervois (Aude)

This small enclosure, situated near the edge of an old terrace overlooking the Laure-Minervois basin, was discovered during an aerial survey by F. Claustre following vine-planting in 1985. It appeared clearly as an open circle of moist black earth, the ditch being 2–4m wide and enclosing a sub-circular space 47–55m in diameter; the entrance, on the eastern side, was 5m wide. No finds were picked up on the surface but a sondage in 1986 yielded two small sherds of pottery and fragments of flint blades and tools. These, and the similarity to the sites of Mourral and Roc d'en Gabit, suggest a final Neolithic date.

Without much doubt, digging ditches of such a size would have required considerable effort from people who had only wooden and stone tools. The ditch material was probably used to raise an imposing bank near to the internal edge of the ditch; this is suggested by the asymmetry of the deposits observed in the trial sections cut at Roc d'en Gabit and Carsac. The scale of these ditched enclosures- a double circuit at Carsac- must have given these sites a monumental appearance contrasting with the complete absence of occupation traces in the interior. While the absence of internal structures is probably related to erosion by deep ploughing, it is still a serious obstacle to our efforts to understand the rôle of these enclosures. The debris found in the lowest layers may suggest that the ditches did serve as dumps and that the sites were therefore occupied. However, the human bone and the remains of burials seen in the two small sondages suggest that they might also have had a funerary function similar to that of British henges.

2 EVIDENCE FROM THE EXCAVATION AT MOURRAL-MILLEGRAND, TRÈBES (AUDE)

This circular enclosure was discovered during an aerial survey carried out over a working quarry in 1993. It was investigated as part of a rescue programme financed by CNRS (UMR 8555), the Ministère de la Recherche et de Communication (Archaeology Section), the Conseil Général de l'Aude, the Archaeological Association for the Aude and the Rivière Company. The excavation took place between 1994 and 1999 in two-month summer seasons with the participation of about a hundred volunteers and students.

The site, on top of a hill overlooking the Aude valley, had not been cultivated since 1940. The outlier of an old alluvial terrace had been subject to little erosion, conditions which favoured good preservation of buried structures and helped in their identification (Fig. 3.7).

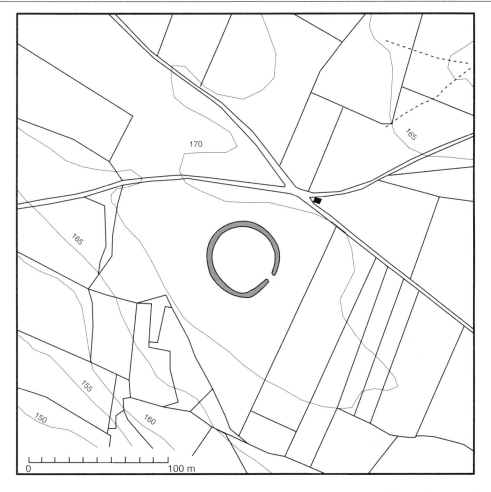

Fig. 3.6: La Serre, Laure-Minervois (Aude). Ground plan of soil anomalies discovered from the air. (Plan: J. Vaquer).

The enclosure consisted of a ditch 66m in diameter and a palisade trench within, having a 4m gap. To the east, the main entrance was marked by a 7m gap in the ditch and a 2m gap in the palisade. The western entrance was originally wider, but was reduced to a narrow opening during the course of occupation. Multiple sondages across the ditch showed that the fill derived mainly from the interior, suggesting that the upcast from the ditch formed an internal bank. The post holes and packing belonging to the palisade showed that the latter consisted of round timbers practically juxtaposed with an average diameter of 0.2m, with larger timbers either side of the two entrances.

Inside, traces of three buildings represented by post holes were distinguished. The largest structure, to the north, had been truncated by the quarry, but appeared to measure more than 29m long by 9m wide. It was a two-aisled building with a spur at right angles and an entrance on the eastern axis represented by two massive posts. Four large axial pits might each have housed several posts supporting the roof-ridge. The front section of the building contained a hearth-scoop which yielded cordoned pottery typical of the final Neolithic. The better-preserved of the side walls was represented towards the rear of the building by a row of regularly-spaced post holes.

To the south, the second building was similarly two-aisled but was trapezoidal in plan. The rows of post holes representing the load-bearing walls survived, as did two large post holes marking an entrance on the eastern axis and one to the west functioning as a roof-support. This arrangement suggests that the entrance must have formed a tall porch structure supporting the roof-beam. The narrowing of the walls towards the rear suggests a terminal apse. Cultural remains from the structures consisted of sherds of final Neolithic pottery. A possible third building was suggested by two post holes in the area of the southern building, but making no architectural sense in terms of the latter. A few Neolithic sherds were retrieved from them but they were atypical and so we do not know whether the structure pre- or post-dated the other two.

Dates obtained from the base of one of the carbonised posts from the large northern building suggest that it is exactly contemporary with the first occupation of the site (the end of the fourth millennium BC). This type of architecture – timber framing with load-bearing walls – is new to the Neolithic of southern France, where little is known aside from the dry stone structures of the Fontbouisse culture which are much smaller. Buildings for collective use or privileged occupation might be

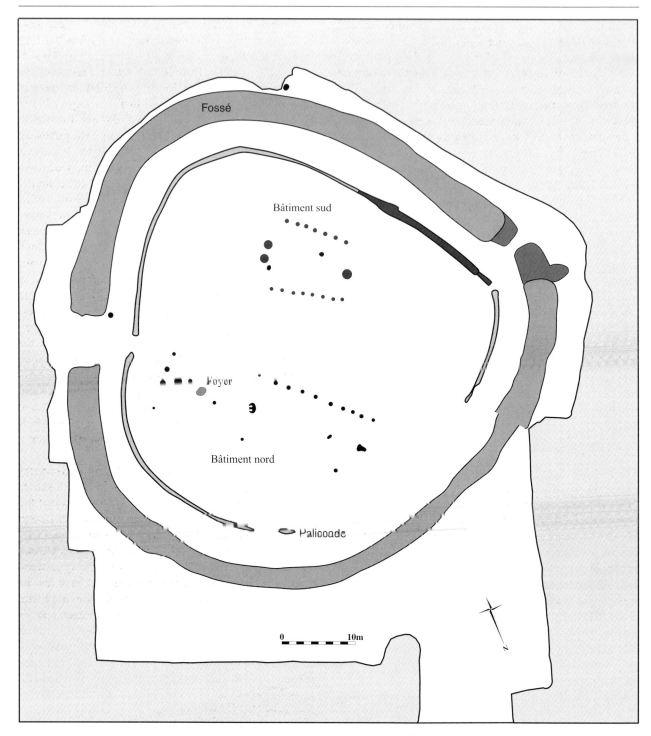

Fig. 3.7: Le Mourral, Trèbes (Aude). Post-excavation plan of site Areas of the palisade and ditch shown in darker tone are those which were recut during the early occupation of the site in order to narrow the western entrance. (Plan: J. Vaquer).

hypothesised for the large structures at Mourral.

Stratigraphic excavation of the ditch fill yielded abundant material which indicates various occupation phases. The earliest, ashy layers contained quantities of butchered animal bone as well as material typical of the local final Neolithic (Saint-Pons group, early Véraza) dated to the end of the fourth millennium BC (Ly 8250: 4480±50 BP/3332–2946 BC). The middle layers contained material of the early Vérazien dated to the third

millennium (Ly 8249: 4225±45 BP/2900–2638 BC). After a gap in time the site was reoccupied by Beaker users, traces of whom were left in the western part of the ditch, by then almost totally filled. This rich deposit contained classic Beaker elements, marking a break in tradition with the local groups preceding: flint barbed and tanged arrowheads, a Palmela point of arsenical copper, variscite beads and much fragmented (but hardly dispersed) pottery. The stratigraphically homogeneous assemblage consisted of All Over Ornamented and Maritime Beakers where the comb decoration was sometimes enhanced by the use of red paint in the plain zones. It is particularly interesting to note that these decorated Beakers were associated with 'accessory' vessels which differed from the indigenous Vérazien wares. Their presence suggests a certain Beaker autonomy from the inception, contradicting the theory that the first Beakers were taken up by indigenous cultures as luxury products, prestige goods or funerary offerings. In another part of the site, a small deposit in the upper fill suggested a later phase of the Bell Beaker complex (scalariform decoration of the Pyrenean style). This marks the last occupation of the site towards 2300 BC.

Food remains are well documented (carbonised grain: *Triticum aestivum/durum, Hordeum vulgare var. nudum*, identified by P. Marinval; fauna: bovines in abundance, goat and pig, currently undergoing study by A. Tresset). There is also good evidence for processing and exchange (much pottery, bone tools and lithics using local or imported materials, ornaments of shell and talc).The domestic remains found at various levels favour a habitation site rather than a ceremonial centre, even though a few human bones were found mixed with the rubbish in the ditch fills.

CONCLUSION

The excavation of the site of Mourral-Millegrand has added much information about this type of enclosure. As at Villeneuve-Tolosane, it demonstrates that the ditch was reinforced internally by an earthen bank and a massive palisade with narrow entrances. One is therefore probably dealing with fortified sites rather than strictly ceremonial or religious monuments. The defensive aspect is emphasised at Mourral by the modifications to the western entrance, where the width was greatly reduced during the early occupation of the site (Fig. 3.7).

Mourral's great novelty is its possession of large timber buildings in the interior; there is however little with which to compare them. There are no convincing plans of domestic units known for the final Neolithic (Saint-Ponien/ Vérazien) in the entire region of its distribution (western Languedoc and Catalonia) – so that it is impossible to know if these great buildings were the norm or not in settlements of the period. Locally, the only published information relates to the site of Dorio, Félines-Minervois (Hérault), but this is difficult to use in that the settlement has not really been excavated, just recorded simply following ploughing. (Arnal, J. and Rodriguez, G. 1971). In fact the only convincing parallels are in western France, where large final Neolithic buildings have recently been discovered (Fouéré, P. 1998). In their general morphology (sizeable, elongated, double-aisled buildings, the side walls with load-bearing posts), the Mourral structures may be compared with those of Airvault (Deux-Sèvres) or with Moulins-sur-Céphons (Indre); however other, better-preserved examples are architecturally more elaborate and show differences in construction techniques or in the positioning of entrances (Douchapt, Dordogne and Antran, Vienne). In fact the outstanding feature of the two Mourral buildings is the presence of an axial entrance in the form of a tall porch which lends a monumental aspect and distinguishes the structures from the Artenac examples. It should be noticed in this context that great size does not exclude domestic use.

The quantity of hearth material, including food remains (animal bone and carbonised grain), mixed with sherds and a variety of bone and stone tools, indicates that the site was occupied and that various activities connected with processing and consumption were carried out there. At the same time the fact that the Mourral enclosure contained only two buildings points to a disparity between the work needed to build the enclosure, its bank and its palisade, and the small number of families living there. There is a similar disparity between the site itself and the

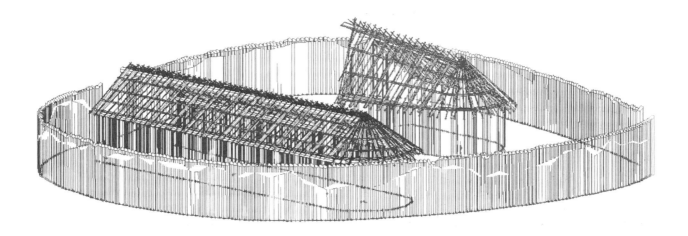

Fig. 3.8: Le Mourral, Trèbes (Aude). Reconstructions of elevations, Neolithic enclosure (by Patrick Perez and Frédéric Lesueur, Ecole d'Architecture de Toulouse).

Fig. 3.9: Le Mourral, Trèbes (Aude). Reconstruction of elevations, final Neolithic enclosure (by Patrick Perez and Frédéric Lesueur, Ecole d'Architecture de Toulouse).

many small contemporary settlements scattered within the region. In fact it is the latter which most often yield rubbish pits, hearths and especially storage pits used for seed corn- absent at Mourral. This tends to identify Mourral as a defended settlement, but one occupied by a social group which did not itself produce everything which it consumed (absence of storage pits).

In the Carcassonne area, which has been intensively surveyed, enclosures of this type mark the course of the Aude every 5 to 7km. They are sited on eminences, facilitating control of territory and of the main axes of communication. It is thus tempting to see them as the dwelling-places of important groups exercising power over the populations occupying these small territories. Their defensive nature is undeniable, together with a fairly long-lived occupation, exploitation of various resources (abundant fauna, especially bovines), long-distance exchange (a great many blades of banded flint from the Alps). The presence of scattered human bone mixed with the faunal remains in the final Neolithic layers of the ditch at Mourral, and in the Beaker layer where it is associated with variscite beads, implies a number of practices involving certain of the dead, unless one is dealing with disturbed burials or exposed corpses placed originally within or on the earthen bank next to the ditch. These factors, as at Roc d'en Gabit, show that the activities taking place at these enclosure sites were not just about domestic economy or temporal power. Were they the burial-places of the inhabitants of these fortified sites? There are doubts concerning the extent to which the remains are residual, found as they were in dumps without any grave-goods.

If these settlements bespeak a probable social hierarchy, this is reflected in tomb-types of the same period, during the course of which appeared large megalithic monuments (end of the fourth and beginning of the third millennium BC). Their construction too required a sizeable work-force and the organisation of funerary practices over a long period. Collective burial was the rite,

but it appears that not every individual qualified for interment in such monuments as many burials in natural shelters and simple pits are also known. In this social context, it is interesting to look at the behaviour of the Beaker population. At Mourral it is clear that an autonomous early Beaker group reoccupied the enclosure, which must by then have fallen largely into disrepair. It is not impossible that they sought to revive the former dominant function of the site, just as they revived the function of many *dolmen*s in western Languedoc.

BIBLIOGRAPHY

Arnal, J. and Rodriguez, G. 1971. Le gisement saintponien de Dorio, Félines-Minervois (Hérault). *Bulletin du Musée d'Anthropologie Préhistorique de Monaco*, fasc. 17, 1971, p. 171–184, 7 fig.

Esperou, J.-L. 1999. Les enceintes chalcolithiques du Languedoc central. *Préhistoire de l'espace habité en France du sud*. Beeching A. et Vital J. dir., Actes des premières Rencontres Méridionales de Préhistoire récente, Valence 1994, Travaux du Centre d'Archéologie Préhistorique de Valence, n° 1 1999, p. 91 100, 7 fig.

Fouéré, P. 1998. Deux grands bâtiments du Néolithique final artenacien à Douchapt (Dordogne). *Production et identité culturelle*. A d'Anna et D Binder dir., Actes des deuxièmes Rencontres méridionales de Préhistoire récente, Arles 1996, éditions ADPCA, Antibes, 1998, p. 311–318, 12 fig.

Guilaine, J. 1967. *La civilisation campaniforme dans les Pyrénées Françaises*. Edition du Groupe Audois d'Etudes Préhistoriques, Carcassonne 1967, 240 p., 52 fig., 9 pl.

Guilaine, J. dir, 1980. *Le groupe de Véraza et la fin des temps néolithiques*. CNRS 1980, Toulouse, 296 p., nb. fig.

Guilaine, J. dir, 1989. *Ornaisons/Médor. Archéologie en Terre d'Aude* et Centre d'Anthropologie Toulouse, 1989, 314 p., nb fig.

Grimal, J. P. 1991. Le gisement ceinturé des Mourguettes (Portiragnes, Hérault). *Le Chalcolithique en Languedoc. Archéologie en Languedoc*, n° 15 1990–1991, actes du colloque en hommage au Dr Jean Arnal, p. 109–113, 5 fig.

Krausz, S., Constantin, C. 1995. Un site d'habitat de la culture d'Artenac à Moulins sur Céphons (Indre). *Bulletin de la Société Préhistorique Française*, T. 92, n°3, 1995, p. 346–352, 11 fig.

Rodriguez, G. 1984, *La grotte de Camprafaud*. Groupe Archéologique Saint-Ponais, 1984. 417 p., 110 fig.

Vaquer, J. 1990. *Le Néolithique en Languedoc Occidental*. Editions du CNRS, Paris 1990, 412 p., 202 fig., 14 photos.

Vaquer, J. 1995, Les enceintes du Néolithique final en Languedoc occidental. *L' Habitat néolithique et proto-historique dans le sud de la France*. Séminaires du Centre d'Anthropologie, Toulouse 1995, pp. 23–26, 4 fig.

Vaquer, J. 1998, Fortifications et pouvoir au Néolithique. *L'Archéologue* n° 35, avril-mai 1998, p. 31–34, 9 fig.

Vaquer, J. 1998. Le Mourral, Trèbes (Aude), a fortified languedocian late neolithic site, reoccupied by bell beakers. In: The Bell Beaker "phenomenon". M. Benz and S. van Willigen (eds), *Proceedings of the 2nd meeting of the 'Association Archéologie et Gobelets'*, Feldberg (Germany) 1997, BAR international series 690, 1998, p. 15–21, 3 fig.

Wainwright, G. 1989. *The Henge Monuments*. Thames and Hudson. Londres 1989, 177 p. et 111 fig.

4 The Late Neolithic settlement of La Hersonnais, Pléchâtel in its regional context

J.-Y. Tinevez

The Neolithic period in the Armorican peninsula is famous for its megalithic heritage. The high density of monuments has produced a research specialisation in this domain, to the detriment of other aspects, notably the remains of settlements which are often more integrated into the landscape and therefore more difficult to locate. Even so, as early as the second half of the 19th century, as the interest in megaliths was growing, early archaeologists decided to consider some of the less obvious remains of settlements. This manifested itself chiefly in survey projects, with some excavations undertaken essentially in the southern coastal area of Brittany, at the end of the nineteenth century and the first half of the twentieth.

After the Second World War, the State decided to gradually take charge of the French archaeological heritage and made it possible to create an institutional organisation. Research found a new lease of life. But most resources were devoted again to the megalithic heritage which benefited from the most significant advances in knowledge. The concern for settlement remains only started growing from the middle of the 1980s with the rise in the number of ground and aerial surveys, planned and preventive excavations and their sometimes spectacular results.

Until the recent discovery and study of the early Neolithic site at St Etienne-en-Cogles (Cassen & *alii*. 1998) in 1995, knowledge of Neolithic settlement in Armorica was limited mainly to the end of the period from the middle of the 4th millennium to the end of the 3rd millennium.

After a short synthesis of the results stemming from early research in this field, this article aims to sum up the discovery and investigation of the site of La Hersonnais at Pléchâtel in its regional context. This site consists of a huge group of settlement structures, unusual in their dimensions and their late Neolithic origin.

EARLY RESEARCH

Until the mid-19th century, research as a whole consisted of surveys and site locating, carried out by scholars who collected information generally recorded in surveys, the reliability and scientific value of which varies from case to case. Despite some inaccuracies, these testimonies are sometimes the first and only information on sites which have been forgotten or destroyed since. Archaeological excavations started only from the second half of the century, initially mainly on megalithic monuments, thanks to the help of the newly created learned societies, such as the Société Polymathique du Morbihan. Towards the end of the century, the interest of early researchers, like F. Gaillard or P. du Chatellier in Finistère (Brittany) also focused on the less obvious remains of settlements. The latter were located during the study of megalithic monuments or thanks to defensive structures still standing. In the first half of the 20th century, these works were completed and developed by Z. Le Rouzic in the area of Carnac on the Morbihan coast.

Most of the sites studied during that period are located within the southern coastal area of Brittany. There are fortified sites, promontory forts or hill forts. The material collected, often found in large quantities, leads us to suppose that the main occupation on these sites can be dated back to the 3rd millennium.

The first important and large-scale investigations were carried out on sites in the Morbihan, such as the Camp du Lizo in Carnac, the headland of Croh-Collé in Quiberon and the islet of Er Yoh at the north-east tip of Houat Island (Fig. 4.1).

The **Camp du Lizo** is an enclosure site built on a granite promontory which overlooks the valley of the river Crac'h in the north-west of the district of Carnac. Research carried out by Z. Le Rouzic between 1922 and 1933 (Le Rouzic 1933) and the recent excavations carried out by Y. Lecerf in 1982 (Lecerf, 1986), have revealed a defensive system of double ramparts which encloses an area of about 2 hectares (100×180m). The quadrangular plan of the enclosure is curved on its northern side, which follows the natural profile of the promontory. Sections recently cut through the rampart have shown the existence of a palisade erected on top of the inner bank. Inside the camp, besides the existence of a passage grave under its mound, Z. Le Rouzic indicates and describes many structures. To these he attributes

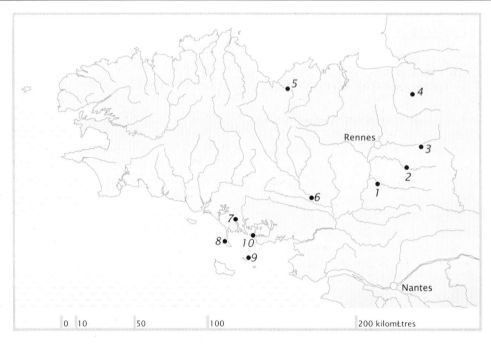

Fig. 4.1: location of settlement sites mentioned in Brittany.

1: Plechâtel, La Hersonnais, 2: Boistrudan, La Trappe, 3: Saint-Aubin- des- Landes, La Charronière, 4: Saint- Étienne -en – Coglès, Le Haut- Mée, 5: Lamballe, Le Val Aubin, 6: Saint- Laurent-sur-Oust, Beaumont, 7: Carnac, Le Lizo, 8: Saint- Pierre- Quiberon, Croh- Collé, 9: Ile de Houat, Er Yoh, 10: Arzon, Bilgroix.

either a domestic role (hut remains, ovens, hearths, etc.) or a funerary role (mounds) but their interpretation remains uncertain. The large quantity of material collected during each excavation is principally dated from the late and final Neolithic, with an especially heavy representation of Croh-Collé and Kerugou ceramic styles.

The **Croh-Collé** headland site on the peninsula of St-Pierre-Quiberon is a typical example of a seacliff promontory fort, violently attacked by the sea and wind erosion. A defensive bank 40m long and 2m high encloses an area no larger than ½ hectare. The rampart and the inner area were explored by Z Le Rouzic at the beginning of the century and restored in 1932. A double facing of upright stone slabs each side of an earthen bank was recognised in the defensive structure. The massive bank covered an axial structure of about 1m×2m in area, built of vertical stones and considered to be a dolmen. The large quantity of material collected from these excavations has rendered this promontory the eponymous site of the Croh Collé culture of the Armorican Late Neolithic (Bailloud 1975; Lejards 1964).

The **Er Yoh** site is also largely eroded by the sea due to its position as a rocky islet detached from the northeast tip of Houat Island in the Morbihan. Described for the first time in 1883, the islet was the subject of archaeological explorations between 1923 and 1925 by Z. Le Rouzic and his team (Le Rouzic 1930). The recorded observations show similar structures to those of the above-mentioned sites. According to the team's observations, the natural topography of the islet may

have been used to create small settlement structures. Most of them were of dry stone construction. A structure built from larger stones could be a defensive element. The Er Yoh site is particularly noted for the density and quality of its material, especially for the exceptional preservation of bone, antler and shell artefacts due to the effects of the coastal dune sand which reduces the usual acidity of the Breton soil.

Information collected from this early research in the south of Brittany is consistent, despite many inaccuracies attributable to methods still in their infancy at that time. First of all, the large quantity of collected material shows that these sites were mainly occupied during the late and final Neolithic, essentially between the end of the 4th millennium and the first half of the 3rd millennium. The pottery is representative of the Croh Collé, Conguel and Kerugou cultures which were well-established in the south of Brittany. The topographical situation of these sites indicates the desire for protection from outside attacks. The natural features of the selected site are reinforced by defensive structures, even if they are poor. Analysis of the inner structure of settlements remains more hypothetical, limited by contemporary knowledge and methods. Nevertheless, the evidence points towards small dry-stone structures, often adjoining the rampart or a natural feature of the site, as at Er Yoh. The existence of a funerary component within the settlement is also a constant feature of these sites either as a structured megalithic monument integrated within the site, or as scattered remains.

RECENT RESEARCH : THE SITE OF BEAUMONT, IN SAINT-LAURENT-SUR-OUST (MORBIHAN)

From 1986 to 1988, excavations to rescue a lateral entrance gallery grave dating to the final Neolithic led to the discovery of a contemporary settlement. The study of this site, carried out from 1988 to 1992, revived regional research on this subject (Tinevez 1988 & 1992). There are close analogies between this site and those recorded earlier. However, its establishment inland differs from the coastal position of the previous sites.

To the south of Saint-Laurent-sur-Oust, about twenty kilometres from the coast as the crow flies, lies the natural promontory of Beaumont. Oriented east-west, it is an ideal defensive site with steep slopes, more than 70m above the Oust valley. The bedrock is composed of weathered schist, with a bed of hard Armorican sandstone forming the ridge. The settlement site is located on the south and south-east promontory edge, at about thirty metres south of the gallery grave. Despite the thick forest vegetation, an area of about 500m² was totally explored. The settlement is clearly delimited by a bank one metre high and 10 metres wide at the base. It is only barely noticeable for 70 metres of its length on top of the southern slope. It is composed of a central core of vertical sandstone and quartz blocks, against which a mixture of earth and schist slabs was piled. Internally the bank is edged by two rows of packing stones in a small foundation trench. These mark the location of two light palisades put up parallel to the bank and reinforced by it at their bases. The stratigraphy (poorly preserved as a result of soil erosion) does not tell us whether we are dealing with two contemporary palisades or with repair work. The distribution of material, especially the numerous pottery sherds in this area, clearly demonstrates the enclosure function of this bank-palisade system. The area thus enclosed is about 1.5 hectares, stretching as far as the end of the natural promontory.

In the eastern part of the promontory, where it is most accessible from the plateau, the defensive bank fades into the landscape. However, a broken line of double post-holes could form some kind of entry-system to the plateau, affording only a narrow throughway which could easily be blocked.

Internally, near the bank, several dug features indicate some domestic occupation in this zone. Well-packed post holes from 0.40 to 0.60m in depth are placed every 2.50m. These are aligned parallel to the palisade and 3m north of it. They form the façade of a small building 3m wide. An 8m length was identified of this structure, which was built against the site fence. Some fragments of wattle and daub discovered near the façade give an insight into the nature of the walls. An alignment of three smaller packing stones perpendicular to the axis of the building probably indicates the existence of a light transverse partition. The eroded remains of small-scale packing, shallow depressions with burnt edges and small ditches represent the last traces of various activities in the area excavated in front of this building.

The existence of domestic activity is confirmed by the distribution of Neolithic material with a heavy concentration along the palisade and particularly within the area of the building.

Ceramics with characteristics clearly dating to the final Neolithic of southern Brittany are most strongly represented amongst the archaeological material, despite erosion and high soil acidity. Small and thin walled vessels are associated with large, thick-walled examples. The fabrics are generally coarse, with various inclusions, and irregularly fired. The forms range from hemispherical bowls and vessels with high carinations to large vessels with vertical walls and flat bases. Ornamentation is rare but vessels with multiperforated rims are common. The lithic material on the site includes equal quantities of imported flint and local substitutes, especially Armorican sandstone which was extracted at the site itself.

The tools found are characteristic of the regional late-final Neolithic with, for example, a combination of trapezoidal tranchet arrowheads and fairly crude barbed and tanged arrowheads. These tools are essentially made on irregular flakes producing mostly small and thick scrapers. Blade elements are rare. Several flakes come from polished flint axes. This shows how often these imported tools were re-used.

The common features, both ceramic and lithic, of these sites show a chronological connection between the collective gallery grave and the nearby settlement site. This is one of the interesting elements of the Beaumont site. This funerary component associated with a settlement was also recognised at the site on the headland of Bilgroix in Arzon (Morbihan) during recent research (Lecornec 1996).

Thus, the Neolithic occupation at Beaumont represents a shift inland of the kind of site revealed by early research in the coastal area.

The characteristics of these sites are as follows:

- a particular choice of site and a system of defences.
- small domestic structures built against the bank/fence.
- similar ceramic and lithic material and a close link to funerary activity.

Recent advances following aerial survey

Aerial survey has been the driving force behind significant progress in the location of archaeological sites and the investigation of settlement over huge areas for many years due to a favourable period at the end of the 1980s. If most of the information concerns more recent periods and the Iron Age in particular, this method has also been beneficial to the Neolithic and notably to the regional late Neolithic.

Some examples of causewayed enclosures:

Aerial surveys make it possible to identify numerous enclosures, some of which date back to the Neolithic.

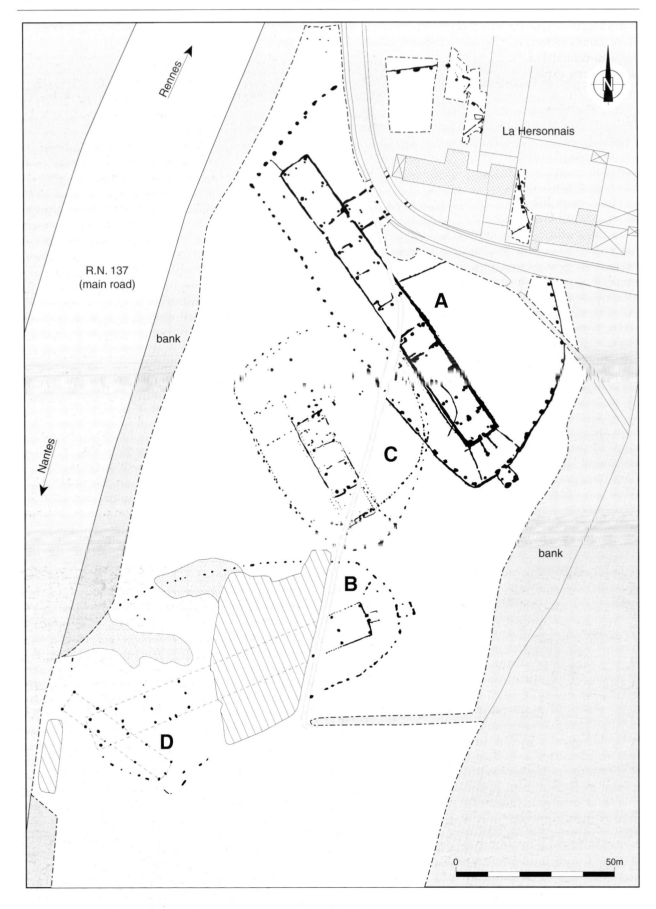

Fig. 4.2: Pléchâtel – La Hersonnais (Ille-et-Vilaine, France): general plan of the neolithic settlement with the four buildings and their enclosures; A to the north, B and D to the south, C in the centre.

Indeed, their morphology is similar to the great number of enclosures known in neighbouring regions and notably the west-central France. However, none of these sites has yet been explored. Only three sites discovered in 1989 have been published (Fig. 4.1).

At **Val Aubin**, in the district of Lamballe (Côtes d'Armor), a ditch forming an arc partially surrounds a triangular promontory overlooking a small river. This markedly curved ditch has several gaps in it. The area including the tip of the promontory is no larger than one hectare (Langouët 1990).

Two sites in Ille-et-Vilaine are more similar to the central western French enclosures (Leroux 1992).

At the locality of **La Trappe** at **Boistrudan**, two concentric ditches demarcate an oval area on the edge of a plateau above the steep slope of a valley. Several gaps in the ditches are visible to the south as well as a large opening to the west. The enclosed area is around 1.20ha. The lithic material collected after a ground survey dates to the Neolithic period.

The enclosure with two concentric ditches of the locality of **La Charronière** at **Saint-Aubin-des-Landes**, with a similar shape and topographical position on the edge of the plateau, is much more extensive with an area larger than 3ha. Many gaps are also visible in the internal and external ditches but they do not really coincide.

The preliminary information on these three sites indicates some coherence between their topographical situation, enclosed area and morphology. But, unlike the hilltop sites described before, there is no evidence of their defensive nature.

The site of La Hersonnais at Pléchâtel (Ille-et-Vilaine)

Due to a long period of drought, 1989 was an exceptional year for carrying out aerial surveys. The discovery of the site of La Hersonnais transformed our regional vision of Neolithic settlement, given the extent of the remains and their original nature.

The hamlet of La Hersonnais is situated on the south-eastern edge of the district of Pléchâtel, less than 30km south of the city of Rennes, towards Nantes. In 1989, the first aerial photographs revealed, with remarkable clearness, the edge of a huge building. The information was quickly spread (Leroux 1992). The first exploratory excavations confirmed that this site dates to the late Neolithic, and show dug features of exceptional dimensions. Between 1992 and 1999, the exhaustive and extensive study of the site was carried out within an area of about 4ha thanks to favourable access conditions.

The topographical environment chosen by the Neolithic builders is a narrow plateau with a very flat and regular relief 50m above sea-level. This natural platform overlooks a wetland zone to the east. The platform is bounded by a deep valley to the west, and the whole is dominated by a hill 100m high. The settlement was thus established on the western edge of the plateau in a very flat and dry area, but next to a small valley giving access to water. Unlike the sites described before, the topography of the place has no defensive nature. On the contrary, the choice of an open area overlooked by a hill seems to indicate that the settlement was intended to be seen from a great distance, in keeping with the ostenta-

Fig. 4.3: Pléchâtel – La Hersonnais (Ille-et-Vilaine, France): aerial view of the site from the east. In the foreground, the monumental entrances of buildings A and B.

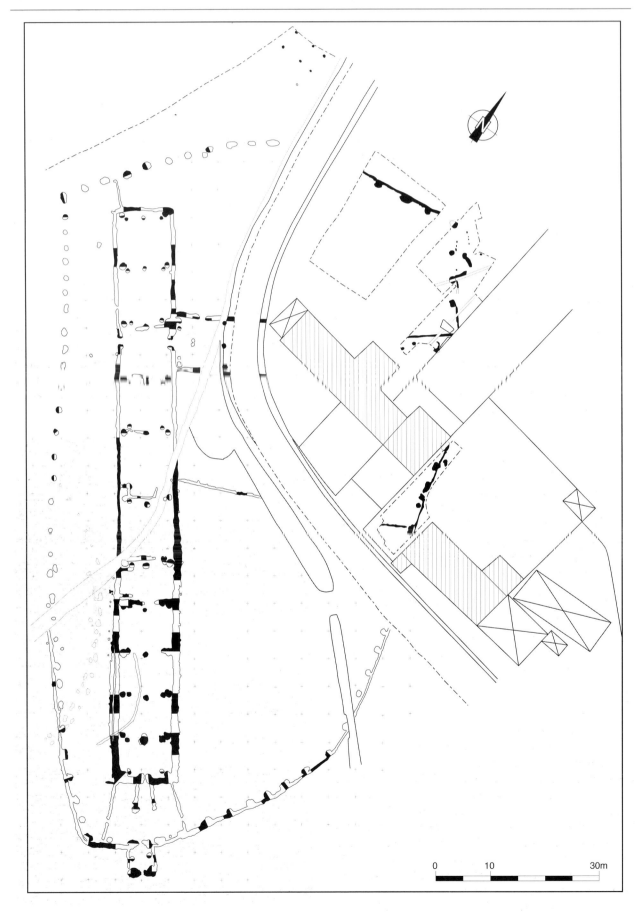

Fig. 4.4: Pléchâtel – La Hersonnais (Ille-et-Vilaine, France): general plan of structure A comprising a long building, a north lateral wing (most under the present hamlet) and the enclosure. Excavated structures shown in black.

tious character of the extremely large buildings.

Over the whole site, the bedrock consists of schist fissured at the surface, but sound and resistant to excavation, except for a few rare areas which are more weathered, in particular at the centre and the north edge of the plateau. The Neolithic occupation levels are not preserved due to previous road works and ploughing. All that remains are the foundations of wooden structures. It was generally difficult to locate remains because of the similar nature of the prehistoric fills and the natural bedrock. Meticulous cleaning of the bedrock was necessary over the whole surface of the site. More than 500 dug features are scattered over a total area of around 3 hectares. These were read as four coherent sites capable of individual study. There is a noticeable lack of pits, grain silos, quarries, burials or any other excavation. Moreover, archaeological interpretation is made easier by the fact the site had not been disturbed during recent times. The hard nature of the bedrock in which the foundations have been dug has resulted in good preservation of the fills. So, the near-systematic detection of the wooden structures (posts, palisades, walls, etc.) is possible either from the dark traces left after the wood had rotted, or from burnt remains.

Four distinct structural groups appear clearly on the general plan of the site and are named A to D in order of discovery (Figs 4.2 and 4.3).

Structure A: (Figs 4.4 and 4.5)

Building A and its enclosure mark the northern limit of the prehistoric site. On a north-west/south-east axis, this structure is situated on the edge of the plateau, the slope of which becomes more pronounced towards the north and west in the direction of the stream.

It was the southeastern end of this building which originally drew attention to the site from the air, due to the deeply dug features favourable to crop marks. Extensive cleaning to the rocky substratum revealed the almost complete plan of a huge building. Its regular, rectangular outline, 102m long by 12m wide, has a flanking wing. A relative chronology of the construction of the various parts of the house can be drawn thanks to the good preservation of the trench fills and their inter-sections.

The three-post supports

Twelve series of three post holes each divide the house internally into eleven modules, the length of which varies from 7m at the south-eastern end to 12.50m in the centre and 10m at the north-west. On the longitudinal axis, the three lines of post holes line up perfectly despite the length of the building. The diameter of lateral post holes varies from 1.20 to 1.50m. They are dug from 1.70m to 1.90m into the schist. The regularity of depth over the whole length of the house shows the builders' desire to give a precise evenness to the main foundations. From the dark traces marking the location of the wooden members, the diameter of the lateral posts varies between 0.40 and 0.50m. They are placed upright and are not

pointed. The distance between the posts is around 8.50m. The central post holes are less massive than the lateral (diameter between 1m and 1.40m, depth from 1.30 to 1.40m). The diameter of the posts is also smaller (0.25 to 0.30m). Towards the east they are noticeably out of line compared with the lateral posts. This disposition is too regular and general to be fortuitous. It can be interpreted as a technical adjustment, making it possible to tie a transverse timber to the central post to support the ridgepole.

The lateral walls

A U- shaped foundation trench 0.80m wide and cut on average 0.80m deep in the schist marks the house plan as a long rectangle. The schist fill, similar to that of the post holes, reveals the traces of a continuous wall composed sometimes of planks, sometimes of logs. It is reinforced approximately every metre by posts of around 0.20m diameter. In several places, this wall is partially preserved as burnt wood showing the violent destruction of the house by fire. Similarly, in the northern trench, several pieces of burnt posts and planks have been collected. However, the absence of burnt clay in the foundations could indicate a wall entirely composed of

Fig. 4.5: Pléchâtel – La Hersonnais (Ille-et-Vilaine, France): aerial view of structure A from the north – west.

wooden members. The intersection of the foundation fill with that of the lateral post holes, particularly in the corners of the house, shows that the peripheral trench was dug after installation of the supporting posts.

The openings

This trench has three gaps: an axial one on the eastern gable and the others opposite each other in the north-east quarter of the main building. These gaps mark three entrances with similar characteristics. The openings, the width of which ranges from 1m to 1.50m, are flanked with either single or double uprights erected in an oval pit set slightly back within the house. The eastern entrance is equipped with a 5m long porch supported by four small posts at the corners.

The internal walls

Deep, narrow trenches indicate the position of internal walls creating five modules in the centre of the building. These walls, of variable length, form passages of varied width between the rooms. Their layout, sometimes complex, suggests internal fittings such as small recesses or structures giving means to the roof timbers. Traces of decayed timbers show again the use of planks in some cases. The existence of inner walls reinforces the hypothesis of domestic units in the central part of the house and larger areas at the ends, with possibly complementary functions.

The secondary posts

The lateral supporting posts are consistently supplemented by additional posts; it can be demonstrated stratigraphically that these post-date the lateral posts and transverse walls. The nature of the fill of these secondary holes contrasts radically with the first ones. It is clear that they were installed in a building already occupied. This could possibly relate to reinforcement of the house frame or re-fitting of roof timbers.

The north lateral wing

The north-west opening gives onto a lateral wing, almost perpendicular to the main building. The foundations of this wing show similar techniques. The building frame is supported by rows of three posts and the side walls are provided with an identical bedding-trench. The junction with the main building is reinforced by the presence of two pairs of posts. An opening on the west wall allows passage to the outside. Mostly covered by the present-day village, the length of this wing can be estimated at between 40 and 50m based on the general plan, with a 10m width quite similar to that of the main building.

The palisaded enclosure (Fig. 4.6)

The first excavations revealed a series of oval pits a few metres away from the west gable. Further research shows the continuation of this series right round the building. Better preserved areas situated to the east and north-east allow us to reconstruct the process of building a sophisticated palisade.

First, a series of vertical supports, either a single post or two parallel squared beams, is put up in large pits two or three metres apart. Then these supports are linked together by a log palisade put up in a shallow V-profile trench. The structure was probably secured by a tie-beam

Fig. 4.6: Pléchâtel – La Hersonnais (Ille-et-Vilaine, France): view from the south – east of the eastern end of structure A. In the foreground, the monumental entrance to the enclosure.

system anchored to the vertical posts. This enclosure formed a huge half circle, distorted in its northern part. Its surface area was estimated at 0.75 ha. Three openings were discovered on its perimeter, two simple entrances on the northern side and a more complex entrance on the eastern side.

The eastern door is flanked on the outside by a building 5.5m square. It is supported by two lateral series of three posts. Because of the strength of these posts and of the facade posts, this may be a monumental door structure or even a tower, controlling access to the enclosure, in line with the building entrance. Moreover, the internal area of the enclosure was divided by several light palisades, thus creating a "lock area" between the eastern gable of the building and the monumental entrance of the enclosure.

Structure B (Fig. 4.7)

Structure B marks the southern limit of the excavated area. Its eastern end had been recognised during the first evaluations in 1992. The dimensions and characteristics of this building are similar to those of the previous one, but are much less well-preserved because of the destruction of the central area by a quarry and by marked weathering of the substratum in the western area. Its

Fig. 4.7: Pléchâtel – La Hersonnais (Ille-et-Vilaine, France): aerial view from the east of structure B. The central area of the building is destroyed by a quarry.

north-east / south-west orientation is quite different from the first building.

Supporting elements

The rectangular plan, 95 metres long by 11 metres wide, also includes several rows of three posts set across the width with a 9m span. In each row, the central post is consistently out of line with the two others towards the east as in building A, probably for similar technical reasons.

Lateral structures

The lateral walls, preserved only at the eastern end, differ from those of building A in the juxtaposition of medium-sized posts (0.20m in diameter), 0.30 to 0.50m apart. The presence of some daub fragments reinforces the hypothesis of a wattle wall on a vertical post framework.

Entrances

Two structures can be considered as entrances. Their position and characteristics are similar to those of the northern building. One is situated in an axial position on the eastern gable and the other one in a lateral position on the southern wall. They are between 1m and 1.20m wide. Their uprights are bedded in large oval pits, slightly inside the building. The eastern entrance is also sheltered by a small porch (3 × 3m) supported by four posts.

Palisaded enclosure

In this area, the extensive excavations have also revealed a string of dug features disposed around the building. Despite the destruction of the central zone, an oval area 105m long and 55m wide is thus defined. Its surface area is over 0.45 ha. The foundations are shallower than those of the northern structure and only the main post pits survive. In this case, the structure appears to consist sometimes of single posts, sometimes of groups of 2 to 4 posts in the same long and narrow pit. At the eastern end, an opening reinforced by two deeper pits is flanked on the outside by a square building supported by six posts, similar to group A. A dividing structure can also be seen between the northeast corner of the building and the enclosure fence.

Structure C: (Fig. 4.8 and 4.9)

In spite of a substratum disturbed in some places and substantially levelled in the central part of the site, it is possible to define another enclosed rectangular building.

Supporting elements

The twelve post holes are strictly in line, arranged in six pairs 7.50 m apart. On the main axis, the distance between the pairs progressively increases from east to west from 6.50m to 9.50 m. Except for their shallower nature, the post holes are similar to those of the previous buildings. The important difference is the absence of a central post.

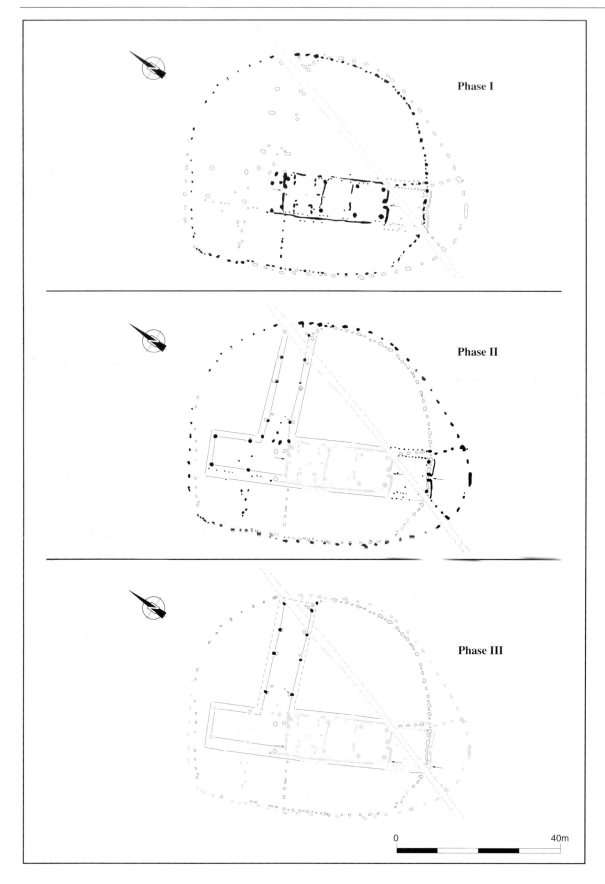

Fig. 4.8: Pléchâtel – La Hersonnais (Ille-et-Vilaine, France): the different phases of structure C. Phase I: a roomed building with enclosure. Phase II: extension from the gables, addition of a north transverse wing and second enclosure. Phase III: replacement of the supporting posts of the lateral wing.

Lateral structures

Because of their shallowness, the foundations of the lateral walls and the gables are poorly preserved, but take an unusual form: the small V-profile trench is edged by two alignments of small post holes laid out in staggered rows 0.50m either side of the trench. The hypothesis of a wall composed of a wooden central frame reinforced with small lateral posts seems to be the most plausible. The base of the wall is 1.50m wide. This hypothetical reconstruction assumes that the material (earth, turf…?) filling the spaces between the wooden structures is not preserved in this type of soil.

A structure built in several phases (Fig. 4.8)

Unlike structures A and B which seem to have been built in a single phase, a detailed study of the architecture shows several expansion phases of the building and its enclosure. Thus, the intersection of the eastern gable and the internal enclosure palisade indicates an expansion of the building to the east. In the same way, after an expansion to the west, a northern transverse wing was built having a plan identical to that of building A. This wing was further modified. Study of the horizontal and vertical stratigraphy suggests the following phases of construction:

Phase I: a primary rectangular building (27m long and 11,50m wide) was built on four pairs of supporting posts. Each well-marked gable presents an axial entrance. Internal walls with light foundations divide the building into three equal-sized rooms, with a surface area of about 100 m². Traces of rectangular seat or bed type fittings can be seen along the lateral walls of the western room.

The internal enclosure belongs to this first phase. This is partitioned by a palisade running between the north-east corner and the eastern fence.

Phase II: the main feature of the second phase is the extension of the building beyond the gables. Two modules were added to the west and one to the east, this new gable standing on the line of the first enclosure. With this addition, the building is 56m long and exactly repeats an eastern gable with axial entrance.

Aside from a 10m extension to the front of the eastern entrance, this second phase is completed by a restoration of the peripheral fence following a plan similar to the previous one. One noticeable feature which is a constant architectural characteristic of this site is the reproduction of partitions between the corners of the building and the palisade. As for the previous groups A and B, a more substantial structure marks the main entrance into the enclosure in front of the eastern gable entrance.

The creation of a lateral wing running north from the west extension could also belong to this phase. This 27m long wing, supported by four pairs of posts, runs up to the northern part of the enclosure. The 5.50m gap between the supporting posts is slightly less than for the main building. A palisade links its north-east corner to the enclosure.

Fig. 4.9: Pléchâtel – La Hersonnais (Ille-et-Vilaine, France): view from the east of structure C. In the foreground, the phase II enclosure. Centre, the east gable of building C of phases II and I.

Phase III: the transverse wing is also transformed by the substitution of the supporting posts by two alignments with a wider gap between. The intersection of the adjacent post-pits shows clearly the relative chronology of the two phases, while the second series has yielded more cultural material by reason of its sealing the occupation soil of the previous phase. As the surface area gained by this alteration is quite small, the hypothesis of a complete restoration of this wing is the most plausible.

The relative dating of structures A and structure C

The northern sector of the enclosure belonging to structure C and the south-eastern sector of that belonging to structure A are superposed and the intersection of several features shows that enclosure C cuts enclosure A. If we admit that each building is contemporary with the enclosure which surrounds it, building A predates the various phases of building C.

Structure D

At the south-western corner of the site, several post holes overlap building B but are not part of it. Their distribution

Fig. 4.10: Pléchâtel – La Hersonnais (Ille-et-Vilaine, France): aerial view from the south – east. In the foreground, eastern entrances of structures A, B and C.

In five pairs, spaced at 6m intervals and with from 8 to 9m between the rows, gives the plan of a rectangular building whose dimensions can be estimated at 40m long and about 10m wide. Despite the poor state of preservation and the absence of peripheral elements, it seems that building D is of a similar type to building C in dimensions and arrangement of the supporting elements.

However, because of the absence of intersecting features, it is not possible to establish the chronological relationship between structures B and D.

The finds
The occupation soils having been destroyed across the whole site, only a small quantity of cultural material survives, which comes exclusively from the fills of the below-ground features. As the soil is highly acidic, the preservation conditions are very unfavourable to perishable materials, except for a few rare bone fragments and charred seeds.

One of the surprising characteristics of La Hersonnais is its great dearth of lithics, especially flint. In spite of fine sieving of the sediments, only a few dozen pieces have been collected and tools are rare. It was only possible to record the presence of a few scrapers and fragments of retouched blades. This thin density might be explained by the manufacture and use of flint tools in areas far away from the buildings.

However, the below-ground structures yielded abundant heavy stone tools made from natural tablets or blocks of Armorican sandstone, of which there are many scattered on the ground on the hill overlooking the site to the west. These tools were reused as packing around the wooden members, and almost all have been flaked at the edges to improve grip, and bear traces of wear and sharpening at the ends. They were clearly used as picks to dig the foundations. Experiments with similar tools on the local bedrock were conclusive. These tools were held in the hand, and had no handles.

Most of the material is represented by ceramics, the characteristics of which are very homogeneous over the whole site. The general poor preservation of the pottery results from contemporary activity in the settlement, the natural acidity of the soil and the poor technology of Armorican late Neolithic ceramics. The pottery is highly fragmentary, frequently weathered, and joins are rare.

From the shapes which it is possible to reconstruct, three basic types can be distinguished: large storage vessels with thick vertical walls and flat bases, often with marked rims, small hemispherical bowls, and bi-conical vessels thinner walled, with high, more or less marked carinations and slightly flattened bases.

Decoration is rare, and appears in this last vessel group. It consists exclusively of incisions, always made before firing on the upper part of the vessel. The most frequent elements are horizontal broken lines, or more rarely oblique strokes, or three irregular rows of isosceles triangles. Handles of any sort are rare, and are restricted to one boss and two lugs.

Morphologically, typologically and technologically, the ceramics of the whole site fit perfectly into the regional late-final Neolithic range. The closest parallels, in shape and decoration, are found in the Conguel and Croh-Collé styles, discovered during early excavations on the Quiberon peninsula.

Radiocarbon dating, charcoal and dendrochronology
A series of nine dates was obtained on charcoal samples from the foundation structures of the three main groups A, B and C. In each group, two were taken from the building and one from the peripheral enclosure.

Group A:
A – building: ① Gif-9119: 4070±50 BP (2865-2466 cal BC)
                 ② Gif-9647: 4290±50 BP (3035-2698 cal BC)
A – enclosure: ③ Gif-10880: 4255±50 BP (3015-2625 cal BC)

Group B:
B – building: ④ Gif-9904: 4090±50 BP (2869-2484 cal BC)
                 ⑤ Gif-9905: 4070±50 BP (2865- 2466 cal BC)
B – enclosure   ⑥ Gif-10881: 4005±45 BP (2619-2400 cal BC)

Group C
C – building   ⑦ Gif-10882: 4030±25 BP (2585-2469 cal BC)
                 ⑧ Gif-10884: 4150±50 BP (2878-2585 cal BC)
                 ⑨ Gif-10883: 3490±80 BP (2025-1543 cal BC)

Except for sample 9 from building C, for which the far later date must result from contamination of the soil, the whole (calibrated) group of dates falls within the first half of the third millennium. These dates are confirmed by the ceramic material.

Moreover, a study of the various charcoal samples taken from the sites has emphasised the use of oak wood, sometimes associated with willow, hazel and holly.

A dendrochronological study is also being carried out and the first results confirm the radiocarbon datings.

Radiocarbon calibrations are based on Stuiver and Reimer 1993; Pearson and Stuiver 1993 and Stuiver and Pearson 1993.

CONCLUSION: THE IMPORTANCE OF LA HERSONNAIS IN ITS REGIONAL CONTEXT AND IN WESTERN FRANCE

After eight years of research, the site of La Hersonnais offers a new vision of the Neolithic during the third millennium in western France. This extensive study, the first in Brittany of a site of this period, shows the size of these architectural complexes, their homogeneity, and the fact that they were occupied over a long period, demonstrated by the sequence of overlapping structural groups of known extent. The absence of later disturbance and the structural layout make it possible to redraw the plan for each building, putting each one in its respective enclosure. From this, four different units appear, with clear common features. These constant features are the regular rectangular plan, and the 10–12m width of the buildings. The position and structure of the entrances are similar for the three best preserved groups. Groups A and C both have a lateral extension. Consistency in architectural tradition is also shown by the way in which each building is closely integrated within its enclosure, notably in the repetition of dividing fences between the eastern gable and the enclosure, and the monumental entrance in the eastern part of the enclosure lining up with the door of the building.

In the same way, the cultural link between these four buildings is attested by the radiocarbon datings, and the homogeneity of the archaeological material.

The excavations show the overlapping of some buildings, which is not compatible with contemporaneous occupation, and in fact demonstrate that group A predates group C. The chronological succession of different units on the same site is matched by a progressive change in architecture towards lighter construction. For example, the overall size and depth of the foundation structures progressively diminish from A to C, without any changes in topographic and technical constraints. In the timber framework, the central post supporting the roof-beam in groups A and B disappears in groups C and D. The progressive improvement in construction techniques and the relative chronology shown by the intersecting dug features seem to indicate successive settlements whose chronology would appear to go from group A to D.

Because of the lack of preservation of the occupation levels, the function of these buildings remains hypothetical, particularly considering the exceptional dimensions of the largest ones. However, domestic use of these buildings may be suggested by certain criteria: the internal organisation of buildings A and C, the peripheral enclosures and their internal divisions suitable for various activities such as stockbreeding and agriculture, and the large storage vessels side by side with smaller ones.

While they are not truly defensive, the size and imposing architecture of these structures points to ostentation, the sign of a social structure developed by a large population well-adapted to its environment.

The archaeological material, particularly the ceramics, fits perfectly into the Armorican late and final Neolithic; however, this type of monumental architecture is unusual in the region. It contrasts strongly with our knowledge of the settlements of this period, which usually consists of smaller structures. Topographically, the choice of site at La Hersonnais also differs from the other promontory sites previously known. These differences may indicate a wide range and a great potential in this region for late Neolithic settlement, the study of which is still in its early stages. The architectural complexes at La Hersonnais are unique in Brittany, but may be compared with others in a large area of west-central France. Over the last few years, several sites have been revealed- by new interpretation of existing data, as in the case of La Croix Verte, Antran [Pautreau 1994], or by aerial detection as in the case of Les Chavis, Vouillé [Ollivier 1994], or by extensive excavations at La Tricherie, Beaumont [Louboutin 1997, 1998], Le Fief Beaudoin, Airvault [Champème 1998], Le Camp, Challignac [Burnez 1995, 1997], Beauclair, Douchapt [Fouéré 1998] and Les Vaux, Moulins-sur-Céphons [Krausz 1995].

As for the site of Pléchâtel, radiocarbon dating and archaeological material, most of which belongs to the Artenac culture, place the occupation of these sites in the third millennium. The monumental aspect of the buildings differs radically from our previous knowledge of settlement at the end of the Neolithic period, which was drawn from data collected in eastern and southern parts of France. The control of lateral thrust in a tall and heavy framework where the building width is an impressive 10–18m shows considerable technical skill. One of the constant features is the long rectangular plan, even if Antran-type buildings (Antran, Vouillé and Douchapt) have more rounded corners. Another common feature is the presence, when it is possible to reconstruct its plan, of a peripheral enclosure with internal divisions. This division of the space inside the enclosure and control of movement between the building and its enclosure is particularly evident at Pléchâtel and the Antran-type structures.

These common features should not hide considerable local variations, in both architecture and material culture. The main distinguishing feature at La Hersonnais is the presence of lateral supporting posts, replaced in other buildings by supporting walls, even in wider buildings such as those of the Antran type. This is also true of wider buildings of Antran type. This feature may show some archaism in the building techniques used at Pléchâtel.

These large wooden Neolithic buildings bring to mind the many ethnographic studies of geographically and culturally diverse societies. The structure and nature of those societies living in large collective buildings open up new possibilities in the exploration of the social relations of prehistoric communities occupying the same type of settlement.

Acknowledgment

Thanks are due to E. Nicolas, M. Batt, A. Rondeau, B. Gruzon, M. Dupré for revising this article and the illustrations.

Note

1. Service Régional de l'Archéologie de Bretagne. U.M.R. 6566 "Civilisations atlantiques et Archéosciences".

BIBLIOGRAPHY.

Bailloud, G. 1975. Les céramiques " cannelées " du Néolithique armoricain. *Bulletin de la Société Préhistorique Française*, 72, pp. 343–367.

Burnez, C., Dassié, J. and Sicaud, F. 1995. L'enceinte artenacienne du "Camp" à Challignac (Charente). *Bulletin de la Société Préhistorique Française*, tome 92, n° 4, pp. 463–478.

Cassen, S. 1998 and al. L'habitat Villeneuve Saint-Germain (Haute-Loire) (Saint-Étienne 88 ?) ... *Bulletin de la Société Préhistorique Française*, 95/1, p. 41–75.

Champême, L.-M. 1998. Le bâtiment sur poteaux du Fief Baudoin (Airvault, Deux-Sèvres). In *Le Néolithique du Centre-Ouest de la France*. Actes du XXIᵉ Colloque interrégional sur le Néolithique, Poitiers, pp. 297–306.

Fouéré, P. 1998. Deux grands bâtiments du Néolithique final artenacien à Douchapt (Dordogne). In: d'Anna A et Binder D – *Production et identité culturelle, actualité de la recherche*. Rencontres méridionales de Préhistoire récente, actes de la 2ᵉᵐᵉ session, Arles, 1996. Antibes, édition APDCA, pp. 311–328.

Krausz, S. and Constantin, C. 1995. Un site d'habitat de la culture d'Artenac à Moulins-sur-Céphons (Indre). *Bulletin de la Société Préhistorique Française*, tome 92, n° 3, pp. 346–352.

Langouët, L. and Andlauer, L. 1990. Les structures archéologiques découvertes en 1989 dans le nord de la Haute-Bretagne. *Les Dossiers du Ce.RAA*, M, 1990, pp. 21–36.

Lecerf, Y. 1986. Une nouvelle intervention archéologique au Camp du Lizo en Carnac (Morbihan). *Revue archéologique de l'Ouest*, 3, pp. 47–58.

Lecornec, J. 1996. L'allée couverte de Bilgroix, Arzon (Morbihan). *Bulletin de la Société Polymathique du Morbihan*, 1996, pp. 15–64.

Lejards, J. 1964. Eperon barré du Croh-Collé en Saint-Pierre-Quiberon (analogies avec l'éperon barré du Coh-Castel en Hoëdic). *Bulletin de la Société Polymathique du Morbihan*, compte-rendu de la 1270ᵉ séance, 1963, pp. 33–34.

Leroux, G. 1992. Découverte de structures d'habitats néolithiques dans le bassin oriental de la Vilaine: l'apport de la prospection aérienne dans le sud-est de l'Ille-et-Vilaine. *Revue Archéologique de l'Ouest*, supplément n° 5, 1992, pp. 79–83.

Le Rouzic, Z. 1930. Carnac. Fouilles faites dans la région. Ilot de Er-Yoh (Le Mulon). Commune de Houat, 1930, Vannes, pp. 1–15.

Le Rouzic, Z. 1933. Premières fouilles au Camp du Lizo. La Revue Archéologique, Librairie Ernest Leroux, Paris, pp. 189–219.

Louboutin, C., Ollivier, A., Constantin, C., Sidera, I., Tresset, A. and Farrugia, J.-P. 1998. La Tricherie, Beaumont (Vienne): un site d'habitat du Néolithique récent. In: *Le Néolithique du Centre-Ouest de la France*. Actes du XXIᵉ Colloque Interrégional sur le Néolithique, Poitiers, pp. 307–326.

Louboutin, C., Burnez, C., Constantin, C. and Sidera, I. 1997. Beaumont – La Tricherie (Vienne) et Challignac (Charente): deux sites d'habitat de la fin du Néolithique. *Antiquités Nationales*, 29, pp. 49–64.

Ollivier, A., Pautreau, J.-P. 1994. Une construction de type Antran: les Chavis à Vouillé. *Bulletin de la Société Préhistorique Française*, 91, 6, nov–déc 1994, pp. 420–421.

Pautreau, J.-P. 1994. Le grand bâtiment d'Antran (Vienne): une nouvelle attribution chronologique. *Bulletin de la Société Préhistorique Française*, tome 91, n° 6.

Polles, R. 1985. Les vases à bord perforé du Néolithique final armoricain. *Bulletin de la Société Préhistorique Française*, 82/7, pp. 218–224.

Polles, R. 1986. Le style de Conguel: nouveaux éléments. *Bulletin de la Société Préhistorique Française*, 83/11–12, pp. 452–469.

Tinevez, J.-Y. 1988. La sépulture à entrée latérale de Beaumont en Saint-Laurent-sur-Oust. *Revue Archéologique de l'Ouest*, 5, pp. 55–78.

Tinevez, J.-Y. 1992. Structures d'habitats du Néolithique et de l'Age du Bronze décelées récemment en Bretagne. In LE ROUX, dir. *Paysans et bâtisseurs. L'émergence du Néolithique atlantique et les origines du Mégalithisme*. Actes du XVIIᵉ Colloque Interrégional sur le Néolithique, Vannes, 1990. *Revue Archéologique de l'Ouest*, supplément n° 5, pp. 71–78.

Tinevez, J.-Y. 1995. La Hersonnais à Pléchâtel (Ille-et-Vilaine): un vaste ensemble du Néolithique final – Résultats préliminaires. In: *Le Néolithique récent et final dans le Bassin parisien et ses marges: état des recherches, essai de définition*. Actes du XXᵉ Colloque Interrégional sur le Néolithique, Evreux, 1993. *Revue Archéologique de l'Ouest*, supplément n° 7, pp. 293–318.

5. The neolithic enclosures of the Tavoliere, south-east Italy

Robin Skeates

INTRODUCTION

The ditched enclosures of the Tavoliere plain in south-east Italy were first identified by British reconnaissance pilots during the Second World War (Bradford & Williams-Hunt 1946; Bradford 1949; 1957), and their aerial photographs of them soon assumed a central place in representations of the Neolithic in the central Mediterranean region, and indeed in Europe. Now, half a century on, new ways of seeing and interpreting the ditched enclosures of the Tavoliere are required. Despite the significant contribution that aerial photography has made to the study of the archaeology of the Tavoliere, it is now high time to replace this bird's-eye view with the more 'down-to-earth' but also complex view of material depositional sequences formed at selected places in the landscape over time and space. The potential of this new approach to reveal new lines of enquiry is immediately evident at the more extensively excavated sites, such as Masseria Candelaro and Passo di Corvo, where a pattern of complex multi-period phases of site-formation emerges, in contrast to the deceptively simple and unified-looking plans of these sites' ditches when seen from the air. By paying due attention to these depositional sequences, it becomes evident that the ditched enclosure sites of the Tavoliere, like similar sites elsewhere in Europe, were never static finished entities: they were always in a dynamic accumulative process of construction and modification, excavation and deposition, and occupation and abandonment (cf. Evans 1988; Tilley 1996, 284). At the same time, new ways of interpreting the ditched enclosures of the Tavoliere are required. Despite the useful contributions of 'traditional' and 'processual' approaches, studies of population density, settlement form, subsistence economy, technology, and social organisation must be replaced by a more dynamic 'ethnographic' emphasis on social relations and social transformations, within which material culture (including ditches) played an active role.

This is, however, easier said than done, particularly considering the relatively poor quality of the published excavation data currently available. For example, few of the excavation reports provide clear and detailed records of excavated features and deposits; only relatively small areas have been investigated at even the most extensively excavated sites; and insufficiently numerous and accurate radiocarbon samples have been obtained from any of the excavated deposits to provide anything but a coarse-grained chronology.

THE SOCIAL DYNAMICS OF ENCLOSURE

Given both these aspirations and these limitations, my intention for this paper is therefore to focus attention on those archaeological contexts that can be reliably dated using the radiocarbon method. (Details of these contexts, including their radiocarbon determinations and primary bibliographic references, are provided in Table 5.1, below.) This obviously excludes many sites, but at the same time it does enable the analysis of a more reliable and detailed chronological sequence for the earlier Neolithic of the sixth millennium cal BC on the Tavoliere. Furthermore, some new and interesting patterns in the data emerge as a result. To this core sequence I have added two essential 'before and after' sections: one on the preceding Mesolithic of the eighth and seventh millennia cal BC, the other on the successive later Neolithic of the fifth and fourth millennia cal BC.

8000–6000 cal BC

Evidence of indigenous people leading a mesolithic, specialised gatherer-fisher-hunter lifestyle in the southern Adriatic region does exist, particularly along the coasts; but it is sparse, and, on the Tavoliere plain, it is perhaps even non-existent (e.g. Whitehouse 1968, 351, 353–4; Barker 1985, 72; Lewthwaite 1986, 64; Chapman & Müller 1990; Biagi 1996, 17, 22; Pluciennik 1994, 55). At the same time, however, it is possible that the southern Adriatic region formed one large but environmentally- and culturally- unified 'interaction zone', throughout which small human groups belonging to a seasonally mobile, boat-using, low-density population exploited a variety of coastal and maritime resources, at the same time as maintaining sizeable social networks of kin-based

Table 5.1: Absolute chronology for the Neolithic of the Tavoliere.

^{14}C sample context	^{14}C sample	cal BC	Associated (traditional) decorated ceramic styles	References
6000–5750 cal BC				
Masseria Giuffreda, Ditch G	MC-2292 7125±200 BP Charcoals	1 [6188](5967)5734 2 [6389]-5585 cal BC	Impressed (fingernail, stick, rocker – 'Archaic')	Simone 1977–82, 160; 1981; Guilaine *et al.* 1981, 155–6
Scaramella S. Vito, Villaggio A, Sounding I, outer ditch, spit 6 (bottom)	R-350 7000±100 BP Charcoal	1 5959(5929,5913, 5849,5816,5813)5711 2 [6067]-5629 cal BC	Impressed & painted	Alessio *et al.* 1969, 486
5750–5500 cal BC				
Ripa Tetta, Area B cobbling, Sectors IN, HN, IM & HM	Beta-47808/ Cams-2681 6890±60 BP Carbonised cereal grains	1 5827(5700)5604 2 5942–5580 cal BC	'Advanced' impressed (finger, point, *Cardium*, rocker – 'Guadone'), incised, & proto-*figulina*	Tozzi & Verola 1991, 47–8; Giampietri *et al.* 1996
Coppa Nevigata, ditch, strata 6-7 (bottom)	OxA-1475 6880±90 BP Carbonised *Hordeum* grains	1 5765(5681)5600 2 5935–5525 cal BC	'Archaic' impressed (finger, stick, point) & 1 sherd impressed/painted	Manfredini 1987, 51; Hedges *et al.* 1989, 226; Whitehouse 1994, 86–7
Coppa Nevigata, ditch, CN II/III (lip)	OxA-1474 6850±80 BP Carbonised grains	1 5797(5726,5722, 5707)5674 Cal 2 5936–5599 cal BC	Impressed (more frequent *Cardium*, 1 sherd 'Guadone'), 1 sherd *figulina*	Hedges *et al.* 1989, 226; Whitehouse 1994, 86–7
Villa Comunale, ditch A (sounding 1), level 8 (spit 14)	MC-2291 6780±70 BP Charcoals & carbonised grains	1 5826(5597)5440 2 [6054]-5268 cal BC	Impressed (fingernail, point, rocker – 'Archaic'), incised (intersecting lines), painted (red lines forming trellis, fish-spine & angular bands 'La Quercia'; red broad bands; white broad bands), 5% *figulina*	Simone 1977–82, 145–8; Guilaine *et al.* 1981, 156
Lagnano da Piede, ditch F-1, Layers 5–7 (bottom)	UB-2271 6790±255 BP Bone collagen	1 5938(5627,5607, 5604)5441 cal 2 [6163]-5224 cal BC	Impressed (fingernail, pinched, triangular point, rocker, feathered – 'Guadone'), incised (long lines lattice & short), painted (medium-wide bands & triangles – 'Lagnano')	Mallory 1984–87, 249–50; Marshall Brown 1984–87, 279–89
Lagnano da Piede, ditch F-1, Layers 3–4 (upper)	UCLA-2148 6700±100 BP Bone collagen	1 5656(5581)5496 2 5730–5436 cal BC	Impressed (triangular point, rocker – 'Guadone'), incised (short), painted (medium-wide bands & triangles – Lagnano & 1 sherd 'La Quercia'), 2 sherds *figulina*	Mallory 1984– 87, 249–50; Marshall Brown 1984–87, 279–89
Masseria Candelaro, later phases	OxA-3684 6640±95 BP Animal bone	1 5593(5570,5530, 5521)5442 2 5677–5350 cal BC	Impressed ('Guadone'); graffiti (frequently filled with white, yellow & red colour); painted (red band *figulina*, rare 'La Quercia')	Skeates 1994, 254–5
5500–5250 cal BC				
Scaramella S. Vito, Villaggio A, Sounding II, inner ditch, spit 7 (bottom layer)	R-351 6540±65 BP Charcoals & burnt earth	1 5521(5442)5387 2 5576–5325 cal BC	Impressed, painted ('La Quercia')	Alessio *et al.* 1969, 486
Masseria Santa Tecchia, C-ditch, spit 4, burial	BM-2414 6520±70 BP Human bone collagen	1 5517(5439)5350 2 5574–5283 cal BC	Impressed (triangular point), painted (red-brown broad bands, filled circle & trellis lines – 'La Quercia'), 18% *figulina*	Cassano & Manfredini eds. 1983, 159; Ambers *et al.* 1989, 27
Masseria Candelaro, later phases	OxA-3685 6510±95 BP Human bone	1 5565(5438)5332 2 5582–5271 cal BC	Impressed (Guadone); graffiti (frequently filled with white, yellow & red colour); painted (red band *figulina*, rare 'La Quercia')	Skeates 1994, 254–5
Masseria Fontanarosa Uliveto, ditch C, level 6a	BM-2415 6490±150 BP Charcoal	1 5571(5436)5278 2 5628–5071 cal BC	Impressed (rocker), painted (red angular bands of lines), 4% *figulina*	Cassano & Manfredini eds. 1983, 141–2; Ambers *et al.* 1989, 27; Whitehouse 1994, 87
5250–5000 cal BC				
Masseria Candelaro, ditch F, burial	OxA-3683 6200±95 BP Human bone	1 5265(5212,5166, 5164,5128,5122,5107,5101 ,5089,5079) 4998 2 5422–4866 cal BC	Painted *figulina* (red angular bands of lines, wavy line & half-filled circles – 'Serra d'Alto')	Cassano & Manfredini 1991, 34; Skeates 1994, 255
Passo di Corvo, Area A, pit at NE C-ditch, 4–6.5m depth	R-846 6140±120 BP Charred plants	1 5256(5207,5180, 5059)4871 2 5415–4764 cal BC	Painted ('Passo di Corvo')	Alessio *et al.* 1976, 333

contact and exchange with each other (Chapman 1988a, 17; 1994, 134, 145; Skeates 1999, 24).

Towards the end of this chronological and cultural phase, the first archaeologically-recorded 'neolithic' ditched site was established near the edge of the southern Adriatic zone. This is the site at Asfaka, in north-west Greece, which has a radiocarbon determination that places it in the late seventh millennium cal BC (5430±240 bc [I-1959], 2 σ 6620 (6182) 5716 BC; Higgs & Vita Finzi 1966, 8). The large standard deviation for this determination leaves it open to question, and very little is known about the character or status of the site, but it does at least provide a (previously overlooked) *possible* precedent for the later ditched enclosures of the Tavoliere. Furthermore, the relatively early date for the Neolithic in this part of the southern Adriatic zone is supported by the even earlier radiocarbon determination for the Early Neolithic site of Sidari on the island of Corfu (5720±120 bc [GXO-772], 2 σ 6704 (6460) 6216 BC; Sordinas 1967, 64).

6000–5750 cal BC

Similar new material components of a 'neolithic agricultural package', including cereals, domesticated animals, blade-based lithic industries, ceramics, and less transitory sites with archaeological features and deposits, appeared more widely throughout the southern Adriatic zone during the first quarter of the sixth millennium cal BC. This 'package' included enclosure ditches, which, although identified predominantly on the Tavoliere and elsewhere in south-east Italy, have also been found occasionally in Dalmatia (Batovic 1975, 152; Bass 1999, 54; cf. Whitehouse 1987, 359).

Well-dated examples of these earliest neolithic enclosure ditches on the Tavoliere come from the sites of Masseria Giuffreda and Villaggio A at Scaramella S. Vito, both of which have radiocarbon dates (see Table). Unfortunately, little detailed information is available about either of them; and all that can be said in general is that they were both located in distinctive raised positions in the landscape, that enclosure ditches were dug at both of them, and that these were filled with material which included burnt deposits and sherds of impressed ware.

I favour an extension of the 'interaction model' (proposed already for the Mesolithic) to help explain these developments (cf. Pluciennik 1997, 53), and resolve many of the old questions and dichotomous interpretative positions relating to the 'Mesolithic-Neolithic transition' in the southern Adriatic region (cf. Whitehouse 1987, 364), and on the Tavoliere in particular (Chapman 1994, 134).

As part of a much broader, Eurasian-scale process, the exotic 'neolithic package' became available to the seasonally mobile indigenous groups in the coastal southern Adriatic zone in the late seventh millennium cal BC. Perhaps as novelties associated with food and the sharing of food (Whittle 1985, 105; 1996, 308; Chapman 1994,

135), these groups began to accept, adopt and disseminate this integrated 'package' throughout the zone, via their pre-existing social networks of contact and exchange, during the first quarter of the sixth millennium cal BC (Chapman 1994, 144). This process involved the exploitation of previously marginal (but already known) parts of the gatherer-fisher-hunter resource zone, including the Tavoliere plain, whose natural resources were well-suited to the practice of early agriculture. It probably also involved a decrease in seasonal residential mobility, and a degree of settling down, at least for a part of the population. But this need not necessarily imply the existence of permanent sedentary settlement from the outset (Chapman 1994, 138; Whittle 1996, 291), nor the total abandonment of seasonal gathering, fishing and hunting.

The adoption of the 'neolithic package' of resources, and its associated novel practices and ideas, by indigenous gatherer-fisher-hunter groups in the southern Adriatic zone, would probably have been accompanied by changes in the way in which those groups organised themselves socially and perceived their landscape. In particular, more prolonged and repeated exploitation of, and aggregation at, selected spaces in the landscape, such as the ecotonal parts of interfluvial rises on the previously marginal Tavoliere (see above), would have led to the adoption of new strategies for controlling social interactions and access to resources at those localities, and new ways of perceiving those localities.

The creation of the first ditched enclosures in selected nodal places on the Tavoliere might be regarded, then, not only as a local adaptation of the neolithic 'package' (Trump 1980, 54), but also as an embodiment of the putting of such new views of society and landscape into practice by local groups, who were participating at that time in an important process of cultural transformation. More specifically, local groups might have constructed these simple but striking 'landmarks' as part of fundamental strategies aimed at the social (and economic) re-definition and re-organisation of themselves and their landscape (cf. Chapman 1994, 133, 135–6; 1998a, 110–1; 1988b). The intended effect would have been both symbolic and practical. The communal digging of these new circular structures and the repeated use of the restricted areas and resources contained in and adjacent to them, would have been intended to focus, intensify, integrate, control and protect the new social identities, values and activities that members of the group practised within them. As a consequence, they would have encouraged the development of a stronger shared sense of local identity, including distinctions between 'insiders' and 'outsiders'; although social fluidity is likely to have continued, and social competition is likely to have been limited at this stage. At the same time, this transformation of fairly neutral 'spaces' into socially meaningful 'places' could have formed a particularly important part of the process of colonising and 'domesticating' the new, or previously marginal, landscape of the Tavoliere (cf. Chapman 1994; 1998a & b; Hodder 1990; Whitehouse 1998, 283–5).

5750–5500 cal BC

During the second quarter of the sixth millennium cal BC, archaeologically-represented cultural material evolved and elaborated in the southern Adriatic region. On the Tavoliere, this is shown, for example, by the decorated pottery that can be assigned to this phase. The earliest 'archaic' Impressed Ware was now joined and gradually replaced by a new range of decorated ceramics. These new styles of ceramics were used and broken (if not also made) at the ditched enclosure sites on the Tavoliere, where further related cultural developments also took place.

Five well-dated ditched enclosure sites on the Tavoliere can be assigned to the chronological phase dating to between 5750 and 5500 cal BC. They are: Ripa Tetta, Coppa Nevigata, Villa Comunale, Lagnano da Piede, and Masseria Candelaro.

These sites are all located on ecotonal rises in the landscape (terraces and low hills), near to bodies of water (streams, rivers and lagoons). Each had at least one major enclosure ditch, which was relatively wide (1.2 to 4.0m deep and 2.0 to 3.5m wide). This was initially dug into the *crusta*, and then remained open at the same time as being gradually filled by layered cultural deposits. The contents of these deposits were mixed and diverse, and included soil, stones, hut plaster fragments (with wood imprints), numerous pottery sherds, stone artefacts, wood charcoal fragments, the carbonised remains of crop plants (cereals, legumes, and weeds of cultivation), animal bones, marine mollusc shells, and the body of an adult man. Further special deposits of organic material, animal bones, and broken pottery vessels (decorated in new styles) were then, in at least one case, added to the filled ditches, via pits and cavities cut into the ditch fills. Within the areas enclosed by these ditches, three other basic structural features commonly existed: C-ditches, huts and cobbled areas. Like the enclosure ditches, one or more C-ditches were also cut into the *crusta*, and then gradually filled by layers of similar mixed cultural deposits. However, they were much smaller in diameter, but also relatively deep (2.75m deep and 1.25m wide). In at least one case the C-ditch deposits included an intentionally deposited assemblage of imported flint artefacts. Also, in at least one case, a C-ditch was modified, when partially filled, by adding a wall of cobbles to its inner side, cutting additional ditch segments, and blocking off the original fill with a stone wall. The old and new ditch segments then continued to be filled. Huts lay either within or outside these C-ditch enclosures. They were small (3–5m long), roughly quadrangular, made of wattle-and-daub with compacted earth floors, and sometimes flanked by stone alignments (possibly low walls) and shallow channels. In one example at least, a raised hearth lay in the corner of a hut. Extensive cobbled areas were also constructed and used, both within and outside the C-ditch enclosures. They were constituted and overlain by: pieces of *crusta* and pebbles (possibly dug from the adjacent ditches), fragments of hut plaster, burnt patches (including carbonised cereals), pottery

sherds, stone artefacts (including a grindstone), and animal bones. No structures appear to have been mounted on top of these cobbled areas. Instead, they appear to have served as open-air areas for the performance of repeated activities, which probably included the processing and preparation of food.

Alasdair Whittle has pointed out that the combined continuity and gradual elaboration of pottery on the Tavoliere seems to go hand in hand with the multiplication and elaboration of ditched enclosures in that area, and has suggested that *'both may have been the product of intensifying social interaction, of gatherings, feasts and social exchanges'* (Whittle 1996, 309). This seems to be a reasonable interpretation, and the archaeological evidence could support it, save for the fact that we know so little about the preceding chronological phase that it is difficult to make reliable comparisons. However, taking the evidence for the second half of the sixth millennium cal BC alone, it does at least reflect the practice of a wide (if not wider) range of social activities taking place at the ditched enclosure sites. New ditched enclosures were established in selected nodal places in the Tavoliere landscape, and their ditches were gradually but repeatedly filled with deposits of cultural material, including not only ceramics and burnt remains, but also a wide range of other cultural material, such as food remains and the bodies of adult men and women. This process of deposition may have become more purposeful over time, to judge from the special pits and cavities that were dug into the top of the previously filled ditch at Masseria Candelaro, and then filled. Within the enclosed area of these outer ditches, a mirror process was taking place, but on a smaller scale, with the digging, cultural filling and modification of smaller but relatively deep and narrow (and therefore, perhaps, more rapidly filled) C-ditches. Small and relatively flimsy huts were also constructed and used to provide people with shelter and warmth (at least), and cobbled areas were laid which appear to have been used as open-air areas for a variety of activities, such as the processing and preparation of food.

As part of this increase in social elaboration and intensification, ritual and related beliefs now appear to have helped to structure the cultural practices carried out repeatedly at the enclosure sites, to judge from the recurrent patterns of ditch digging and their filling with cultural deposits, some of which are clearly 'special' (cf. Evans 1988, 94; Chapman 1998, 110). The intentional placing of the body of a deceased adult in one of the enclosure ditches, for example, may have ritually reinforced and highlighted the physical and conceptual boundaries already marked out by that ditch, including, of course, boundaries between the living and the dead (cf. Pluciennik 1997, 51, 67).

The main social purposes underlying the construction and occupation of these ditched enclosure sites may also have continued and developed. On the one hand, the formation of these sites may have continued to serve as part of the cultural process of colonising and 'domesticating' the landscape of the Tavoliere, by transforming relatively neutral 'spaces' into socially meaningful 'places' (see above). On the other hand, they may also have been used, like the ceramics, to encourage the development and reproduction of less fluid, more integrated, local social groups, with a stronger sense of shared identity (see above; cf. Chapman 1988b; 1994: 138; Pluciennik 1997, 53; Morter & Robb 1998, 87–8). The ritual elaboration of the ditches as liminal boundaries, in which the bones of the ancestors were embedded, may also have enhanced distinctions between 'insiders' and 'outsiders'. However, in more detail, the functions and uses of these sites are likely to have been multiple, varied and socially negotiable (cf. Whittle 1988; Evans 1988).

Alasdair Whittle has also argued that it is unlikely that there was prolonged, large or intensive occupation of these ditched enclosure sites on the Tavoliere, including the sites at Ripa Tetta and Coppa Nevigata, and that instead, the archaeological features and deposits identified at them might suggest impermanence and movement (Whittle 1996). He develops this point by suggesting that the assigning of the label of '*villages*' to these sites is probably unhelpful, with its connotations of a '*classic early agrarian landscape*' on the Tavoliere, and of enclosures representing concentrations of population, '*anchors for a sedentary existence*', and the '*staking out fixed territories and resources*' (*ibid.,* 307). Instead, he suggests that the enclosures were probably '*rarely permanently occupied, either through the year or from year to year for generation after generation*' (*ibid.,* 311), and that they '*may mark points of coming and going*', places of fixed interest in a fluid, more mobile, landscape (*ibid.,* 299), '*chosen for gatherings and aggregations of people, for social negotiation and transaction as much as the meeting of subsistence needs*' (*ibid.,* 311). He bases his new interpretations on claims of: the absence of '*obvious structures surviving*' (*ibid.,* 295), '*what seem to be modest amounts of material in the ditches*' (*ibid,* 298), and the presence of what '*seem to have been incomplete skeletons, with crania and major limb bones most prominent*' suggestive of '*selected remains of the dead carried by the living on their circuits*' (*ibid.,* 312). None of these claims are valid. Evidence of obvious structures *does* now exist, in the form of huts; large amounts of cultural material *have* been found in the ditches; and whole bodies *were* deposited in the ditches. Similarly, Whittle bases his interpretation on claims that the subsistence economy practised by the occupants of the enclosures was one based on the exploitation of '*a broad spectrum of resources ... over the whole of the landscape*', from the coast, through the Tavoliere to the Apennines, which was characterised by extensive herding and foraging and limited cultivation (*ibid.,* 299). Again, the current archaeological evidence does not support this view: subsistence practices appear to have been locally adapted, with not only the seasonal gathering, fishing and hunting of specific local resources (including molluscs and possibly deer) and the raising of domesticated animals (including sheep, goat, cattle, pig and dog), but also the cultivation of crops on adjacent cultivable soils (including peas, emmer wheat, barley and lentil), the remains of which have been found in the ditches in significant quantities. Whittle also argues that '*too many enclosures were abandoned or altered for them to serve as the equivalent of tells in the Balkans and Greece*' (*ibid,* 312). Such analogies are obviously inappropriate for the ditched enclosures of the Tavoliere, and have never actually been made, but neither are analogies to the British Neolithic, which appears to be the starting point for Whittle's interpretative model that he then applies to the rest of 'Neolithic Europe'.

Alasdair Whittle's new claims of impermanence and movement in the occupation of the ditched enclosures and landscape of the Tavoliere should, then, be treated with caution; but that is not to say that they should be rejected outright. The ditched enclosure sites of the Tavoliere have been inappropriately labelled as '*villages*', and traces of modification, impermanence, seasonality and even abandonment can be seen at them (see above; cf. Chapman 1998, 111; Evans 1988). However, to my mind, one of the active roles played by the enclosures during the first half of the sixth millennium Cal BC was to encourage groups of people to settle down and form more fixed and unified agricultural communities within them. The occupation of these sites, therefore, lies somewhere between the two neolithic extremes of the Balkan tells, on the one hand, and the British hunter-pastoralists' enclosures, on the other.

5500–5250 cal BC

Four well-dated ditched enclosure sites on the Tavoliere can be assigned to the chronological phase dating to between 5500 and 5250 cal BC. They are: Villaggio A at Scaramella S. Vito; Masseria Santa Tecchia, Masseria Candelaro; and Masseria Fontanarosa Uliveto.

These sites were again located on ecotonal rises in the landscape, close to water. They also continued to be modified. Their enclosure ditches continued to be gradually filled with stratified cultural deposits, which included charcoal and burnt earth, the remains of locally grown crop plants, and pottery sherds. Even when filled, or partially filled, these ditches still seem to have retained a special significance. For example, at Scaramella S. Vito a new enclosure ditch was dug within the area of, and concentric to the line of, an earlier and at least partially filled outer enclosure ditch, and at Masseria Candelaro a cavity was dug on the line of an earlier filled enclosure ditch and used as a multiple grave for adult men and women. Smaller C-ditches also continued to be filled with mixed cultural deposits, which included occasional 'special' deposits. At Masseria Santa Tecchia, for example, a cavity was cut into the wall of a C-ditch, filled with the disarticulated remains of adult men and women, and then flanked (in the ditch fill proper) by a concentration of pottery sherds, mollusc shells, and crop plant remains.

In this phase, the social and symbolic significance of the ditched enclosures on the Tavoliere also appears to have been maintained and enhanced. The process of frequentation and modification continued at them, with, for example, the enclosure- and C-ditches continuing to be gradually filled with stratified, mixed, cultural deposits. However, the 'special', symbolic, and in particular mortuary-related significance of at least parts of these ditches and their deposits seems to have increased slightly at this time. At Masseria Santa Tecchia, for example, a cavity was cut into the wall of a C-ditch, filled with the disarticulated remains of adult men and women, and then flanked (in the ditch fill proper) by a concentration of pottery sherds, mollusc shells, and crop plant remains. Also, even when filled or partially filled, the enclosure ditches seem to have retained a special significance. For example, at Scaramella S. Vito a new enclosure ditch was dug within the area of, and concentric to the line of, an earlier and at least partially filled outer enclosure ditch, and at Masseria Candelaro a cavity was dug on the line of an earlier, filled enclosure ditch and used as a multiple grave for adult men and women. This elaboration of depositional practices and of the symbolic demarcation of space might reflect an increased attempt (perhaps on the part of local group elders), to focus attention on the definition and strengthening of social and conceptual boundaries and identities, particularly between locally significant categories such as '*insiders*' and '*outsiders*'; the living, the ancestors and the supernatural, and landscape spaces and ancestral places. Although the enclosure sites may now have been occupied by at least part of a group on a daily basis, these special practices are likely to have taken place only on special occasions, marked seasonally for example by feasts, funerals and the communal digging of concentric ditches.

5250–5000 cal BC

Just two well-dated ditched enclosure sites on the Tavoliere can be assigned to the chronological phase dating to between 5250 and 5000 cal BC. They are Masseria Candelaro and Passo di Corvo.

At both sites, traditional structures such as enclosure and C-ditches, were now accompanied by a variety of new structures (variously described as 'hollows', 'cavities' and 'pits') which were cut into the *crusta* within the enclosures, and in some cases also delineated by walls and cordons of stone and clay. All of these features were then gradually filled by even richer mixed cultural deposits. These included more numerous mortuary deposits, represented by primary inhumation burials in artificial cavities, and by a mixture of possibly intentionally disturbed inhumation burials and secondary burials of selected body parts in open pits and piles, perhaps especially of adult males, and occasionally accompanied by distinctive (and quite possibly imported) painted *figulina* flasks and jugs decorated in the 'Serra d'Alto' style. The deposits also included large quantities of food remains (represented by animal bones, mollusc shells, and carbonised crop plants), and a more-or-less unique pair of clay figurines.

Material culture appears to have taken on a more symbolic role and seems to have been used in a more specialised manner during the last quarter of the sixth millennium cal BC in south-east Italy. This is reflected on the Tavoliere by developments in ceramics and at the ditched enclosure sites where they were consumed. Amongst the ceramics, a more distinctive category of painted fineware emerged, including *figulina* storage vessels painted in the (early) 'Serra d'Alto' style, small numbers of which were probably imported from outside the region via exchanges of social and symbolic significance. The relatively high value ascribed to these decorated fineware vessels is reflected in their occasional deposition in special mortuary deposits at the ditched enclosure sites. Such deposits formed just one part of a more general elaboration of the ditched enclosure sites, which now seem to have been used in a more intensive and formalised manner for the treatment of the dead and for rituals and ceremonies of various kinds (cf. Chapman 1988b; Bradley 1998, 17). At these sites, the traditional ditches were now associated with a variety of new special-purpose structures, all of which were filled by even richer mixed cultural deposits. These included more numerous mortuary deposits, formed as a result of both of primary and secondary burial practices; larger deposits of food remains, which might be interpreted as the residues of feasts; a wider range of storage and serving vessels, including the exotic-looking 'Serra d'Alto' style painted *figulina* storage vessels and clay figurines, which might be interpreted as new elements of ritual paraphernalia.

The general picture appears to be one of increasing elaboration of material culture and related ritual practices occurring at key traditional places in the landscape. More specifically, increasing attention seems to have been focused on the remains of the ancestors (and perhaps especially adult male ancestors). It is tempting to suggest, with reference to ethnographic generalisations about small-scale agricultural societies, that emergent groups of elders (possible male) may have lain behind these developments (Skeates 1999, 32–3). Institutionalised social control and power in such societies tend to be held by a group of elders, who emphasise and exploit a principle of anteriority in social relations, which encourages the dependency of '*those who come after*' upon '*those who come before*'. Furthermore, social control based upon this principle of anteriority is often legitimated and extended by its religious and ritual incorporation within a cosmos that is anthropomorphised as an extension of the world of the living, with the wealth and prosperity of the living conceptualised as being controlled by the supernatural spirits which are linked directly through the ancestors to the elders, who act as ritual mediators. Through the continued ritual elaboration of activities at ancestral ditched enclosure sites (which seem to have included, on special occasions, feasts, mortuary rituals, and the symbolic demarcation of space), such elders might, therefore, have continued to attempt to enhance the identity and cohesiveness of their local groups, and to strengthen their control over them.

5000–3000 cal BC

The long-term cultural patterns and processes established in the sixth millennium at ditched enclosure sites on the Tavoliere and elsewhere in the southern Adriatic region continued to develop throughout the fifth and fourth millennia cal BC. John Chapman's concise summary of developments in the fifth millennium cal BC makes this point well: '*The archaeological evidence for the 7th MBP in the Mediterranean is unambiguous on the development of wider exchange networks incorporating a greater variety of raw materials, especially exotic items. There is also evidence for increasing intensities of ritual activities. ... The implication of wider alliance structures, partly based on ritual links to the ancestors, is hard to resist.*' (Chapman 1988a, 18; cf. Skeates 1993, 110–3; 1995, 291).

Related developments can be seen at the ditched enclosure sites on the Tavoliere. Although the old tradition of ditch digging appears to have been abandoned, these sites probably still remained visible as earthworked landmarks situated on rises in the landscape, and new features continued to be established on top of them on special occasions. Continuing the trend established in the sixth millennium cal BC, these new features now appear to have been even more specialised in nature, with an even greater emphasis on mortuary-related deposits and practices. A notable recurrent feature is the 'Diana-Bellavista' form of burial, typically consisting of slab cists (about 0.5m high and 1m long) containing flexed skeletons (sometimes multiple), grave goods (including new styles of fineware) and ochre, and associated with burnt deposits (Robb 1994, 42). John Robb has plausibly interpreted these features as communal tombs that were placed by groups at the sites of their ancestral homes, both of which served as physical repositories and markers of the common histories and territories of those groups (Robb 1994; cf. Whittle 1988; Bradley 1998). However, his claim that this development was associated with a shift to a more mobile pattern of resource exploitation and to a more dispersed pattern of settlement, and that the Tavoliere became a '*landscape of the dead*', still needs to be demonstrated through a detailed examination of the whole of the archaeological record for this period (and not just mortuary deposits), and therefore remains open to question (see above).

SUGGESTIONS FOR FUTURE STUDIES

These interpretations stretch the available data to the limit, and new high quality data are now required. The production of large numbers of high quality radiocarbon determinations and the detailed publication of vertical and horizontal stratigraphic sequences must now be regarded as essential prerequisites for any new excavation projects carried out at the neolithic ditched enclosures of the Tavoliere. Only then will we be able to consider seriously the development of these sites, including the sequences of their ditch construction and their abandonment.

Acknowledgements

I would like to thank Ruth Whitehouse and Brian Bass for discussing some of the ideas that I have included in this paper. I would also like to thank Valentina Vulpi for her support during the writing of this paper.

REFERENCES

Alessio, M., Bella, F., Cortesi, C. & Turi, B. 1969. University of Rome Carbon-14 dates VII. *Radiocarbon*, 11, 482–98.

Alessio, M., Bella, F., Improta, S., Belluomini, G., Calderoni, G., Cortesi, C. & Turi, B. 1976. University of Rome Carbon-14 dates XIV. *Radiocarbon*, 18, 321–49.

Ambers, J., Matthews, K. & Bowman, S. 1989. British Museum natural radiocarbon measurements XXI. *Radiocarbon*, 31, 15–32.

Barker, G. 1985. *Prehistoric farming in Europe*. Cambridge. Cambridge University Press.

Bass, B. 1999. Early Neolithic offshore accounts: remote islands, maritime exploitations, and the trans-Adriatic cultural network. *Journal of Mediterranean Archaeology*, 11.2, 37–62.

Batovic, S. 1975. Le relazioni tra la Dannia e la sponda orientale dell'Adriatico. In S. Tiné (ed.), *Civiltà Preistoriche e Protostoriche della Annia. Atti del Colloquio Internazionale di Preistoria e Protostaria della Dannia, Foggia (24–29 aprile 1973). Firenze.* Istituto Italiano di Preistoria e Profostaria. 149–57.

Biagi, P. 1996. North eastern Italy in the seventh millennium BP: a bridge between the Balkans and the West? In *The Vinca culture: its role and cultural connections. International Symposium on the Vinca Culture and its role and cultural connections. Timisoara, Romania, October 1995.* Timisoara. The Museum of Banat. 9–22.

Bradford, J. 1949. 'Buried landscapes' in southern Italy. *Antiquity*, 90, 58–72.

Bradford, J. 1957. *Ancient landscapes: studies in field archaeology*. London. G. Bell & Sons Ltd.

Bradford, J. & Williams-Hunt, P. R. 1946. Siticulosa Apulia. *Antiquity*, 80, 191–200.

Bradley, R. 1998. *The significance of monuments: on the shaping of human experience in Neolithic and Bronze Age Europe*. London. Routledge.

Cassano, SM, & Manfredini, A, (eds) 1983. *Studi sul neolitico del Tavoliere della Puglia: indagine territoriale in un'area-campione*. Oxford. BAR, International Series, 160.

Cassano, S. M. & Manfredini, A. 1991. Rinvenimento di una sepoltura Serra D'Alto a Masseria Candelaro: scavo 1990. In Clemente, G. (ed.), *Atti del 12° Convegno Nazionale sulla Preistoria – Protostoria – Storia della Daunia. 14–15–16 dicembre 1990. Volume 1.* San Severo. Archeoclub d'Italia, Sede di San Severo. 21–30.

Chapman, J. C. 1988a. Ceramic production and social differentiation: the Dalmatian Neolithic and the western Mediterranean. *Journal of Mediterranean Archaeology*, 1.2, 3–25.

Chapman, J, 1988b. From "space" to "place": a model of dispersed settlement and neolithic society. In C. Burgess, P. Topping, C. Mordant, & M. Maddison (eds), *Enclosures and Defences in the Neolithic of Western Europe*. Oxford. British Archaeological Reports, International Series, 403. 21–46.

Chapman, J. 1994. The origins of farming in south east Europe. *Préhistoire Européenne*, 6, 133–56.

Chapman, J. 1998. Objectification, embodiment and the value of places and things. In D. Bailey (ed), *The archaeology of value: essays on prestige and the processes of valuation*. Oxford. British Archaeological Reports, International Series, 730. 106–30.

Chapman, J. & Müller, J. 1990. Early farmers in the Mediterranean basin: the Dalmatian evidence. *Antiquity*, 64, 127–34.

Evans, C. 1988. Acts of enclosure: a consideration of concentrically-organised causewayed enclosures. In J. C. Barrett & I. A. Kinnes (eds), *The archaeology of context in the Neolithic and Bronze Age: recent trends*. Sheffield. Department of Archaeology and Prehistory, University of Sheffield. 85–96.

Giampietri, A., Grifoni, R., Radi, G., Tozzi, C., Verola, M. L. & Wilkens, B. 1996. Torre Sabea, Trasano, Ripatetta, Santo Stefano. In V. Tiné (ed.), *Forme e tempi della neolitizzazione in Italia meridionale e in Sicilia. Atti del Seminario Internazionale Rossano 1994*.

Guilaine, J, Simone, L., Thommeret, J. & Thommeret, Y. 1981. Datations C14 pour le Néolithique du Tavoliere Italie. *Bulletin de la Société Préhistorique Française*, 78.5, 154–60.

Hedges, R. E. M., Housley, R., Law, I. A. & Bronk, C. R. 1989. Radiocarbon dates from the Oxford AMS system: *Archaeometric* datelist 9. *Archaeometry*, 31, 207–34.

Higgs, E. S. & Vita Finzi, C. 1966. The climate, environment and industries of Stone Age Greece: Part II. *Proceedings of the Prehistoric Society*, 32, 1–29.

Hodder, I. 1990. *The domestication of Europe: structure and contingency in neolithic societies*. Oxford. Basil Blackwell.

Lewthwaite, J. 1986. The transition to food production: a Mediterranean perspective. In M. Zvelebil (ed.), *Hunters in transition: Mesolithic societies in temperate Eurasia and their transition to farming*. Cambridge. Cambridge University Press. 53–66.

Mallory, J. P. 1984–87. Lagnano da Piede I – an Early Neolithic village in the Tavoliere. *Origini*, 13, 193–290.

Manfredini, A. 1987. Coppa Nevigata. In S. M. Cassano, A. Cazzella, A. Manfredini & M. Moscoloni (eds), *Coppa Nevigata e il suo territorio: testimonianze archeologiche dal VII al II millennio a.C.* Roma. Quasar. 48–55.

Marshall Brown, L. 1984–87. Catalogue. In J. P. Mallory, Lagnano da Piede I – an Early Neolithic village in the Tavoliere. *Origini*, 13, 279–89.

Morter, J. & Robb, J. 1998. Space, gender and architecture in the southern Italian Neolithic. In R. D. Whitehouse (ed.), *Gender in Italian archaeology: challenging the stereotypes*. London. Accordia Specialist Studies on Italy, 7. 83–94.

Pluciennik, M. 1994. Holocene hunter-gatherers in Italy. In R. Skeates and R. Whitehouse (eds), *Radiocarbon dating and Italian prehistory*. London. Archaeological Monographs of the British School at Rome 8 and Accordia Specialist Studies on Italy 3. 45–59.

Pluciennik, M. Z. 1997. Historical, geographical and anthropological imaginations: early ceramics in southern Italy. In C. G. Cumberpatch & P. W. Blinkhorn (eds), *Not so much a pot, more a way of life: current approaches to artefact analysis in archaeology*. Oxford. Oxbow Books. 37–56.

Simone, L. 1977–82. Il villaggio neolitico della Villa Comunale di Foggia. *Origini*, 11, 129–81.

Simone, L. 1981. I villaggi neolitici di Masseria Guiffreda e Masseria Russo (Foggia). *Taras*, I.2, 279–84.

Skeates, R. 1993. Neolithic exchange in central and southern Italy. In C. Scarre & F. Healy (eds), *Trade and exchange in prehistoric Europe: proceedings of a conference held at the University of Bristol, April 1992*. Oxford. Oxbow Books. 109–14.

Skeates, R. 1994. A radiocarbon date-list for prehistoric Italy (c. 46,400 BP – 2450 BP/400 cal. BC). In R. Skeates & R. Whitehouse (eds), *Radiocarbon dating and Italian prehistory*. London. Accordia Research Centre and British School at Rome. 147–288.

Skeates, R. 1995. Animate objects: a biography of prehistoric 'axe-amulets' in the central Mediterranean region. *Proceedings of the Prehistoric Society*, 61, 279–301.

Skeates, R. 1999. Unveiling inequality: social life and social change in the Mesolithic and Early Neolithic of east-central Italy. In R. H. Tykot, J. Morter & J. E. Robb (eds), *Social dynamics of the prehistoric central Mediterranean*. London. Accordia Research Institute, Specialist Studies on the Mediterranean, 3. 15–45.

Sordinas, A. 1967. Radiocarbon dates from Corfu. *Antiquity*, 51, 64.

Tilley, C. 1996. *An ethnography of the Neolithic: early prehistoric societies in southern Scandinavia*. Cambridge. Cambridge University Press.

Tinè, S. 1983. Problemi relativi al Neolitico e all'Età del Bronzo in Italia e rapporti tra le due sponde Adriatiche. In *L'Adriatico tra Mediterraneo e penisola balcanica nell'antichità*. Taranto. Istituto per la Storia e l'Archeologia della Magna Grecia. 25–44.

Tozzi, C. & Verola, M. L. 1991. La campagna di scavo 1990 a Ripatetta (Lucera, Foggia). In G. Clemente (ed), *Atti del 12° Convegno Nazionale sulla Preistoria – Protostoria – Storia della Daunia. 14–15–16 dicembre 1990. Volume 1*. San Severo. Archeoclub d'Italia, Sede di San Severo. 37–48.

Trump, D. H. 1980. *The prehistory of the Mediterranean*. London. Yale University Press.

Whitehouse, R. D. 1968. Settlement and economy in southern Italy in the Neothermal period. *Proceedings of the Prehistoric Society*, 34, 332–366.

Whitehouse, R. 1987. The first farmers in the Adriatic and their position in the Neolithic of the Mediterranean. In J. Guilaine, J. Courtin, J.-L. Roudil & J.-L. Vernet (eds), *Premières communautés paysannes en Méditerranée occidentale. Actes du Colloque International du C.N.R.S. Montpellier, 26–29 avril 1983*. Paris. Centre National de la Recherche Scientifique. 357–65.

Whitehouse, R. 1994. The British Museum 14C programme for Italian prehistory. In R. Skeates & R. Whitehouse (eds), *Radiocarbon dating and Italian prehistory*. London. Archaeological Monographs of the British School at Rome 8 and Accordia Specialist Studies on Italy 3. 85–98.

Whitehouse, R. D., 1998. Società ed economia nel neolitico italiano: la problematica dei fossati. In S. Tusa (ed.), *La preistoria del Basso Belice e della Sicilia meridionale nel quadro della preistoria siciliana e mediterranea*. Palermo. Società Siciliana di Storia Patria. 275–85.

Whittle, A. 1985. *Neolithic Europe: a survey*. Cambridge. Cambridge University Press.

Whittle, A. 1988. Contexts, activities, events – aspects of Neolithic and Copper Age enclosures in central and western Europe. In C. Burgess, P. Topping, C. Mordant & M. Maddison (eds), *Enclosures and Defences in the Neolithic of Western Europe: Part i*. Oxford. British Archaeological Reports, International Series, 403. 1–46.

Whittle, A. 1996. *Europe in the Neolithic: the creation of new worlds*. Cambridge. Cambridge University Press.

6. An interrupted ditch alignment at Rivoli, Italy, in the context of Neolithic interrupted ditch/pit systems

Lawrence Barfield

INTRODUCTION

A distinctive feature of most of the ditched enclosures in northern Europe is their construction in discrete sections which has led to the use of the name 'interrupted ditched' or 'causewayed' enclosures (Burgess et al. 1988). Whereas the enclosure may be explained in various ways, cattle kraal or seasonal meeting place, ritual centre or burial site, the interrupted ditch requires in itself a different explanation which is no less certain. Is this method of construction of itself symbolic or is it purely functional? Are we dealing with multiple entrances or are the diggings the result of work gang allocated quarries for the construction of a continuous embankment?

Another type of Neolithic site with similar problems of interpretation are the regular arrangements of lines of equally spaced, and uniform sized pits found at St Michel du Touch and Villeneuve Tolosane on the Upper Garonne belonging to the southern French Chassey culture (Vaquer 1990). These are themselves set within ditched enclosures. These are certainly very different structures from the ditches of causewayed camps since they are filled with fire-cracked stones and are generally interpreted as communal feasting places at times of social aggregation. However, they do occur within a similar time frame and like causewayed ditches we do not have a satisfactory explanation as to why they are spaced or aligned in the way they are.

THE ROCCA DI RIVOLI

We can bring into this discussion another Neolithic site, this time in northern Italy on the Rocca di Rivoli, Verona (Barfield & Bagolini 1976). This is a Neolithic settlement occupying a limestone-surrounded 'dolina' field belonging to the middle and late phases of the Square Mouthed Pottery Culture (VBQ II and III) with absolute dating somewhere in the second half of the 5th millennium BC. The main structural features from the site were round or oval pits filled with settlement debris of the type that are characteristic of the north Italian Neolithic from the Early period through to the end of the VBQ (Fig. 6.1). Only one posthole was recognised, but then the absence of

postholes is another feature of most north Italian Neolithic sites.

On the site there was also an interrupted linear ditch which ran across the site for a distance of 22m, effectively cutting the settlement in half on a north-south axis (Fig. 6.1) (Barfield & Bagolini 1976, 17). This ditch consisted of some ten equal-sized sections. The individual sections were uniform, measuring between 1.25m and 1.75m in length and 0.35m to 0.50m in width. They had rounded ends and profiles and their surviving depth seldom reached more than 0.20m. The spacing between the ends of the ditches was also regular ranging from 0.15m to 0.40m. They appear to have been dug after the associated Neolithic pits, but at a time when these were in use, or still visible, since their spacing was interrupted to avoid cutting into pits O, M and S. Unlike the Neolithic pits, which were full of settlement debris, the ditch fill was almost devoid of finds as well as the dark organic material characteristic of the pit fills. The uncontaminated nature of the pit fill also excludes that they were dug after the Neolithic period. The few sherds recovered were also in a fresh condition and all Neolithic. There were no postholes or evidence from the fill that it had ever held posts, nor would they in their present state have been deep enough to have held them. Truncation of the original depth is however possible and the clean nature of the contents suggests a back-filling carried out soon after digging. At the time of publication the interpretation of this feature was uncertain but it was suggested in the absence of any visible post holes along the ditch that it once held some kind of fence made up of standard sized woven hurdles.

DISCUSSION

In the light of evidence, both material and theoretical, available since the 1970s, we are in a position to widen the discussion of this ditch alignment.

1. The idea of a wattle fence would still seem the most probable explanation, especially in the light of what we now know about the widespread use of wattle panels in Neolithic and later prehistoric Europe (Coles & Orme 1977, 29). Also if we take the spaces

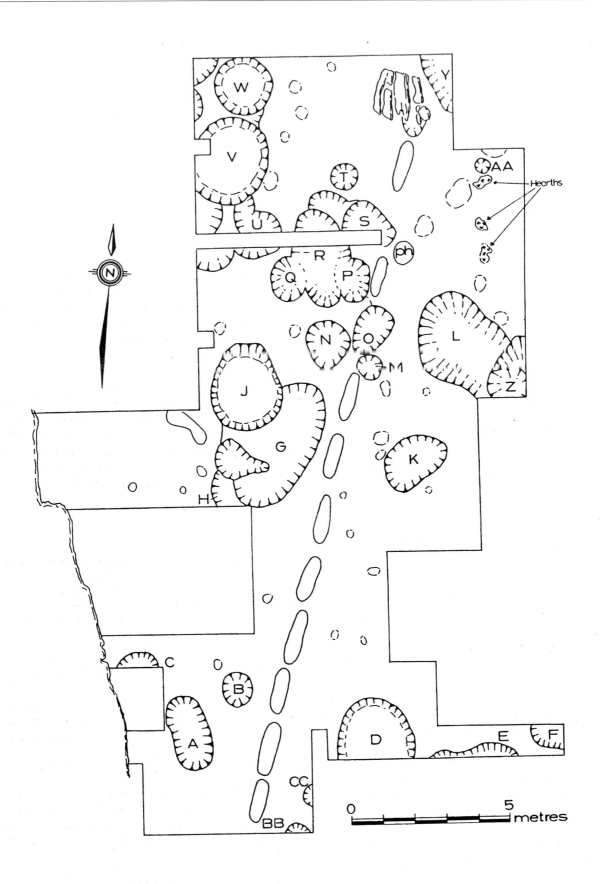

Fig. 6.1: Plan of settlement area on the Rocca di Rivoli, Verona, Italy (from Barfield & Bagolini 1976)

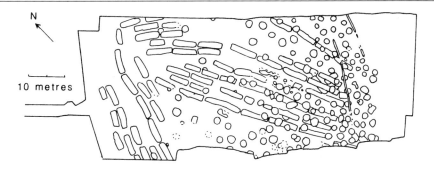

Fig 6.2: Pit alignments at Villeneuve-Tolosane, France (after Vaquer 1990)

between our ditches as part of the total length of putative hurdles, these would match the lengths of at least the shorter panels used in the Neolithic Walton track from the Somerset levels, which measured between 1.50m and 2.7m in length (Coles & Orme 1977, 14).

2. The ditch alignment can alternatively now be compared with the alignments of similarly spaced shallow pits found on Chassey sites in southeastern France such as St Michel du Touch and Villeneuve Tolosane (Fig. 6.2). These are generally longer (more than 5m) and wider than the Rivoli alignment and are filled with fire-cracked stones. Their current interpretation is as sites for cooking in association with periodic feasting at a seasonal central site. Their linear layout, however, has not yet been successfully explained.

Stone-filled pits of the same type are also a feature of Neolithic Italy (Mileto (Sarti & Martini 1993), and St Andrea di Travo (Bernabo Brea et al 1994), etc) (Barfield in press). These again have been seen as cooking sites, although Mileto has been interpreted unconvincingly as a pottery kiln (Sarti & Martini 1993). Unlike the Chassey sites cited earlier these usually occur singly or in smaller groupings and are not in linear lay outs. The Rivoli features, because of their small size, would not have been suited to be cooking pits, nor were fire-cracked stones found in them.

The alignment of the ditch line at Rivoli, approximately north-south, is probably not significant. Although some of the pits at Villeneuve-Tolosane are on the same alignment others are not (Fig. 6.2).

If we stick to the interpretations we have just discussed between Rivoli on the one hand and St Michel du Touch and Villeneuve-Tolosane on the other, we see different functions yet a comparison in the linear arrangement and spacing. If at Rivoli we do have a fence the problem of its interpretation remains. Most probably it was been a boundary feature. It is very straight and regular, whereas the disposition of the pits is irregular, and its line also runs through the pits at the same time as respecting them. It also cuts the settlement area into two equal halves. So may this be a symbolic boundary, perhaps a linear boundary into two moieties within the settlement.

The main purpose of this article has been to describe and discuss the unique ditch alignment at Rivoli. There may be no link between this, the Chassey stone pits and causewayed camps, yet they all encapsulate the same concept of an interrupted ditch and all are Neolithic. It is hoped that comparison can illuminate interpretation or at the very least stimulate discussion.

Endnote

Since going to press we have received information about two, straight, interrupted ditch systems from Central Italy, that are similar to the one at Rivoli. These at Fossacesia (Chieti) (Cremonesi 1990p. 59, tav 10a), which is on a slightly zig-zag alignment, and misano S. Monica, Riccione (Cremonesi 1990 p. 60). Both are on Neolithic sites of a comparable date to Rivoli.

REFERENCES

Barfield, L. H. & Bagolini, B. 1976. *The Excavation on the Rocca di Rivoli, Verona, 1963–1968*, Memorie del Museo Civico di Storia Naturale di Verona (II serie), No. 1.

Barfield, L. H. (in press). European once hot stones. *Symposium on 'Once Hot Stones'*, American Archaeological Association Conference, Nashville 1997.

Bernabò Brea, M. Cattani, M. & Farello, P. 1994. Una struttura insediativa del neolitico superiore a S. Andrea di Travo. *Quaderni del Museo Archeologico Etnologico di Modena*, 1, 55–87.

Burgess, C., Topping, P., Mordant, D. and Maddison, M. (eds) 1988. *Enclosures and Defences in the Neolithic of Western Europe*. Oxford. British Archaeological Reports, International Series, 403. 21–46.

Coles, J. & Orme, B. 1977. *Somerset Levels Papers, 3*. Cambridge and Exeter.

Cremonesi, G. 1990. Il villaggio neolitico di Fossacesia. In: E. Giannitrapani, L. Simone and S. Tine. *Interpretazione funzionale dei "fondi di capanna" di eta preistorica, Milano 1989*, Sovraintendenza Archeologica della Lombardia, pp. 59–62.

Sarti, L. & Martini, F. 1993. *Costruire la memoria, archeologia preistorica a Sesto Fiorentino (1982–1992)*. Montelupo Fiorentino. Garlatti and Razzai.

Vaquer, J. 1990. *Le Néolithique du Languedoc Occidentale*. Paris. Editions du CNRF.

7. Aerial Survey and Neolithic Enclosures in Central Europe

Otto Braasch

No statement on aerial survey for archaeology in Europe should be made without mentioning that this technique, in contrast to all other archaeological exploration methods, still has to overcome antiquated aviation laws in European countries which pretend to share a common European archaeological heritage. Following World War II most western countries had little or no restrictions on private flying and air photography, however, there were very few possibilities for aerial archaeology in the former Soviet Bloc states for 50 years, from 1939/1940 until the political changes in 1989/1990. This has led to a totally unbalanced view of archaeological sites and landscapes in Europe and in our understanding of site distributions. Aerial survey, when properly implemented and resourced, is capable of transforming our knowledge of sites buried beneath the soil (as well as those above ground) throughout Europe. When restrictions in some central and east European countries were abolished after 1990, and the first modern flights (for archaeology) could be made, archaeological sites were discovered at an explosive rate. Thus confirming the immense bias in archaeological research and proving once again the value of aerial reconnaissance for archaeological investigation.

Even so, the present aviation authorities in Belgium, Greece, Portugal and Spain still maintain restrictions on aerial photography for archaeology as prior military permission is required. For 75 years in Italy (from 11 March 1925 to 29 September 2000) stringent regulations were in force, which kept aerial archaeology from being introduced as an accepted, standard survey method at universities and regional archaeological offices as had been practiced in Britain and a few other European states. The Italian situation was particularly frustrating as JSP Bradford (Bradford 1957), stationed at Foggia (in southeast Italy) as an officer of the British Army in the Second World War, recorded a wealth of Neolithic and Roman sites on the Tavoliere through aerial photography with the help of the RAF. Succeeding researchers in this area, for example Barri Jones (Jones 1987) and Derrick Riley (Riley 1992), had to battle with peacetime bureaucracy just to get into the air at all. Fortunately a high ranking military officer, an Italian Air Force General, G . Schmiedt, had the foresight to set up the well known archaeological air photo archive after the war (in Rome – *Aerofototeca del Ministero per i Beni Culturali e Ambientali*).

In a remarkable contrast to the situation in Italy and other western states, restrictions on private flying and air photography were removed in the Baltic states after 1990, in Poland, the Czech and Slovak Republics, Slovenia and Hungary, with only Romania and Bulgaria maintaining bureaucratic impediments to aerial archaeology (Bewley, Braasch & Palmer 1996).

Aerial reconnaissance and photography for archaeology is an extremely cost-effective and rapid technique, especially in finding and recording buried enclosure sites. New information about the discovery of new sites is slow to filter through because of national, federal (or imagined) boundaries amongst researchers. Different traditions of monument recognition, protection and access to information as well as the difficulties of many European languages have hampered a more rapid development of the subject within European archaeology. The printing costs and speed of traditional publication methods have not helped the rapid dissemination of results.

The author, as an aviator and observer of this situation is under the impression that European archaeological research and heritage protection proceeds at a very slow pace and that its executioners seem to think that there is all the time in the world. Aerial survey has shown that time is not on our side and these sites (especially those recorded as cropmarks) are under threat from ploughing, road and pipeline construction and other forms of development.

Archaeologists are still having to draw conclusions by comparing single monuments which are many kilometres apart, while in fact there is a large number in closer proximity which had been detected many years before, but still await dissemination or publication (Geschwinde & Raetzel-Fabian 1998). When aerial archaeology was finally established in southern Germany in Bayern and Baden-Wuerttemberg during the early 1980s it soon became obvious, that in the long term, a strategic approach for the dissemination, understanding and management of

*Fig. 7.1: A double ditched enclosure (*Grabenwerk*) near Wittmar, Niedersachsen, resembles a site of almost the same size and similar shape further south at Calden, Hessen, Germany. The ditches at Wittmar have been cut 2 metres deep into limestone with the outer one measuring 1,274 meters in length. Provisional dating suggests the site dates from 4200–3500 BC, as there are other Michelsberger and Baalberger Neolithic sites in the region (Geschwinde & Raetzel-Fabian 1998).*

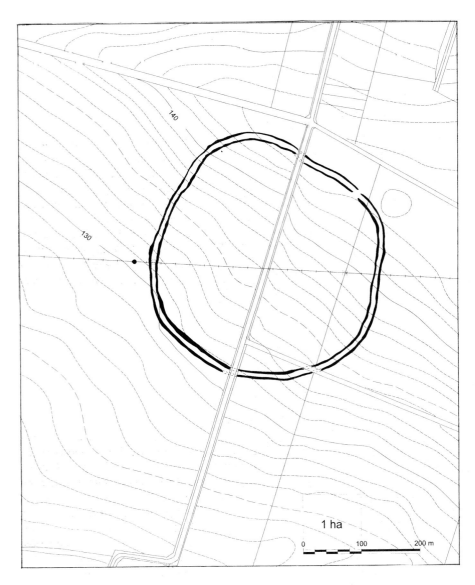

Fig 7.1a: Plan of the Wittmar enclosure (see Fig. 7.1) from the rectified air photograph taken on 12 July 1993 overlain on a topographical map. Interpretative drawings, using standards that have been developed in Britain, with a descriptive text could also be linked to other plans (e.g. field survey and geophysical surveys) and would make up the bulk of an European archaeological archive on sites and archaeological landscapes generated through air survey. The inclusion of actual air photographs should be kept to a minimum to save on storage costs.

Fig 7.2: A single-ditch enclosure near Zehbitz, Sachsen-Anhalt, photographed 29 May 1992. Iron Age surface finds underline the need to develop reliable dating methods for features detected from the air (Braasch 1996, Schwarz 1997).

Fig. 7.3: North of Boerssum on the eastern bank of the Oker river and close to Heiningen, Niedersachsen, Germany (see Fig. 7.4), a single-ditched enclosure with multiple entrances has not yet been dated. Surface finds from other sites and the single ditch might indicate a later date (Bronze or Iron Age) but more information is required to date this site.

Fig. 7.4: Through sample trenches in this Neolithic causewayed enclosure at Heiningen, Niedersachsen, could be dated to the period 4200 to 3500 BC (Braasch & Moeller 1994, Geschwinde & Raetzel-Fabian 1998). Obviously the river Oker, canalised in a straight ditch visible at the top of the photograph, has partially covered the site with a layer of sediments, which conceal at least half the enclosure.

Fig. 7.5: In 1999 a double-ditched enclosure showed for the first time at the village of Ohrum, Niedersachsen. This site lies a few kilometres further downstream along the Oker from the enclosure at Heiningen (see Fig. 7.4). Additional features include two parallel pipelines cutting the monument and traces of erosion heading from the right to the bank of the river on the left, passing a small cluster of pits near the road.

Fig. 7.6: Over north-western Hungary on 18 June 2000, when ripening crops were already losing contrast, three Neolithic enclosures were found, overlying each other. Traces of houses were visible within two of the enclosures, (probably less visible now as a result of the printing process), dating these sites to the early Neolithic phase of the Linearbandkeramik.

Fig. 7.7: This huge Neolithic enclosure at Plate, south of Schwerin, lies in the state of Mecklenburg-Vorpommern. Shape and dimensions resemble many sites found since 1989 further south in the Elbe-Saale area around Halle, Leipzig and Erfurt and in the eastern part of Niedersachsen.

Fig. 7.8: The multiple-ditched enclosure of Berge, Brandenburg, is one of the few archaeological sites detected through cropmarks on vertical photographs so far discovered in Germany (Wetzel 2001). No wonder its huge shape and striking image did not escape the British archaeologist Anthony Harding, University of Durham, who screened the area from an airliner shortly after takeoff when flying home from Berlin-Tegel in June 1999. Harding immediately and laudably reported his find via email to Germany (Harding 1999).

Fig. 7.9: The henge near Goseck, Sachsen-Anhalt, was the first of more than 14 henge-type enclosures which were detected from the air after the ban on air photography in the former German Democratic Republic had been removed in 1990; prior to these discoveries only one henge was known (and excavated) in that part of Germany.

the rapidly growing information on new sites would be the major problem – with airborne survey remaining the easier part (Braasch 1983).

There is still a misconception amongst some archaeologists that all enclosures should be excavated; the large and still increasing numbers of the sites, and the excavation costs involved make this prohibitively expensive (Braasch & Kaufmann 1992). Instead agreed methods of presenting, describing and comparing sites with a minimum of destruction through excavation or small-scale excavation have to be developed and practiced in concert with other non-destructive survey methods. In Germany, Helmut Becker has pioneered joint aerial and geophysical survey through combining the results of aerial photography with high speed high resolution Caesium magnetometry through digital imaging (Becker 1996).

Neolithic enclosures with ditches and pit alignments in close proximity are one of the most significant and monumental of site types, which have recently been recorded through aerial photography in increasing numbers in the former communist states in central and eastern Europe. They provide a good example of the new information which aerial survey has brought to light and which is transforming our understanding of Neolithic settlement and land use in Europe.

To assist the flow of information world wide, but especially in Europe, an international image database of sites should be created. This could be a research tool, going beyond all current political and administrative boundaries so that information and experiences can be shared to allow for better understanding of the sites and landscapes which have been recorded. In 2000/2001 the European Commission, through its Culture 2000 programme has funded a *Conservation through Aerial Archaeology* project which will pave the way for the creation of an aerial survey database, through the existing networks which have been created. If the research bodies and heritage managers agree then it might be possible to have the database fully implemented within the next few years.

This international digital pictorial database, as an initiative of a combined European research and heritage effort (on the Internet), would be ideally suited to identify and to overcome the many persisting, mostly bureaucratic, obstacles and to effectively unveil and overcome present provincial type barriers. It should contain images and information on monumental enclosures and the traces of archaeological landscapes (e.g. ditches and pit align-

ments) because those are easy to find and compare. The technological, administrative and legal aspects of such an enterprise have been tested by several projects so the prospects for an European archaeological air photo archive should be good. To succeed it will require the support of archaeological research institutions and heritage managers at all levels to make it happen.

Illustration credits
All photographs were taken by the author; Figure 7.1a was drawn by Winfried Gerstner.

REFERENCES

Becker, H. 1996. Kombination von Luftbild und Geophysik in digitaler Bildverarbeitung. *Archaeologische Prospektion – Luftbild und Geophysik*, Arbeitshefte des Bayerischen Landesamtes fuer Denkmalpflege 59, 77–81.

Bewley R. H., Braasch O. and Palmer R. An Aerial Archaeology Training Week, 15–22 June 1996, near Siofok, Lake Balaton, Hungary. *Antiquity,* 70, 745–750.

Braasch, O. 1983. Luftbildarchaeologie in Sueddeutschland. *Kleine Schriften zur Kenntnis der roemischen Besetzungsgeschichte Suedwestdeutschlands*, Nr. 30, 56.

Braasch, O. & Kaufmann, D. 1992. Zum Beginn archaeologischer Flugprospektion in Sachsen-Anhalt. *Ausgrabungen und Funde*, 37, 186–205.

Braasch, O. & Moeller, J. 1994. Zum Stand der archaeologischen Flugprospektion in Niedersachsen. *Berichte zur Denkmalpflege in Niedersachsen*, 14, 2–8.

Braasch, O. 1996. Zur archaeologischen Flugprospektion .... *Archaeologisches Nachrichtenblatt*, 1, 16–34.

Geschwinde, M. & Raetzel-Fabian, D. 1998. Monumental-Architektur aus Holz und Erde. Archaeologische Erdwerksforschung in Suedniedersachsen. *Archaeologie in Niedersachsen*, 1, 34–37.

Bradford, J. S. P. 1957. *Ancient Landscapes. Studies in Field Archaeology*. Bell & Sons.

Harding, A. 1999. Email dated 9 June 1999, 13:05:13.

Jones, G. D. B. 1987. *Apulia. Volume 1: Neoltihic Settlement in the Tavioliere*. Report of the Research Committee of the Society of Antiquaries, 44.

Riley, D. N. 1992. New Aerial Reconnaissance in Apulia. *Papers of the British School at Rome*, 60, 291–307.

Schwarz, R. 1997. Luftbildarchaeologie in Sachsen-Anhalt. *Begleitband zur Sonderausstellung Landesmuseum fuer Vorgeschichte Halle*. 61.

Wetzel, G. 2001. Grabenanlagen und Doppelkreisgrabenanlagen des Neolithikums. *Luftbildarchaeologie, Denkmalpflege in Brandenburg*. (In press).

8. From Lilliput to Brobdingnag: the traditions of enclosure in the Irish Neolithic

Gabriel Cooney

INTRODUCTION

The title of the paper is taken from the names of two of the places that Lemuel Gulliver travels to in Jonathan Swift's prose satire, *Gulliver's Travels* (1726). In Lilliput Gulliver is referred to as the 'man-mountain' by the diminutive inhabitants, while in Brobdingnag it is Gulliver who is diminutive and the Brobdingnagians gigantic. It struck the author that these two contrasting situations in which Swift placed Gulliver were a useful analogy for the evidence of enclosure that we have in the Irish Neolithic. There are large enclosures, which have an element of monumentality, involving significant construction and landscape change. But there are also some very small enclosures whose context is very much a local one in the wider setting of the socialised landscape. From a spatial and architectural perspective it appears as if through the large enclosures people were concerned with creating places that were much greater than the human scale. In making small enclosures they created places within and around which activities were carried out, in what may have been seen as a more familiar, intimate, small-scale arena.

Because of the paucity of evidence of causewayed enclosures in Ireland, it is sometimes assumed that enclosure was not an important characteristic of the Irish Neolithic. What I wish to suggest here is that we can see the act and process of enclosure being carried out at a variety of scales and in different settings during the Neolithic. The concept of enclosure being employed in particular locations at a range of scales – nested enclosures – and perhaps with different symbolic overtones is also something that can be identified. The best known elements of the tradition of enclosure in the Irish Neolithic are the hengiform monuments and related sites as documented by Stout (1991) and Condit and Simpson (1998). The variability and complexity of this tradition is demonstrated at particular complexes such as Bally-nahatty, Co. Down (Hartwell 1998) and Brú na Boinne, Co. Meath (Sweetman 1985; 1987; Eogan & Roche 1997; Condit & Cooney 1997). However it is clear that these form a later part of a long-lived tradition of enclosure that began early in the Neolithic. For example, Gibson

(1999, 156) has pointed out that the construction of palisaded enclosures in Ireland and Britain takes us from the earlier Neolithic to the massive palisaded circles of the Late Neolithic. The latter in turn can be seen as related to the hengiform tradition. Perhaps we have been too inclined to box off categories of enclosures as being unrelated or of different dates and functions, rather than recognising the potency and symbolism of the act of enclosure itself, as has been commented on with reference to causewayed enclosures (e.g. Evans 1988; Whittle 1988; Edmonds 1993; Bradley 1998). Enclosure creates a bounded zone which may have symbolised a range of different spatial and social relationships.

In this review I have assembled evidence from a range of sites (Fig. 8.1), based on published excavation reports but also mentioning significant sites where research is ongoing. Some of the material has been considered by others, but generally under a number of different headings and contexts (e.g. Waddell 1998). What I want to emphasise is that we can identify a varied but widespread pattern of enclosure within the Irish Neolithic and raise questions about other possible sites that have not been considered as Neolithic enclosures. The significance of the enclosure tradition can only be discussed when we have some appreciation of its character.

A CAUSEWAYED ENCLOSURE AND POSSIBLE PALISADED ENCLOSURES

What is recognised as the only *'classic'* causewayed enclosure in Ireland is at Donegore Hill, Co. Antrim, excavated by Mallory (Mallory & Hartwell 1984; Mallory 1993). The site is located on the summit of a hill at 234m OD on the northern side of the Six Mile Water valley (Fig. 8.2). Four to five per cent of the site was excavated. There is evidence for two interrupted ditches and two timber palisades. The ditches are about 3m across and 1m deep. The outer ditch encloses an area of 2.6ha (6.4 acres), measuring 219m × 175m. The inner ditch encloses an area 2ha (4.8 acres). Radiocarbon dates suggest that the outer ditch may be earlier, dating to 4000–3700 BC. The inner ditch appears to date to between 3800–3400 BC. Dates

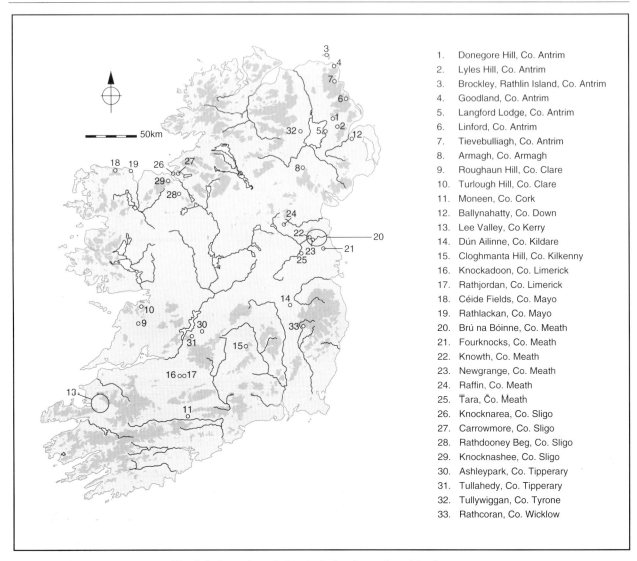

1. Donegore Hill, Co. Antrim
2. Lyles Hill, Co. Antrim
3. Brockley, Rathlin Island, Co. Antrim
4. Goodland, Co. Antrim
5. Langford Lodge, Co. Antrim
6. Linford, Co. Antrim
7. Tievebulliagh, Co. Antrim
8. Armagh, Co. Armagh
9. Roughaun Hill, Co. Clare
10. Turlough Hill, Co. Clare
11. Moneen, Co. Cork
12. Ballynahatty, Co. Down
13. Lee Valley, Co Kerry
14. Dún Ailinne, Co. Kildare
15. Cloghmanta Hill, Co. Kilkenny
16. Knockadoon, Co. Limerick
17. Rathjordan, Co. Limerick
18. Céide Fields, Co. Mayo
19. Rathlackan, Co. Mayo
20. Brú na Bóinne, Co. Meath
21. Fourknocks, Co. Meath
22. Knowth, Co. Meath
23. Newgrange, Co. Meath
24. Raffin, Co. Meath
25. Tara, Co. Meath
26. Knocknarea, Co. Sligo
27. Carrowmore, Co. Sligo
28. Rathdooney Beg, Co. Sligo
29. Knocknashee, Co. Sligo
30. Ashleypark, Co. Tipperary
31. Tullahedy, Co. Tipperary
32. Tullywiggan, Co. Tyrone
33. Rathcoran, Co. Wicklow

Fig. 8.1: Location of sites in Ireland mentioned in the text.

from activity in the interior range from 3900–3200 BC. Site occupation may have been as short as 300 years or as long as 900 years. In the interim publications Mallory has suggested that there may have been settlement activity in the interior although it had been badly disturbed by ploughing. Here there are pits, post holes and hearths. There also appear to be deliberate patterns of material culture use and deposition. For example, porcellanite axes from sources at Tievebulliagh and Brockley, Rathlin Island, 30km and 50km respectively to the north-east, seem to be deliberately broken. The ground and polished surfaces are partially removed by flaking. The very large quantity of pottery from the site, 45,000 sherds of carinated bowl (Sheridan 1995, 7) and the range of lithics suggest either prolonged small scale deposition or more episodic activity.

Looking south-eastwards from Donegore Hill across the Six Mile Water there is the prominent landmark of Lyles Hill, Co. Antrim, with a hilltop enclosure. Within the enclosure is a cairn just below the summit of the hill, which is 225m OD. Lyles Hill is about seven kilometres

from Donegore Hill (Figs 8.2 and 8.3a). This site was originally excavated by Evans (1953) with additional excavation by Simpson and Gibson in the 1980s (Gibson & Simpson 1987; Simpson & Gibson 1989). Roughly following the 210m contour and enclosing the top of the hill is a bank about 9m wide and nowhere more than a metre in height enclosing an area of 5.2ha (12.5 acres). Set into the top of the bank there was an irregular setting of postholes. There is no ditch and there appeared to be a single entrance at the north-west. Evans (1953) was convinced that the earthwork was Neolithic on a number of grounds, particularly because the buried soil and the core of the bank produced only Neolithic material. The recent excavations produced Bronze Age and Iron Age dates from the buried soil, bank and post-holes, supporting the view that the Lyles Hill bank represents a later Prehistoric hillfort incorporating residual Neolithic material (see discussion in Simpson & Gibson 1989).

However, in the course of the recent excavations two roughly parallel lines of palisade trench were uncovered in the south-east of the interior about 40m inside the later

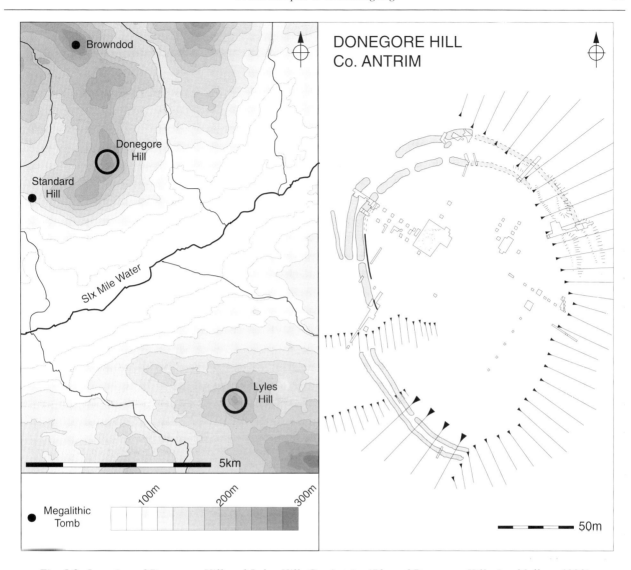

Fig. 8.2: Location of Donegore Hill and Lyles Hill, Co. Antrim (Plan of Donegore Hill after Mallory 1993).

prehistoric earthen bank. These are set between 3m to 6m apart and a length of about 25m was uncovered. Both trenches contained stone packing and large quantities of unweathered carinated bowl pottery. There appears to be Neolithic activity both inside and outside the palisade trenches. Radiocarbon dating of charcoal suggests a date of 3330–2920 BC for the inner palisade and a date of 2600–2350 BC for the outer palisade. A hearth containing carbonised barley was dated to 3650–3250 BC. The outer palisade certainly extends to the north-east and south-west beyond the area of excavation and while the inner palisade has a terminal at its north-east end it too continues to the south-west. If they are part of an enclosure and the 25m excavated length was extended around the hill, then the inner palisade could represent an enclosure of about 70m in diameter while the outer palisade could be part of an enclosure with a diameter in excess of 110m. These would incorporate the cairn and the summit of the hill. On the other hand the trenches could relate to structures and it requires further work to establish if they are part of an enclosure (Gibson, pers. comm.).

This cairn is the visible focus of Neolithic activity at Lyles Hill. It was about 21m in diameter and less than a metre in height. Here initially eight pits were dug and material (pottery sherds and cremated bone) placed deliberately in them. The pits were covered with a sealing layer of heavily burnt, occupation-type material incorporating a very large quantity of pottery sherds (sherds representing more that a thousand pots come from the cairn deposits) and lithics. As at Donegore it would appear that axes and other material were deliberately slighted or broken. Placed upon this layer were the basal stones of the cairn that was contained within a kerb, over 11m in diameter. On the north-east side of the kerb there was what Evans (1953) described as a *'dummy entrance'* with a decorated stone between the two largest orthostats. The centre of the cairn was free of stones and was just over 1m across and lined with slabs set on edge. Here the cremated bones of a child and numerous sherds of Neolithic bowl had been placed. Further deposits of burnt bone were scattered through the mound. Around the edge of the cairn were three Bronze Age burials.

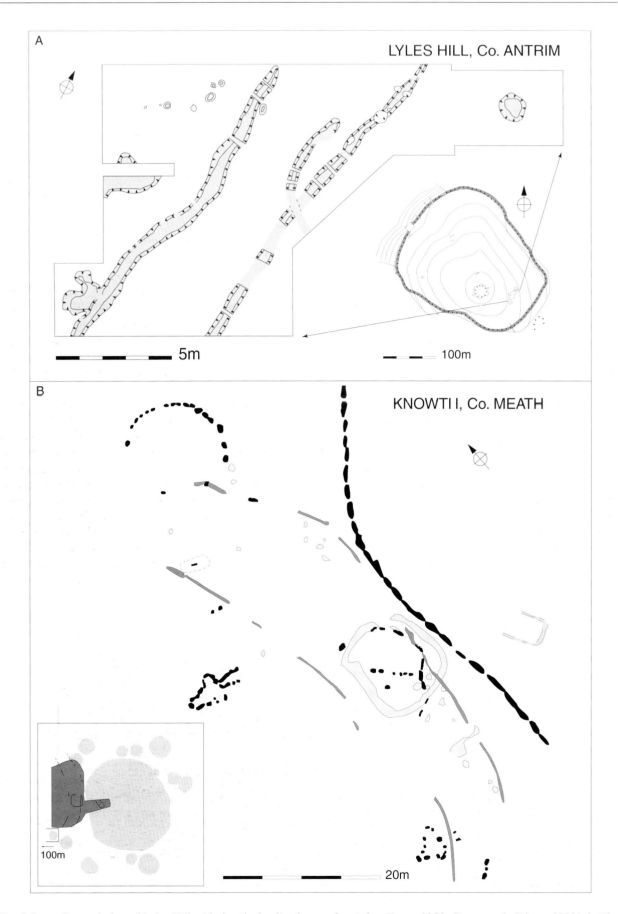

Fig. 8.3: a, General plan of Lyles Hill with detail of palisade trenches (after Evans 1953; Simpson & Gibson 1989). b, The palisade trenches at Knowth, Co. Meath (after Eogan 1984).

Based on the ceramic assemblage it would appear that there is an association between the cairn activity and the possible palisaded enclosure, or whatever other activity may be represented by the two palisade trenches to the south-east of the cairn. The radiocarbon dates might be read as suggesting that the palisade trenches at Lyles Hill are later than the ditches at Donegore and that activity began earlier at Donegore. However, there is a degree of overlap in the dates from the two sites and the pottery assemblage from them is very similar (see Mallory & McNeill 1991, 36; Sheridan 1995, 7). It seems likely that both hilltops were foci of activity during the Neolithic, whatever the chronological relationship between the enclosing elements on both sites. If the palisade trenches at Lyles Hill do form part of an enclosure, it would be significantly smaller than the Donegore Hill enclosure.

A good parallel for the palisade trenches at Lyles Hill comes from Knowth, Co. Meath (Fig. 8.3b). Here as part of the Early Neolithic phases of activity two curved palisade trenches were found. They overlie earlier activity and in turn are overlain by a number of passage tombs dating to the Middle Neolithic passage tomb phase of the site sequence. The edge of the main passage tomb mound is just to the east of the trenches. The trenches have a length of almost 60m (Eogan 1984; Eogan & Roche 1997). They held upright posts that were closely spaced and averaged 25cm in diameter. They were between 8–11m apart and there were some gaps along the trenches. The most definite of these was mid-way along the western (inner) trench that was over 3m wide and was pebbled. In between the palisades there were features such as pits, pebbling and an area where flint knapping took place. There was also a distinct area of pebbling within the western trench. The eastern trench (outer) overlies a sub-rectangular structure.

In the excavation reports of the site there has been a change in emphasis by the excavators regarding the interpretation of the palisade trenches. In the first monograph (Eogan 1984, 219–24) the features are treated as stretches of trenches, but in the second, (Eogan & Roche 1997, 44–5, 48–50), the clear suggestion is that the trenches form part of a palisade enclosure which has been subjected to differential preservation. It is argued that the trenches in the area further to the west may have been removed by ploughing. The structural sequence suggested by Eogan and Roche (1997) is that the western (inner) trench forms part of a primary circular enclosure that was about 70m in diameter. Subsequently this was enlarged with the construction of the eastern (outer) trench that would have been part of an enclosure with a diameter of about 100m. This eastern palisade trench cuts across the sub-rectangular structure. There is a date for a pit within this sub-rectangular building with a range of 3780–3385 BC. The earliest dates for Neolithic rectangular structures at Knowth are from around 4000 BC, suggesting activity from early in the Neolithic. Hence the possible enclosure was built within an area where there was already substantial activity.

During the excavation of the Mound of the Hostages passage tomb at Tara, Co. Meath (de Paor 1957; de Valera 1961), part of what has been discussed as a possible palisaded Neolithic enclosure was found. It was represented by a trench over 18.3m in length, dug prior to the construction of the tomb, and was dated to 3030–2190 BC (Watts 1960, 115; Newman 1997, 74, 146–7, 225–6). A burnt area on the old ground surface beneath the cairn gave a date of 3350–2470 BC. The ditch was about 0.6m deep and was described as following a broad arc and as appearing to represent an enclosure extending a consider-

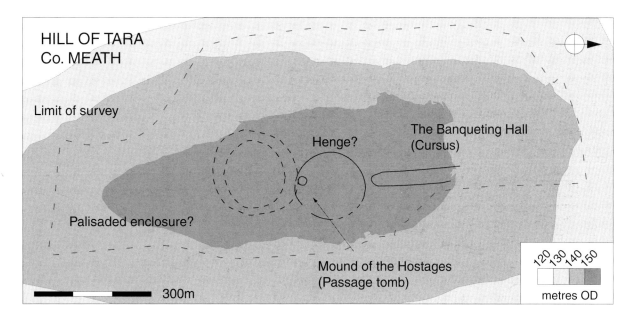

Fig. 8.4: Possible palisaded enclosure and henge-related enclosure at Tara, Co. Meath (based upon Newman 1997; Fenwick & Newman 1998).

able distance to the west of the mound (de Valera 1961, 28). Our understanding of Neolithic activity on the Hill of Tara has been greatly augmented by the Discovery Programme's research there in recent years. Geophysical survey of a number of areas within the large central enclosure at Tara, Ráith na Ríg, which itself has been dated to the late prehistoric period through recent excavation (Roche 1999), has revealed traces of one or possibly two linear features. These are 15–17m apart. The 'outer' of the features has been discussed as a possible continuation of the trench revealed by excavation (Newman 1997, 75). Newman, recognising the tentative nature of the evidence, suggested that the geophysical anomalies and the length of excavated trench may be part of an enclosure. This would be oval in ground plan and would measure approximately 180m in maximum diameter, with traces of a smaller enclosing ring inside. He pointed out that this arrangement would parallel that at Donegore Hill and the possible smaller enclosures at Lyles Hill and Knowth (Newman 1997, 146–7). However, the link between the pre-tomb ditch and the geophysical evidence can now be disounted and there seems to be a considerable question mark about this possible palisaded enclosure (Newman, pers. comm.).

Geophysical survey continues at Tara and in 1998 work in the area to the east of Ráith na Ríg and west of the Tech Midchúarta (the Banqueting Hall), the latter interpreted as a cursus monument (Condit 1995; Newman 1997, 103–11, 150- 3, 226–7; 1999, 143–4), indicated the presence of an enclosure defined by a ditch 3m wide flanked on either side by spaced post-holes (Fenwick & Newman 1998; Fig. 8.4). This enclosure seems to fit best within the tradition of late Neolithic palisaded enclosures, as at Newgrange (Sweetman 1985) and Ballynahatty (Hartwell 1998).

LARGE UPLAND ENCLOSURES

Apart from the Donegore Hill enclosure and the possible enclosures at Lyles Hill, Knowth and Tara there are a number of very large hill-top enclosures which may be Neolithic in date. Here the problem is not so much the nature and extent of these sites, but establishing their date. Important support for the practice of creating large upland enclosures in the Neolithic comes from Bergh's ongoing project on Knocknarea, Co. Sligo. Following on his earlier analysis and interpretation of the Cúil Irra landscape (Bergh 1995), Bergh has focussed on Knocknarea, the dominant landscape feature in the area, a limestone plateau overlooking the Carrowmore complex of passage tombs to the east and with a linear arrangement of passage tombs on the summit. Bergh (1995, 87–90) has demonstrated that the northern tomb of this arrangement has an encircling bank, as has the central monument, Maeve's Cairn (Miosgán Meadhbha). On the north-east side of Knocknarea, about 300m from the summit, there is a group of hut or house sites and three

were excavated as part of the Carrowmore project (Burenhult 1984; Bengtsson & Bergh 1984).

Recent survey and excavation by Bergh (2000) has shown that below the hut sites there are three or four roughly parallel lengths of discontinuous bank running downslope with scoops/terraces on the inner side. There is Neolithic material (pottery and lithics) associated with both the construction of the banks and the terrace activity. These banks follow a course from an altitude of about 290m OD down to about 240m OD. Along the 260/250m contour line there is a discontinuous bank/rubble wall following the length of the eastern face of Knockarea, a distance of over 2km. At the southern end one of several hut sites with Neolithic material overlies the wall (Bergh 2000) Bearing in mind that further work on the project will undoubtedly amplify and alter the brief summary presented here, what is clear is there is an association between the monuments on top of Knocknarea, the partial enclosure and other activity on the eastern slopes and that this overlooks the Carrowmore complex. In a broader context Bergh's research is also very significant in that it challenges the assumption that large upland enclosures in Ireland necessarily date to the later prehistoric period. Many of these enclose or incorporate earlier hilltop monuments. Could some of these enclosures be Neolithic in date?

One such enclosure is situated at the northern end of Turlough Hill on the north-east escarpment of the Burren in Co. Clare, at 240m OD (Fig. 8.5). The striking feature of this site is the interrupted nature of the enclosing wall. In 1905 as part of his monumental survey of the archaeology of the Burren, Thomas J Westropp described the multiple, intentional breaks in the stone wall that forms the enclosure. The wall is 1.00m–1.75m high and 1–4m wide. Internally it measures 200m from north to south by 220m east to west. The wall outline reflects the local topography as it follows the shape of the edge of a limestone pavement that then drops very steeply with a cliff-face between 2–10m in height. This incorporation of the topography can also be seen in the main entrance from the east, which is through an existing gully/depression giving access from the lower limestone pavement. There appears to be between nine to twelve interruptions in the enclosure wall. The sides of the gaps are faced with vertical slabs, although those on the western side have no facing. There are a number of semi-circular hut sites adjoining the wall but otherwise there are no traces of structures in the interior. Outside the enclosure on higher ground to the south-west there is a large hilltop cairn with many circular hut sites lying immediately to the north-east.

A question that arises from a consideration of Turlough Hill is whether it may be an expression in stone of a form of interrupted enclosure normally represented as an earthwork. It stands apart, typologically, from the continuous nature of the enclosing elements of Irish hillforts (Raftery 1994). Another intriguing site in this regard is the bivallate hillfort at Rathcoran, Baltinglass, Co.

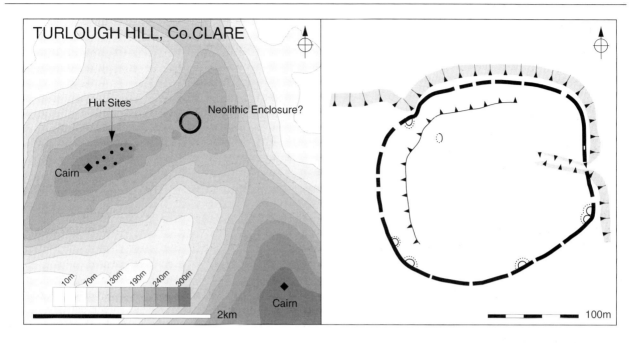

Fig. 8.5: Location of Turlough Hill, Co. Clare and sketch plan of enclosure (based upon Westropp 1905).

Wicklow (Raftery 1994, 44, fig. 26; Condit 1998, 14). This is 10.5ha (25.9 acres) in size and there is a passage tomb on the summit in the southern part of the site. On the north and east the outer rampart is discontinuous and between the two ramparts in these areas is a series of small depressions with mounds at their edges. This is interpreted as an unfinished hillfort with the depressions representing quarry scoops (Raftery 1994, 44). Is it may be possible that the interruptions in the rampart were deliberate and that we are looking at a site more akin to Turlough Hill?

A relatively recently discovered site that is normally considered a hillfort is Knocknashee, Co. Sligo (Condit *et al.* 1991; Raftery 1994). The site is located on a limestone table-top plateau. An area of some 22ha (53 acres) is enclosed by an earth and stone rampart with a partial outer rampart on the south and eastern side. The inner rampart survives to a height of 1.5m and width of 3.8m. It appears to have been constructed from quarry hollows on the inner side of the wall. At the north-east the outer rampart turns downslope. There are two large cairns, perhaps passage tombs, at the northern end of the enclosed area (see Bergh 1995, 89). Along the eastern side of the interior there are some 30 circular house sites with stone foundations, surrounded by rock-cut ditches with a narrow entrance facing to the south-east. There is a strong suggestion of more extensive occupation within the enclosure (Condit *et al.* 1991, 61). Given the evidence from Knocknarea (16km to the north-east) of the Neolithic date for an enclosing element, circular house sites as well as passage tombs, it seems plausible to suggest that a similar set of relationships may have existed at Knocknashee. More broadly we perhaps need to re-examine the proposal that hill-top enclosures in Ireland should be assumed in the first instance to be later

prehistoric in date (see comments in Waddell 1991, 72; Condit 1998, 20–1). A site that gives an interesting perspective on this problem is Cloghmanta Hill, Co. Kilkenny. Here there is a summit cairn 21m in diameter with a massive central cist. Ryan (1981, 142) listed it as a probable example of a particular Irish type of Neolithic burial mound, a Linkardstown-type tomb. What Condit and Gibbons (1988) have drawn attention to is that the cairn is at the centre of a hilltop enclosure, suggesting that the enclosure may have been laid out with reference to and perhaps at the same time as when the cairn was built.

ENCLOSURES IN A DOMESTIC CONTEXT

In recent discussions of the British and European evidence there has been a tendency to play down the possibility of enclosures having a domestic dimension (e.g. Andersen 1997; Thomas 1999). This is a view expressed with particular reference to causewayed enclosures (but for a contrary view see for example Mercer 1981; 1990; Dixon 1988), and also reflects a current emphasis on a more mobile, dispersed pattern of life in the Neolithic (e.g. Whittle 1996). The evidence from Ireland suggests a more complex picture. In some areas we have evidence for the transformation of the landscape into field systems, in itself a form of enclosure, and in other cases occupation sites suggesting a considerable degree of sedentary settlement. In both of these types of contexts enclosures occur around what appear to be residential buildings. For example, at Céide Fields, Co. Mayo there is a number of small stone-walled, circular or oval enclosures. These are set within a system of large rectangular fields dating to between 3700–3200

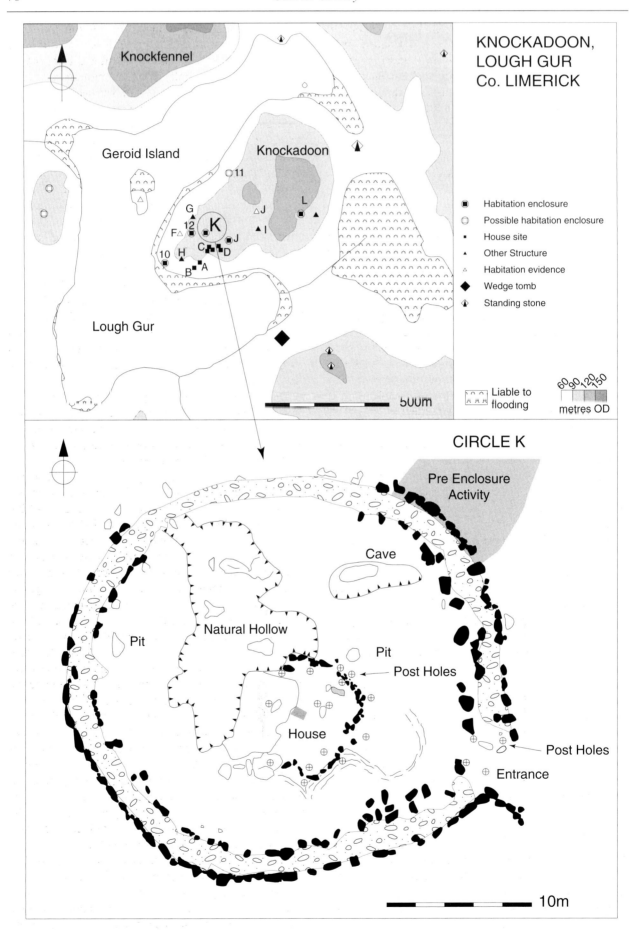

Fig. 8.6: The settlement site at Knockadoon, Lough Gur, Co. Limerick with detailed plan of one of the enclosed sites, Circle K (after Grogan & Eogan 1987).

BC and extending over an area of at least 400ha (1,000 acres) (Caulfield *et al.* 1998; Molloy & O'Connell 1995; Cooney 2000, 25–29). Excavation of one of these, an oval enclosure 22m by 25m, produced evidence for a small circular house structure about 6m in diameter with a date of around 3200 BC (Caulfield 1978; 1988). There are other oval or circular enclosures defined by stone walls within field systems of varying organisation and date. For example at Rathlackan, Co. Mayo (Middle Neolithic; Byrne 1986; 1994) east of the Céide Fields there is evidence of activity from the mid-fourth millennium BC. At Roughan Hill on the Burren in Co. Clare (Jones 1998; 1999) a settlement dating to the mid-third millennium BC is set in an kidney-shaped enclosure about a hectare in extent, in turn this lies within a larger field system, defined by a curving terminal wall (Jones 1998; 1999).

In other cases enclosures can be identified around buildings on settlement sites. The best example of this occurs at Knockadoon, Lough Gur, Co. Limerick (Fig. 8.6). Here on a limestone peninsula jutting out into the lake there is a focus of Neolithic settlement with a series of house sites that have no evidence of being enclosed and five definite enclosed habitation sites (Ó Ríordáin 1954; Grogan & Eogan 1987). The latter, such as Circle K, consist of a circular area, about 25–30m across with a wall consisting of an inner and outer facing of stones and a rubble core. There is a well-defined entrance and inside a house of rectangular or oval form. Some of the locations had clearly been occupied prior to the construction of the enclosure. In the case of Circle K there was an earlier house on the north-east side of the site and the enclosure wall followed the rim of a depression which may have been a focus of earlier activity. Grogan and Eogan (1987, 470–1) argue that the enclosures delimit the home of a family or household and that the contemporaneity of the open and enclosed sites, along with the patterning of material culture, suggest that the enclosures may be indicative of social status. The complexity of this domestic world is indicated by the contemporary burial of people on Knockadoon. For example, the remains of 14 individuals, mostly children, were found in Circle K (Grogan & Eogan 1987, 471), some predating the construction of the enclosure. In terms of the concept of enclosure being employed at different scales and perhaps with different symbolic overtones, it is perhaps relevant to mention that Knockadoon was probably an island in Lough Gur, rather than a peninsula, during the Neolithic (Ó Ríordáin 1954, 448; Grogan & Eogan 1987, 487).

ENCLOSING AND DEFINING MONUMENTS

Another aspect of the use of enclosures in the Irish Neolithic that needs to be highlighted is that they were employed to define a range of monument types. We can perhaps better understand this practice by drawing together two ideas from the discussion above. Firstly, there is the concept mentioned in relation to Lough Gur of the

enclosure standing in metaphoric relationship to an island, set apart from the outer world. Secondly, in some of the hilltop sites, such as Lyles Hill and Knocknarea, we have seen a link between monumental and depositional activity going on within an enclosure. These linkages may be specifically referenced where ditches are used to enclose and define the edges of monuments. At Rathdooney Beg, Co. Sligo, on the summit of a drumlin ridge there is a mound just over 6m in height and 24.5m in diameter with a possible boulder kerb and surrounded by a wide fosse. Just to the north of the site is a bowl barrow with a saucer barrow built onto the west side. The barrows date to the Iron Age (Mount 1998). Excavation demonstrated that the mound dates to the Early Neolithic. The ditch of the mound is 6.7m wide and 2.1m deep and in turn is enclosed by an external bank 2.4m wide. Seeds from the waterlogged lower fill of the ditch provided a date between 3930–3520 BC. Whatever monumental tradition the mound belongs to (see discussion in Mount 1998), it is clear from Rathdooney Beg that the concept of using a ditch to set a monument apart was present from early in the Irish Neolithic.

On the ridge at Newgrange in the Brú na Bóinne complex there are two smaller passage tombs to the west of Newgrange and one, possibly two sites to the east of it, creating a distinct linear arrangement (O'Kelly *et al.* 1978; Cooney 2000, 153–8). Site K is the most westerly and seems to have been initially surrounded by a penannular ditch, enclosing an area of about 12m diameter. The ditch itself was 1.3–1.5m in width and 1.0–1.2m deep and was located at a distance of 1–1.5m from the kerb of the monument. The ditch extended out from the mound to terminate on either side of the outer end of the passage leading into the tomb chamber. At some later stage the monument was re-modelled, the passage extended and a larger mound constructed over the primary ditch. However, it seems that the ditch was recut from the surface of the enlarged mound, almost on the same line as the first cut (O'Kelly *et al.* 1978, 276–83), stressing the symbolic importance of the enclosing ditch, now however incorporated into rather than defining the edge of the monument. Another monument in the passage tomb tradition where we can see the use of enclosure as a crucial element in the history of the site is Fourknocks II, Co. Meath (Hartnett 1971). Here a small cairn enclosed within an annular ditch and a cremation trench 14m to the north-east were placed within a penannular ditch enclosing an area 28m by 24m. The ditch terminals respected a roofed passage leading to the edge of the cremation trench and the ditch defined the edge of a covering mound (Cooney 2000, 106–8).

A variation on this theme of ditches being used to define the edges of monuments can be seen at the Linkardstown-type tomb at Ashleypark, Co. Tipperary (Manning 1985). Here there was a megalithic structure containing the disarticulated remains of an elderly adult male and two children under a cairn and covering mound of clay 26m in diameter and 5m high. This was surrounded by a low, wide outer bank with two internal ditches separated by a penannular ring of undug ground. The inner ditch was interrupted in the south where there were large limestone blocks on the surface. The megalithic structure was made by splitting a limestone block. It could be argued that the ditches both served to separate the mound from the outer world and by highlighting the visible limestone blocks acted as a reminder of the way in which an existing landmark had been transformed to create a monument to the dead (Cooney 2000, 97–9).

ENCLOSURES AS A FOCUS OF DEPOSITION

What has been emphasised above is the variety of ways in which enclosures were used in Ireland during the Neolithic. Far less focus has been placed on the depositional practices both within the sites and in their ditches, a topic that would be to the fore in other areas of western Europe where enclosures occur. The fact that patterns of deliberate, structured deposition are best seen in a number of small enclosures (Fig. 8.7) stresses the point that the tradition of enclosure was used in a specific, local way in Ireland.

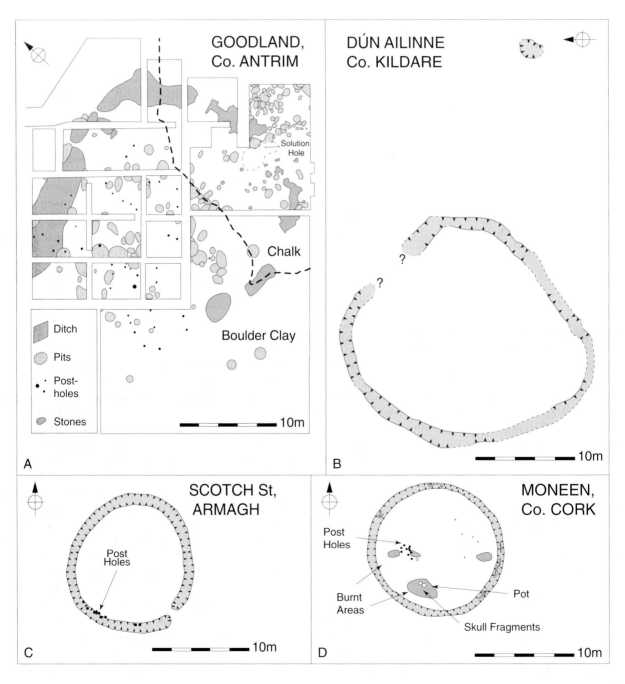

Fig. 8.7: Plans of enclosures, (a) Goodland, Co. Antrim (after Case 1973); (b) Dún Ailinne, Co. Kildare (after Wailes 1990); (c) Scotch Street, Co. Armagh (after Lynn 1988); (d) Moneen, Co. Cork (after O'Kelly 1952).

These small enclosures are sometimes referred to as Goodland-type enclosures, after the type-site in Co. Antrim (Case 1973). Here (see Fig. 8.7a), associated with small-scale extraction of flint from a chalk surface at an altitude of 240m OD, a segmented ditched enclosure about 21m in maximum dimension was created. In the ditch segments and in a large number of pits in the interior there were deposits of flint, quartz, porcellanite and pottery. These appear to have been packed around boulders and the pits were left as low cairns. Case (1973) suggested that this material and the associated charcoal-rich sediment were placed as a fertility offering.

There are a number of sites that seem to show affinities with Goodland and others where there are strong indications of links between an enclosure and patterns of deliberate, formal deposition. At Scotch Street in Armagh (Fig. 8.7c) excavation revealed a penannular ditch, enclosing an area of about 12m diameter with an entrance in the south-east. The ditch was just over a metre in width and depth. In the fill there were hundreds of small sherds of Neolithic pottery representing several dozen vessels of a range of styles associated with charcoal. There were also lithics and animal teeth in the ditch fill. Radiocarbon assay indicates a date for the site around 3000 BC (Lynn 1988; see also ApSimon 1985/6, 10). Scatters of joining sherds suggest a pattern of deliberate deposition, perhaps over a short period of time. Stake-holes following the curve of the ditch were inserted after the ditch had filled up. At Rathjordan, Co. Limerick, east of Lough Gur, there are a number of sites where Neolithic depositional activity involving the placement of pottery, axe fragments, animal bone and charcoal in and around pits was then commemorated by being encircled by a ditch 10–15m in diameter (in some cases with an outer bank) which provided material for a low covering mound between (Ó Ríordáin 1947; 1948).

A Bronze Age cemetery mound was placed over a ditched enclosure at Moneen, Co. Cork (O'Kelly 1952). The enclosure (Fig. 8.7d) had an internal diameter of 15.8m and enclosed pits, stake-holes and spreads of charcoal. There were a number of flint flakes, some quartz and fresh, unweathered sherds from more than a dozen pots of Late Neolithic/Beaker affinity. One large pot was found crushed flat, embedded in a charcoal spread with portions of a human skull close by. Charcoal from the spread provided a date of between 2850–2280 BC (O'Kelly 1989, 350). That the enclosing ditch continued to have a significance into the Bronze Age is indicated by the construction of a cemetery cairn within it, the placement of one burial to the south-west of and just outside the ditch and the addition of a specially dug annex to enclose a later burial abutting the exterior of the partially silted ditch.

At Dún Ailinne, Co. Kildare (Fig. 8.7b), the earliest of a range of prehistoric features was a sub-rectangular ditch enclosing an area at least 23.5m in maximum dimension (Wailes 1990; Johnston 1990). Because of the amount of disturbance by later activity it is unclear whether the ditch was continuous; there may have been

an entrance on the north-west side. There were a few boulders within the enclosure and there were some lithic finds of Neolithic date in the ditch. Some eighteen metres east of this enclosure there was a pit containing a decorated Neolithic bipartite bowl and a stone disc bead which may have accompanied a burial deposit (Herity 1982, 298). Newman (1997, 147) has suggested that the Dún Ailinne enclosure can be compared to what appears to be a sub-rectangular hilltop enclosure at Raffin, Co. Meath (Newman 1995). Here the southern and eastern sides of the enclosure (about 20m by 30m) were revealed; the ditch was 3m wide, 1.8m deep and a deposit in the fill was dated to 3300–2920 BC.

Other relevant sites include Tullywiggan, Co. Tyrone (Bamford 1972), where there are indications of Neolithic activity outside a stretch of ditch about 4–5m wide and 1.5m deep. The ditch cut a large pit which appears to have contained deliberate deposits of pottery and flint and to have been focused on a central slot. One of the first sites with which Goodland was compared was Langford Lodge, Co. Antrim (Waterman 1963). The Neolithic evidence consisted of pits, stake-holes and stone settings in an area about 8m in maximum diameter. This may have been enclosed by a ditch, of which however only a short length could be excavated, about 10m east of the pits and other features. It was suggested by Waterman that the Neolithic features were deliberately sealed with a sediment containing charcoal, sherds, struck flint and quartz, the same range of material found in the pits. A recently excavated site in Antrim that appears to have close parallels with Goodland is Linford (Doyle & Moore 1997; Williams & Moore forthcoming).

CONCLUSION

While the discussion above may be more descriptive and less discursive than the author would prefer, it seemed appropriate to provide data to support the contention that enclosure was a widely used practice and tradition during the Neolithic in Ireland. With the increasing pace of archaeological work in Ireland enclosures are turning up in areas where there had previously been little visible Neolithic archaeology, as in the Lee valley east of Tralee in Co. Kerry (Connolly & Condit 1998; Connolly 1999). Also new kinds of Neolithic enclosures are being recognised such as Tullahedy, Co. Tipperary, where the higher parts of a wetland glacial knoll were enclosed with a combination of ditch, posts and pits (McConway, pers. comm.; O'Brien 2001). A series of palisaded enclosures have been uncovered at Thornhill, Co. Derry (Logue 2001).

While enclosures of a variety of forms as well as scales occur in Ireland, evidence for causewayed enclosures like those occurring in southern Britain and western Europe is rare. As Mallory (1993, 415) put it, *'until the recent discovery and excavation of Donegore Hill, the pattern of Neolithic ditched enclosures, known from central and western Europe, has not extended as far west as Ireland'.*

On the other hand, if a wider definition of enclosures is used, to include ditches, banks and walls as enclosing elements, then clearly there were a range of different kinds of enclosures in use from early in the Neolithic. It is recognised that a variety of different activities mark the construction and use of causewayed enclosures (Whittle 1988; Whittle & Pollard 1998; Edmonds 1993; 1999). In Ireland while there is some evidence for a range of activities taking place at particular locales, the more widespread pattern seems to be that the act of enclosure was used at different scales, in different contexts and different places to define areas as being distinctive. Enclosure was thus used to define and differentiate areas of occupation, areas of monumental activity and areas of deposition. Like 'islands' enclosures achieve the effect of worlds with defined edges and the activities that went on within helped to establish the character of enclosures as being special, in some cases these were places of transformation (Thomas 1999). This idea of increasing differentiation also fits with the evidence that enclosures often appear to have been created in places that already had a history of Neolithic activity.

The Donegore causewayed enclosure and the possible palisaded enclosures have to be seen as an integral part of a wider tradition of enclosure, which may incorporate such variation as we have seen at Knocknarea and certainly includes the creation of much smaller sites. We also have to see enclosure as part of a number of wider traditions, for example the domestic domain, the construction of monuments and the deliberate deposition of material (Cooney 2000). The Irish evidence is somewhat fragmented and there has been an understandable tendency to consider different types of enclosures as separate entities. However, this overlooks the linkages and similarities between what may initially appear to be very different sites. For instance, ApSimon (1985/6, 10) has pointed out the close comparability of the enclosures at Newgrange, Site K and Scotch Street, Armagh. On a similar note Condit and Simpson (1998), in their recent examination of the evidence for Irish hengiform enclosures and related monuments, have suggested that a great variety of monuments in Ireland can be encompassed within the henge category. Indeed just as the hengiform tradition in Ireland has distinctive characteristics, so has the background of the use of enclosures in Ireland from early in the Neolithic. We can certainly suggest that enclosures were central to how people in Neolithic Ireland constructed their worlds.

BIBLIOGRAPHY

Andersen, N. H. 1997. *The Sarup Enclosures*. Moesgaard. Jutland Archaeological Society.

ApSimon, A. 1985/6. Chronological contexts for Irish megalithic tombs. *Journal of Irish Archaeology*, 3, 5–15.

Bamford, H. 1972. Tullywiggan. In T. Delaney (ed.), *Excavations 1971*. Belfast. Association of Young Irish Archaeologists. 24.

Bengtsson, H. & Bergh, S. 1984. The hut sites at Knockarea North. In G. Burenhult, *The archaeology of Carrowmore: Environmental archaeology and the megalithic tradition at Carrowmore, Co. Sligo, Ireland*. Stockholm. University of Stockholm, Institute of Archaeology (Theses and Papers in North-European Archaeology #14). 216–318.

Bergh, S. 1995. *Landscape of the monuments*. Stockholm. Riksantikvarieämbet Arkeologiska Undersöknigar.

Bergh, S. 2000. Transforming Knocknarea – The archaeology of a mountain. *Archaeology Ireland*, 52, 14–18.

Bradley, R. 1998. *The significance of monuments*. London. Routledge.

Burenhult, G. 1984. *The Archaeology of Carrowmore: Environmental Archaeology and the Megalithic Tradition at Carrowmore, Co Sligo, Ireland*. Stockholm. University of Stockholm, Institute of Archaeology (Theses and Papers in North-European Archaeology #14).

Byrne, G. 1986. *The Pre-Bog Archaeology of the Ballycastle – Palmerstown area of North Mayo*. University College Dublin. Unpublished MA thesis.

Byrne, G. 1994. Rathlackan, Co. Mayo. In I. Bennett (ed.), *Excavations 1993*. Dublin. Wordwell. 61–2.

Case, H. J. 1973. A ritual site in north-east Ireland. In G. Daniel and P. Kjaerum (eds), *Megalithic Graves and Ritual*. Moesgaard. Jutland Archaeological Society. 173–96

Caulfield, S. 1978. Neolithic fields: the Irish evidence. In H. C. Bowen and P. J. Fowler (eds), *Early Land Allotment*. Oxford. British Archaeological Reports, British Series 48. 137–44.

Caulfield, S. 1988. *Céide Fields and Belderrig Beg Guide*. Killala. Morrigan Book Company.

Caulfield, S., O'Donnell, R. G. & Mitchell, P. I. 1998. Radiocarbon dating of a Neolithic field system at Céide Fields, County Mayo, Ireland. *Radiocarbon*, 40, 629–40.

Condit, T. 1995. Avenues for research. *Archaeology Ireland*, 34, 16–8.

Condit, T. 1998. Observations on aspects of the Baltinglass hillfort complex. *Wicklow Archaeology and History*, 1, 9–25.

Condit, T. & Cooney, G. (eds) 1997. *Brú na Bóinne*. Dublin. Archaeology Ireland.

Condit, T. & Gibbons, M. 1988. Two little known hillforts in Co. Kilkenny. *Decies*, 37, 47–54.

Condit, T. & Simpson, D. D. A. 1998. Irish Hengiform Enclosures and Related Monuments: A Review. In A. Gibson & D. D. A. Simpson (eds), *Prehistoric Ritual and Religion*. Stroud. Sutton Publishing. 45–61.

Condit, T., Gibbons, M. & Timoney, M. 1991. Hillforts in Sligo and Leitrim. *Emania*, 7, 59–62.

Connolly, M. & Condit, T. 1998. Ritual enclosures in the Lee Valley, Co. Kerry. *Archaeology Ireland*, 46, 8–12.

Connolly, M.1999. *Discovering the Neolithic in County Kerry: A passage tomb at Ballycarty*. Dublin. Wordwell.

Cooney, G. 2000. *Landscapes of Neolithic Ireland*. London. Routledge.

de Paor, M. 1957. Mound of the Hostages, Tara, Co. Meath. *Proceedings of the Prehistoric Society*, 23, 220–221.

de Valera, R. 1961. Excavations of the Mound of the Hostages: supplementary note. In SPO Ríordáin, *Tara: The monuments on the hill* (1961 edition). Dundalk. Tempest.

Dixon, P. 1988. The Neolithic settlements on Crickley Hill. In C. Burgess, P. Topping, C. Mordant & M. Maddison (eds), *Enclosures and Defences in the Neolithic of Western*

Europe. Oxford. British Archaeological Reports, International Series 403. 75–87.

Doyle, L. & Moore, D. G. 1997. *Antrim Coasts and Glens: A Preliminary Assessment of the Archaeology*. Belfast. Queen's University Belfast / Environment and Heritage Service, DOENI.

Edmonds, M. 1993. Interpreting causewayed enclosures in the past and present. In C. Tilley (ed.), *Interpretative Archaeology*. Oxford. Berg. 99–142.

Edmonds, M. 1999. *Ancestral Geographies of the Neolithic: Landscapes, monuments and memory*. London. Routledge.

Eogan, G. 1984. *Excavations at Knowth 1*. Dublin. Royal Irish Academy.

Eogan, G. & Roche, H. 1997. *Excavations at Knowth 2*. Dublin. Royal Irish Academy.

Evans, C. 1988. Monuments and analogy: the interpretation of causewayed enclosures. In C. Burgess, P. Topping, C. Mordant & M. Maddison (eds), *Enclosures and Defences in the Neolithic of Western Europe*. Oxford. British Archaeological Reports, International Series 403. 47–73.

Evans, E. E. 1953. *Lyles Hill, A Late Neolithic Site in County Antrim*. Belfast. HMSO.

Fenwick, J. & Newman, C. 1998. *Geophysical survey at Tara*. Unpublished report prepared for the Discovery Programme.

Gibson, A. M. 1999. *The Walton Basin Project: Excavation and survey in a prehistoric landscape 1993–7*. London. Council for British Archaaeology, Research Report 118.

Gibson, A. M. & Simpson, D. D. A. 1987. Lyles Hill, Co. Antrim. *Archaeology Ireland*, 2, 7–25.

Grogan, E. & Eogan, G. 1987. Lough Gur excavations by Séan P. Ó Ríordáin: further Neolithic and Beaker habitations on Knockadoon. *Proceedings of the Royal Irish Acaemy*, 87C, 299–506.

Hartnett, P. J. 1971. The excavation of two tumuli at Fourknocks (sites II and III), Co. Meath. *Proceedings of the Royal Irish Academy*, 71C, 35–89

Hartwell, B. 1998. The Ballynahatty Complex. In A. Gibson & D. D. A. Simpson (eds), *Prehistoric Ritual and Religion*. Stroud. Sutton Publishing. 32–44

Herity, M. 1982. Irish decorated Neolithic pottery. *Proceedings of the Royal Irish Academy*, 82C, 247–404.

Johnston, S. A. 1990. The Neolithic and Bronze Age activity at Dún Ailinne. *Emania*, 7, 26–31.

Jones, C. 1998. The Discovery and Dating of the Prehistoric Landscape of Roughan Hill in Co. Clare. *Journal of Irish Archaeology*, 9, 27–44.

Jones, C. 1999. Roughan Hill, a Final Neolithic / Early Bronze Age landscape revealed. *Archaeology Ireland*, 47, 30–2.

Logue, P. 2001. Ballynashallog and Ballynagard, Co. Derry, Neolithic settlement. In I. Bennett (ed.) *Excavations 2000*. Dublin. Wordwell. 53–4.

Lynn, C. J. 1988. Armagh in 3000 BC: 39–41 Scotch Street, Armagh City. In A. Hamlin & C. Lynn (eds), *Pieces of the Past*. Belfast. HMSO. 8–10.

Mallory, J. P. 1993. A Neolithic ditched enclosure in Northern Ireland. In J Pavúk (ed), *Actes de XII Congrès International des Sciences Préhistoriques et Protohistoriques*. Nitra. UIPPS. 415–8.

Mallory, J. P. & Hartwell, B. 1984. Donegore Hill. *Current Archaeology*, 92, 271–4.

Mallory, J. P. & McNeill, T. E. 1991. *The Archaeology of Ulster*. Belfast. Queens's University Belfast, Institute of Irish Studies.

Manning, C. 1985. A Neolithic burial mound at Ashleypark, Co Tipperary. *Proceedings of the Royal Irish Academy*, 85 C, 61–100.

Mercer, R. 1981. Excavations at Carn Brea, Illogan, Cornwall 1970–73. *Cornish Archaeology*, 20, 1–204.

Mercer, R. 1990. *Causewayed Enclosures*. Princes Risborough. Shire.

Molloy, K. & O'Connell, M. 1995. Palaeoecological investigations towards the reconstruction of environment and land-use changes during prehistory at Céide Fields, western Ireland. *Probleme der Küstenforschung im südlichen Nordseegebiet*, 23, 187–225.

Mount, C. 1998. Ritual, landscape and continuity in prehistoric County Sligo. *Archaeology Ireland*, 45, 18–21.

Newman, C. 1995. Raffin Fort, Co. Meath: Neolithic and Bronze Age activity. In E. Grogan & C. Mount (eds), *Annus Archaeologiae*. Dublin. Office of Public Works and Organisation of Irish Archaeologists. 55–66.

Newman, C. 1997. *Tara: An Archaeological Survey*. Dublin. Discovery Programme and the Royal Irish Academy: Discovery Programme Monograph #2.

Newman, C. 1999. Notes on four cursus-like monuments in County Meath, Ireland. In A. Barclay & J. Harding (eds), *Pathways and Ceremonies: The cursus monuments of Britain and Ireland*. Oxford. Oxbow. 141–7.

O'Brien, R. 2001. Nenagh by-pass excavations, 1998–1999. *Tipperary Historical Journal*, 2001, 175–188.

O'Kelly, M. J. 1952. Excavation of a cairn at Moneen, Co. Cork. *Proceedings of the Royal Irish Academy*, 54C, 79–93.

O'Kelly, M. J. 1989. *Early Ireland: An Introduction to Irish Prehistory*. Cambridge. Cambridge University Press.

O'Kelly, M. J., Lynch, F. M. & O'Kelly, C. 1978. Three passage graves at Newgrange, Co. Meath. *Proceedings of the Royal Irish Academy*, 78C, 249–352.

Ó Ríordáin, S. P. 1947. The excavation of a barrow at Rathjordan, Co. Limerick. *Journal of the Cork Historical and Archaeological Society*, 52, 1–4

Ó Ríordáin, S. P. 1948. Further barrows at Rathjordan, Co. Limerick. *Journal of the Cork Historical and Archaeological Society*, 53, 19–31.

Ó Ríordáin, S. P. 1954. Lough Gur Excavations: Neolithic and Bronze Age houses on Knockadoon. *Proceedings of the Royal Irish Academy*, 56C, 297–459.

Raftery, B. 1994. *Pagan Celtic Ireland: The Enigma of the Irish Iron Age*. London. Thames and Hudson.

Roche, H. 1999. Late Iron Age activity at Tara, Co. Meath. *Ríocht na Midhe*, 10, 18–30.

Ryan, M. 1981. Poulawack, Co Clare: the affinities of the central burial structure. In DO Corráin (ed), *Irish Antiquity*. Cork. Tower Books. 134–46.

Sheridan, A. 1995. Irish Neolithic pottery: the story in 1995. In I. A. Kinnes & G. Varndall (eds), *Unbaked Urns of Rudely Shape*. Oxford. Oxbow Monograph #55. 3–22.

Simpson, D. D. A. & Gibson, A. M. 1989. Lyles Hill. *Current Archaeology*, 114, 214–5.

Stout, G. 1991. Embanked enclosures of the Boyne region. *Procedings of the Royal Irish Academy*, 91C, 245–84.

Sweetman, P. D. 1985. A Late Neolithic/Early Bronze Age pit circle at Newgrange, Co Meath. *Proceedings of the Royal Irish Academy*, 85C, 195–221.

Sweetman, P. D. 1987. Excavation of a Late Neolithic/Early Bronze Age site at Newgrange, Co. Meath. *Proceedings of the Royal Irish Academy*, 87C, 283–98.

Swift, J. 1726. *Gulliver's Travels*, London.

Thomas, J. 1999. *Understanding the Neolithic*. London. Routledge.

Waddell, J. 1991. The First People, The Prehistoric Burren. In J. W. O'Connell & A. Korff (eds), *The Book of the Burren*. Kinvara. Tír Eolas. 59–76.

Waddell, J. 1998. *The Prehistoric Archaeology of Ireland*. Galway. Galway University Press.

Wailes, B. 1990. Dún Ailinne: A summary excavation report. *Emania*, 7, 10–21.

Waterman, D. M. 1963. A Neolithic and Dark Age site at Langford Lodge, Co. Antrim. *Ulster Journal of Archaeology*, 26, 43–54.

Watts, W. A. 1960. C14 dating and the Neolithic in Ireland. *Antiquity*, 34, 111–6.

Westropp, T. J. 1905. The Eastern Border West Corcomroe Glasha Group. *Journal of the Royal Society of Antiquaries of Ireland*, 35.

Whittle, A. 1988. Contexts, Activities, Events – Aspects of Neolithic and Copper Age Enclosures in Central and Western Europe. In C. Burgess, P. Topping, C. Mordant & M. Maddison (eds), *Enclosures and Defences in the Neolithic of Western Europe*. Oxford. British Archaeological Reports, International Series 403. 1–19.

Whittle, A. 1996. *Europe in the Neolithic, the creation of new worlds*. Cambridge. Cambridge University Press.

Whittle, A. & Pollard, J. 1998. Windmill Hill Causewayed Enclosure: The Harmony of Symbols. In M. Edmonds & C. Richards (eds), *Understanding the Neolithic of north-western Europe*. Glasgow. Cruithne Press. 231–47.

Williams, B. B. & Moore, D. (forthcoming). Linford site 4, Co. Tipperary. *Ulster Journal of Archaeology*.

Postscript/acknowledgements

Brief mention was made in the text to recent and ongoing work by Stefan Bergh (Knocknarea), Paul Logue (Thornhill) and Cia McConway (Tullahedy) and I am pleased to have been able to refer to these very important sites. I am inebted to Conor Brady and Barbara Leon for the illustrations. My thanks to Dr Stefan Bergh, Tom Condit, Professor George Eogan, Dr Alex Gibson, Professor Jim Mallory, Dr Charles Mount, Conor Newman, Professor Barry Raftery, Dr Alison Sheridan and Professor Simpson for their comments on the text from which I have greatly benefited. The views expressed and any errors are of course the sole responsibility of the author.

9. Billown Neolithic Enclosures, Isle of Man

Timothy Darvill

INTRODUCTION

Although the Isle of Man has long been known for its ensemble of megalithic tombs and related monuments (Megaw 1938; Daniel 1950, 179–81; Henshall 1978) it is only since the early 1990s that the full range of its Neolithic cultural assemblages and monuments began to be fully recognized (Burrow 1997). In 1995 a series of ditched enclosures was discovered at the Billown Quarry Site near Castletown in the southern part of the Island. This short paper provides a brief introduction to the enclosures and their wider relationships. Investigations at the site are expected to continue until 2002/3 and thus the present report must be considered provisional and interim.

NEOLITHIC MAN AND THE BILLOWN PROJECT

The Isle of Man is a small but geographically varied island of about 570 square kilometres. It lies in the middle of the Irish Sea, variously influenced and culturally connected to coastal and inland communities living around the Irish Sea basin in what is now Scotland, England, Wales and Ireland (Fig. 9.1). Tidal flows and currents within the Irish Sea favoured two directions of movement through historic and prehistoric times (Bowen 1970; Davies 1946, 41). South to north movements from Cornwall, south-east Ireland, and the west coast of Wales relate to the south-eastern shores of the Island, but north to south influences from Antrim and Galloway relate to the north-western coastlands.

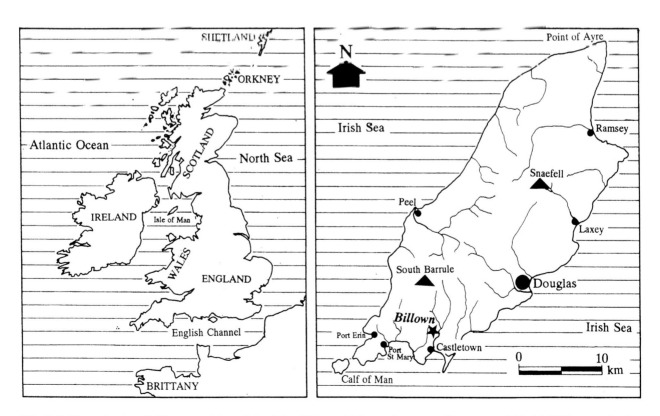

Fig. 9.1: Map showing (left) the position of the Isle of Man within north-western Europe, and (right) Billown and other places mentioned in the text within the Isle of Man.

The Neolithic period in Man divides into two main cultural-historical phases (Darvill 2000). The earlier Neolithic spans the later fifth and fourth millennia BC, and is conventionally characterized by round-bottomed pottery of Mull-Hill tradition (Piggott 1932) together with long barrows and passage graves that allow links to be proposed with the more widespread Clyde-Carlingford traditions (Clark 1935, 75–81; Piggott 1954, 157; Burrow 1997, 11–17). The later Neolithic, broadly the third millennium BC, is distinctive to the Isle of Man and was defined as the Ronaldsway Culture by Basil Megaw following the excavation of a Neolithic house at Ronaldsway Airport in 1943 and a cemetery at Ballateare in 1946 (Bruce *et al.* 1947; Bersu 1947; Piggott 1954, 346–51; Moffatt 1978; Burrow 1997, 19–31; Burrow & Darvill 1997).

Billown is situated in the southern part of the Isle of Man, approximately 2.5km north of Castletown and 1.2km west of Ballasalla, in the parish of Malew, sheading of Rushen (Fig. 9.1). The Billown Quarry Site is centred at national grid reference SC 268 702 and occupies slightly elevated ground (*c.*40m OD) within a generally undulating plain. It lies on a narrow interfluve between the Silver Burn to the east and a stream from Chibbyr Unjin to the west. Both watercourses run southwards, emptying into the Irish Sea at Castletown and Poyll Vaaish respectively. On a clear day there are good views from the site. To the north is upland, dominated by South Barrule with its hillfort crowned summit at 483m OD. To the north-west and west are further hills, many rising to over 200m OD, while to the south-west it is possible to see the coast with the Irish Sea beyond. Views south and east are more restricted, but in general look out over the coastal plain and the valley of the Silver Burn.

The Billown Neolithic Landscape Project is a joint venture by Bournemouth University's School of Conservation Science in association with Manx National Heritage. It began in the summer of 1995 following the discovery, two years earlier, of pits, postholes and gullies containing early and middle Neolithic pottery and flintwork within an area of land identified for stone quarrying. The rationale of the Project involves three main strands: 'rescue' excavation of an extensive site prior to its destruction by quarrying; research into the evolution and development of a tract of land during a critical period in the early history of occupation on the Island, namely the later Mesolithic through to the later Bronze Age; and training and the provision of opportunities to participate in the process of archaeological excavation and survey. Between 1995 and 1998 open area excavations have examined 0.5ha while geophysical and geochemical surveys of the surrounding landscape provide information for an area of about 1km.[2] Annual interim reports have been published (Darvill 1996a; 1997; 1998; 1999a) together with general overviews of progress (Darvill 1996b; 1999b).

THE NEOLITHIC ENCLOSURES

Geophysical surveys in 1995 revealed a series of anomalies provisionally identified as the braided course of a curved causewayed ditch. This was evaluated in the same season and confirmed as a series of intercutting Neolithic ditches (Darvill 1996a). Excavations in subsequent seasons, especially between 1996 and 1998, allowed the detailed investigation of a 45m length of the main enclosure boundary together with associated features and antenna ditches connected to the main boundary. Geophysical surveys over the same period allow a provisional interpretation of the surviving portion of the enclosure and its boundaries, although this is based on the identification of what are currently considered contiguous anomalies; parts of the circuit have yet to be tested through excavation.

As currently understood the main enclosure is D-shaped in plan, at least 240m north to south and more than 220m east to west with an area in excess of 4ha (Fig. 9.2). The flat perimeter, in fact slightly concave, faces to the west, and may have had an entrance more or less in the centre. A large white quartz standing stone, The Boolievane Stone, stands about 40m west of the enclosure, again more or less central to the western boundary. The eastern part of the enclosure has been partly cut away by quarrying over the last few centuries.[1] Geophysical surveys suggest the presence of a small penannular enclosure about 14m in diameter with an entrance facing south-east immediately inside the enclosure about mid-way along the western side (Darvill 1998, 25–6). As a whole the enclosure occupied all of a low gently rounded hilltop; the internal penannular enclosure stands on the highest ground within the bounded area. The ground outside the enclosure to the west, around the Boolievane Stone is notably poor in geophysical anomalies.

Excavation of the enclosure has been confined to the northern boundary and part of the interior on the north side. Here at least two main phases are represented, in some cases involving sufficient remodelling as to suggest a succession of enclosures on more or less the same area (Fig. 9.3). The earliest phase is represented as a continuous linear ditch about 1m wide and up to 0.5m deep running on a north-east to south-west alignment for a distance of about 25m (F14/F28) before turning sharply north-west and continuing on a generally westward curving course for a distance of about 90m (F17/F272/F297/F400). This line is broken by two wide gaps, one of which contains a mini-henge structure. This northward projecting arm of ditch probably continues into areas yet to be explored, and perhaps forms a northern annex of some kind. About 1.5m south of the sharp corner already referred to is a second continuous ditch (F68) which continues the general line of the first ditch in a south-westerly direction. The gap between the two ditches is interpreted as an entrance allowing communication between the interior of the main enclosure and the northern annex or exterior to the north. All of these ditches show some evidence of re-cutting, and the fills

Billown, Isle of Man

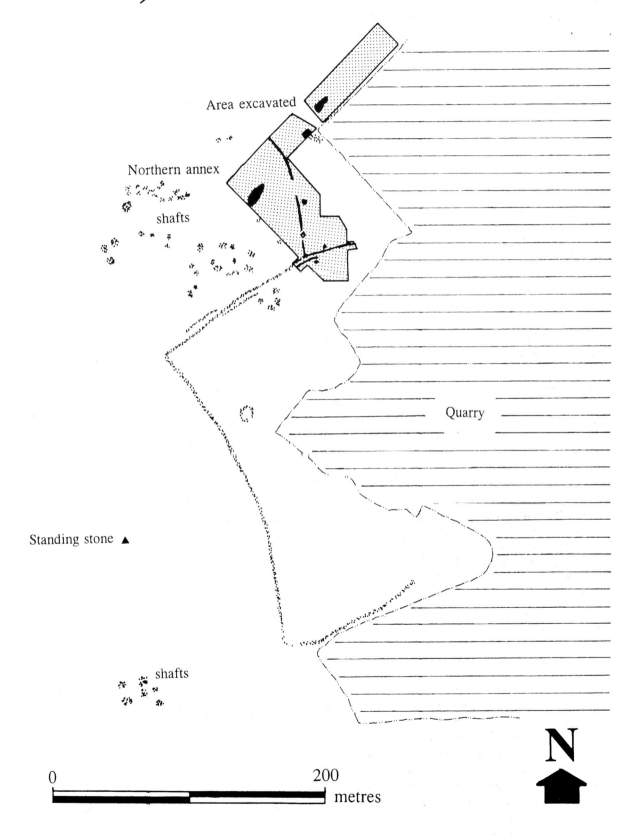

Fig 9.2: Plan showing the provisional outline of the Billown enclosures and associated features in relation to the area excavated 1995–98.

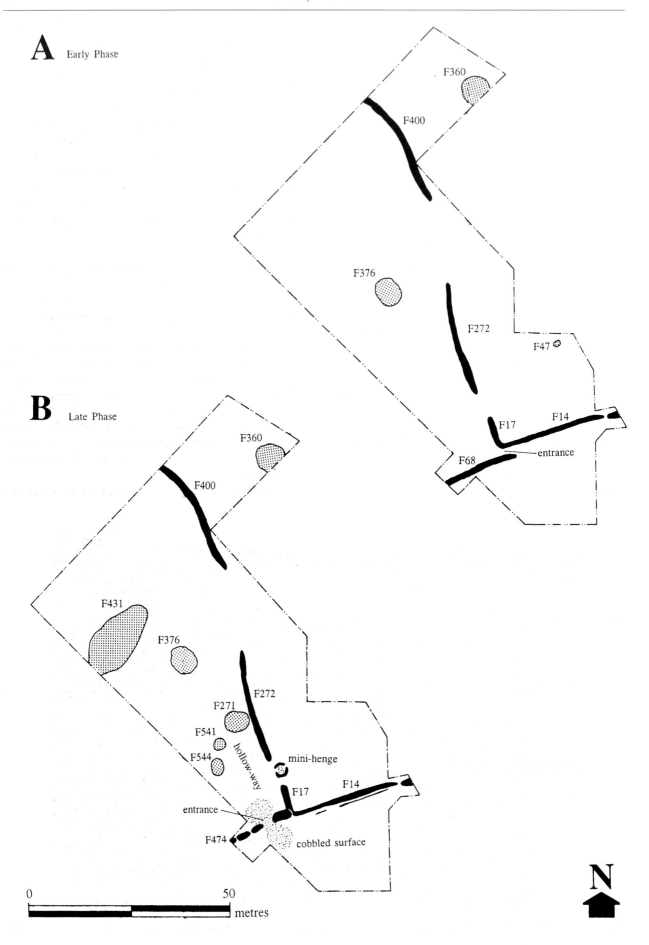

Fig. 9.3: Provisional phase plans of the northern entrance area of the main enclosure based on excavations 1995–98.

contain Neolithic pottery and numerous complete leaf-shaped arrowheads. Whether the ditches were ever flanked by a bank is not known; certainly none survives within the excavated areas. For much of its course, especially north of the sharp turn northwards, the ditch profile is asymmetrical, with a steeper northern side and a more shallow southern side.

The southerly of these early ditches, F68, appears to have been deliberately in-filled fairly soon after being dug. It was sealed by a layer of stones packed into its upper fill. This fill was in turn overlaid by a thin layer of soil, possibly the result of excavating a new line of ditches some 1.5m to the north. This new line was causewayed in form. One segment (F127) joined (and stratigraphically cut) the corner of ditch F17/F28 while others (F281 and F474) continued the line. Overall, the alignment of the causewayed ditch extends the line of the non-causewayed ditch F28/F14 south-westwards.

The gap between segments F127 and F281 in the causewayed ditch is about 2.5m wide and appears to have formed an entrance, presumably replacing the one that had been in filled and covered when the ditches were remodelled. A sequence of three postholes on the east side and six on the west side suggests some elaboration and periodic reconstruction. A cobbled stone surface extending for over 7m either side of the entrance, sealing the earlier ditch F68, is further evidence that this entrance received heavy usage. Moreover, the natural surface north of the entrance appears to have been eroded in the form of a slight hollow-way leading into the centre of

space (?annex) defined by the ditches west of F272 and south of F400.

The causewayed ditch segments were re-cut on at least three occasions. In its last phase, the most easterly, F127, had a narrow slot cut along its southern edge. Stone slabs were set upright in the slot, a large granite erratic being set in the slot adjacent to the entrance (Fig. 9.4). A second similar stone may have been set on the other side of the entrance, perhaps as a final replacement for the earlier wooden setting, but only the stone socket survived at the time this area was excavated. The ditch fills contained small amounts or bowl-style Neolithic pottery, flintwork including numerous leaf-shaped arrowheads, and white quartz pebbles that seem to have mainly been placed on or near the bottom of the ditch segments. Small quantities of carbonized plant remains, including cereals, have been recovered from the ditch fills. Bone is not preserved on the site so it is not known whether animal or human body parts were also included in the ditch fills.

The area excavated within the main enclosure revealed few features: a small stone cairn (Darvill 1996a, 20), a series of undated postholes, a short length of gully (F222), a scoop (F233), and a narrow gully (F231) running parallel to the main ditch F14. The topsoil in this area is rather deeper than to the north of the ditch system, suggesting perhaps that the areas either side of this boundary were subject to differential land-use at some stage.

North and north-west of the main enclosure, in the

Fig. 9.4: Photograph showing the second-phase northern entrance to the main enclosure with the cobbled surface in the entranceway part excavated and the stone settings in the final recut still in place.

area tentatively identified as the northern annex, and beyond, are a series of scoops, pits and shafts. Some of these features are extremely large and most preserve evidence for occasional visits that involved lighting fires and perhaps cooking and eating. F376, for example, was a large pit in the bottom of which was a shaft. The pit was about 6m in diameter with gently sloping sides. In the upper fill was a hearth in which lay the remains of three early Neolithic bowls (Darvill 1998, 17); charred plant remains include cereals and hazlenut shells. Under the hearth was what turned out to be the burnt remains of a series of planks. A radiocarbon date on the charcoal from one of these timbers suggests that the tree from which the plank was made was cut down about 4899–4719 cal BC (5910±70 BP (Beta-110691)). Below the planks was the top of a circular shaft extending downwards from the bottom of the pit for a distance of 2.5m. By contrast, F431 was an extensive scoop, 25m long and up to 15m wide, probably dug in a series of episodes with pits dug in the bottom of the scoop. Charcoal from a hearth in the central part of the scoop, at a depth of about 1.2m below the ground surface, provided a radiocarbon date of 2886–2586 BC (4170±90 BP; Beta-129019). Fourteen pits, scoops and shafts of Neolithic date have so far been excavated; geophysical survey suggests that these are part of a scatter of perhaps 70 such structures, all but three or four outside the main enclosure (see Darvill 1999a, 71).

All these scoops, pits, and shafts were accessible from the entrance through the northern boundary of the main enclosure, and as already noted a hollow way had formed immediately north of the cobbled area in the entranceway suggesting fairly heavy usage. In passing through the northern entrance in a northerly direction the field of view is dominated by the second highest mountain on the Island, South Barrule, which rises to 483m above sea level.[2] Its peak is 5.7km from the Billown Quarry Site and is topped by a clearly visible round stone cairn of unknown date (Megaw 1938, 237).

The northern entrance to the main enclosure appears to coincide with a scatter of flintwork of the heavy blade industries traditionally assigned to the later Mesolithic of the Island (Woodman 1978). Charcoal from pre-enclosure pit F526 has been dated to 4542–4464 BC (5680±40 BP; Beta-125767), the earliest ditch fill (F69) to 4713–4549 BC (5780±40 BP; Beta-125768), and the latest ditch re-cut, which includes the stone setting referred to above (F127), to 1973–1884 BC (3590±40 BP; Beta-125766). This provisional dating is broadly confirmed by the range of cultural material recovered, and shows that the use of the site spans what is conventionally regarded as the earlier and later Neolithic.

DISCUSSION

The Billown enclosures extend the distribution of recorded examples into new territory; they are also the first to be found on any of the small islands within the British Isles archipelago. As currently interpreted the focus of the sites was a large D-shaped enclosure that underwent several phases of reconstruction, each with episodes of boundary re-cutting, over a period of up to 2000 years. Throughout its history there was an entrance in the north side of the enclosure boundary giving access to an area of pit/shaft digging, possibly within a smaller northern enclosure or annex, or at least in an area subdivided by ditches connected to the main enclosure boundary. This area outside the main enclosure to the north and north-west appears to have been the focus of pit-digging. Available radiocarbon dates suggest that construction of the first enclosure lies back in the fifth millennium BC making it amongst the earliest in the British Isles.[3]

Although the outline of the Billown main enclosure must be regarded as provisional pending further investigation and verification of the detail, the emergent plan is not without parallels, especially in central and eastern England. At Haddenham, Cambridgeshire, the outline of the 8.5ha enclosure is very close in plan and scale. Here too there is a curved west-facing 'front' with an oval enclosure behind (Evans 1988). D-shaped plans to Neolithic monuments are fairly widely known, and can be seen also in the form of the inner ditch at Windmill Hill, Wiltshire (Smith 1965), and at a much smaller scale at the Grendon Barrow, Northamptonshire (Gibson 1985). Mention may also be made of the undated ditched enclosure that appears to pre-date the massive stone circle known as Long Meg and Her Daughters, Cumbria (Soffe & Clare 1988). Although slightly more irregular in plan than either Haddenham or Billown appears to be, there is a south facing slightly concave 'front' with a centrally placed main entrance and the standing stone of Long Meg directly in front of the entrance at a distance of about 100m. The apparently later stone circle fits between the enclosure and the standing stone.

The complexity of the Neolithic boundary works, the final recut slot containing carefully packed stones dating to the early second millennium BC, and the abundance of arrowheads allows parallels to be drawn with the complex at Hambledon Hill, Dorset (Mercer 1980; 1988). The presence of human crania on the floor of the enclosure ditches at the main enclosure at Hambledon Hill also has certain similarities with the placement of white quartz pebbles on the ditch floors at Billown (cf. Mercer 1980, 32). Other comparisons may be made with enclosures in southern and especially south-western England including the presence of pits outside the boundary on the north side of Robin Hood's Ball, Wiltshire, (Richards 1990, 61–5) and the relatively high proportion of leaf-shaped arrowheads in assemblages from Carn Brae, Cornwall (Saville in Mercer 1981,124), Hembury, Devon (Liddell 1935, 162), and Crickley Hill, Gloucestershire (Dixon 1988, 83) amongst other sites. To what extent some of these similarities can be attributed to connections facilitated by maritime links along the western seaways is a matter that deserves further investigation.

Notes

1. Quarrying at Billown is believed to extend back to at least the 12th century AD when limestone was extracted to build the keep of the castle in Castletown.

2. Sadly, the place-name evidence does not provide any clues to the special character of this hill. The name "South Barrule" is interpreted by Gelling (1970, 131) as being a survival from the Norse language meaning the southern 'watch fell': a place from which a lookout was kept.

3. Support for an early date can be found in evidence for an elm decline at 4235–4042 BC (5313 38 BP; UB-3555) in the Dhoo valley, Glen Vine, in the central part of the Island (Innes 1995).

BIBLIOGRAPHY

Bersu, G. 1947. A cemetery of the Ronaldsway Culture at Ballateare, Jurby, Isle of Man. *Proceedings of the Prehistoric Society*, 13, 161–169.

Bowen, E. G. 1970. Britain and the British Seas. In D. Moore (ed), *The Irish Sea Province in archaeology and history*. Cardiff. Cambrian Archaeological Association. 13 28.

Bruce, J. R., Megaw, E. M. & Megaw, B. R. S. 1947. A Neolithic site at Ronaldsway, Isle of Man. *Proceedings of the Prehistoric Society*, 13, 139–160.

Burrow, S. 1997. *The Neolithic culture of the Isle of Man. A study of sites and pottery*. Oxford. Archaeopress (British Archaeological Reports, British Series 263).

Burrow, S. & Darvill, T. 1997. AMS dating of the Ronaldsway Culture of the Isle of Man. *Antiquity*, 71, 412–19.

Clark, G. 1935. The prehistory of the Isle of Man. *Proceedings of the Prehistoric Society*, 1, 70–92.

Daniel, G. E. 1950. *The prehistoric chambered tombs of England and Wales*. Cambridge. Cambridge University Press

Darvill, T. 1996a. *Billown Neolithic Landscape Project, Isle of Man, 1995*. Bournemouth and Douglas Bournemouth University and Manx National Heritage (School of Conservation Sciences Research Report 1).

Darvill, T. 1996b. Billown, Isle of Man. *Current Archaeology*, 13.6 (No. 150), 232–37.

Darvill, T. 1997. *Billown Neolithic Landscape Project, Isle of Man, 1996*. Bournemouth and Douglas. Bournemouth University and Manx National Heritage (School of Conservation Sciences Research Report 3).

Darvill, T. 1998. *Billown Neolithic Landscape Project, Isle of Man. Third Report: 1997*. Bournemouth and Douglas. Bournemouth University and Manx National Heritage (School of Conservation Science, Research Report 4).

Darvill, T. 1999a. *Billown Neolithic Landscape Project, Isle of Man. Fourth Report: 1998*. Bournemouth and Douglas. Bournemouth University and Manx National Heritage (School of Conservation Science, Research Report 5).

Darvill, T. 1999b. Billown Neolithic Landscape Project 1995–1997. In PJ Davey (ed.), *Recent archaeological research on the Isle of Man*. Oxford. Archaeopress (British Archaeological Reports, British Series 278). 13–26.

Darvill, T. 2000. Neolithic Mann in context. In A Ritchie (ed.), *Neolithic Orkney in its European context*. Cambridge. McDonald Institute Monographs, 371–85.

Davies, M. 1946. The diffusion and distribution pattern of the megalithic monuments of the Irish Sea and North Channel coastlands. *Antiquaries Journal*, 26, 38–60.

Dixon, P. 1988. The Neolithic settlements on Crickley Hill, Gloucestershire. In C. Burgess, P. Topping, C. Mordant & M. Maddison (eds), *Enclosures and defences in the Neolithic of Western Europe*. Oxford. British Archaeological Reports, International Series 403. I, 75–88.

Evans, C. 1988. Excavations at Haddenham, Cambridgeshire: a "planned" enclosure and its regional affinities. In C. Burgess, P. Topping, C. Mordant & M. Maddison (eds), *Enclosures and defences in the Neolithic of Western Europe*. Oxford. British Archaeological Reports, International Series 403. I, 127–148.

Gelling, M. 1970. The place-names of the Isle of Man. *Journal of the Manx Museum*, 7 (No. 86), 130–39.

Gibson, A. 1985. A Neolithic enclosure at Grendon, Northamptonshire. *Antiquity*, 49, 213–9.

Henshall, A. 1978. Manx Megaliths again: An attempt at structural analysis. In P. Davey (ed.), *Man and Environment in the Isle of Man*. Oxford. British Archaeological Reports, British Series 54. 171–176.

Innes, J. B. 1995. *The Dhoo Valley, Isle of Man: a palaeoenvironmental assessment*. Douglas. Centre for Manx Studies (Centre for Manx Studies, Research Report 2).

Liddell, D. M. 1935. Report on the excavations at Hembury Fort (1934 and 1935). *Proceedings of the Devon Archaeological Exploration Society*, 2.3, 135–75.

Megaw, B. R. S. 1938. Manx megaliths and their ancestry. *Proceedings of the Isle of Man Natural History and Antiquarian Society*, 4.2, 219–39.

Mercer, R. 1980. *Hambledon Hill. A Neolithic landscape*. Edinburgh. Edinburgh University Press.

Mercer, R. 1981. Excavations at Carn Brea, Illogan, Cornwall, 1970–73. *Cornish Archaeology*, 20, 1–204.

Mercer, R. 1988. Hambledon Hill, Dorset, England. In C. Burgess, P. Topping, C. Mordant & M. Maddison (eds), *Enclosures and defences in the Neolithic of Western Europe*. Oxford. British Archaeological Reports, International Series 403. I, 89–106.

Moffatt, P. J. 1978. The Ronaldsway Culture: A review. In P. Davey (ed.), *Man and environment in the Isle of Man*. Oxford. British Archaeological Reports, British Series 54. I, 177–215.

Piggott, S. 1932. The Mull Hill Circle, Isle of Man, and its pottery. *Antiquaries Journal*, 12, 146–157.

Piggott, S. 1954. *Neolithic Cultures of the British Isles*. Cambridge. Cambridge University Press.

Richards, J, 1990. *The Stonehenge Environs Project*. London. English Heritage, Archaeological Report 16.

Smith, I. F. 1965. *Windmill Hill and Avebury*. Oxford. Clarendon Press.

Soffe, G. & Clare, T. 1988. New evidence of ritual monuments at Long Meg and Her Daughters, Cumbria. *Antiquity*, 62, 552–557.

Woodman, P. 1978. A re-appraisal of the Manx Mesolithic. In P. J. Davey (ed.), *Man and environment in the Isle of Man*. Oxford. British Archaeological Reports, British Series 54. I, 119–140.

10. Lithic Artefacts from Neolithic Causewayed Enclosures: Character and Meaning

Alan Saville

INTRODUCTION

This paper focuses on practical problems associated with contexting and characterizing flaked lithic artefacts from causewayed enclosures and on how these types of lithic artefacts may or may not add to understanding of the nature and function of such sites. My own research in this area has been concerned largely with the struck flint artefacts from the causewayed enclosures on Hambledon Hill, Dorset, England (Saville 1990a). In what follows, however, the problems addressed are not specific to the archaeology of Hambledon Hill or other causewayed enclosures, but have general applicability for the study of lithic artefacts from the same period.

The excavation of a causewayed enclosure will normally produce a substantial collection of struck lithic artefacts. However, lithic artefacts are virtually indestructible, and hence have a high propensity for residuality. It is also the case that later prehistoric lithic artefacts are often in themselves chronologically insensitive and difficult to date other than in very general period terms, which in Britain can often mean simply post-Mesolithic. A further given is that causewayed enclosures are generally extensive – normally larger than one hectare and up to almost ten hectares in terms of maximum area (Palmer 1976, fig.10) – and relatively poorly preserved, often as a result of long-term overploughing.

Taken together, these statements would suggest at the outset a need for considerable caution when attempting to interpret lithic finds from these enclosures. The taphonomy of any finds from such sites is liable to be complex and problematic, but with lithic artefacts the norms of archaeological phasing by context are always potentially compromised by the residuality factor.

To flesh this out, imagine that Neolithic activity of some kind took place at a location before an enclosure was constructed. The lithic residues from that activity would almost inevitably become incorporated, to a lesser or greater extent, in the subsequent ditch fills of the enclosure. The same would apply to the residues of any construction-stage, occupational, or post-enclosure activity, for as long as deposits were able to accumulate in the ditch fills. As for attempting to phase ditch infill

horizons, there is considerable potential for incremental admixture from the residues of each previous phase or phases. This would be exacerbated, of course, by any recutting of ditch infills, an apparently recurrent feature at such sites (Smith 1971, 98). Archaeologists are accustomed to regard lithic collections from ploughsoil as potential, if not undoubted, admixtures, and it should be accepted that lithic collections from ditch fills are equally prone to unknown, and unknowable, conflation (cf. Smith 1965, 15).

Internal enclosure features – usually pits and scoops of various sizes – are often regarded as of higher integrity as contexts than ditches, but these are equally susceptible in terms of artefact content to the problems of residuality. Also, unlike the enclosure ditches, these features are frequently enigmatic in terms of specific site chronology, since they usually lack any straightforward stratigraphic link with the enclosure within which they are found or with any other features in or around the enclosure.

Residuality is therefore a factor which crucially affects lithic artefact evidence, though only rarely has it been acknowledged in studies of causewayed enclosures (Edmonds & Bellamy 1991, 215; Smith 1971, 98). However, residuality is only one aspect of the difficulties involved in being able to assess, let alone fully understand, the nature of lithic artefact discard and its contribution to site formation processes.

The distinction between lithic implements and waste is generally made on the basis of 'types' and the presence, character and location of their secondary retouch. This practice continues, despite the fact that use-wear studies have shown that many artefacts which would in this way be classified as waste are in fact implements (e.g. Jensen 1986; van Gijn 1998, 341). Thus, while on the one hand the assumption is usually made that implements and waste will have undergone different patterns of use and discard, on the other hand the knowledge that this differentiation will be undermined by the unknown proportion of unrecognized implements among the 'waste' is tacitly ignored.

Neither is it clear at what point in their individual histories implements become 'waste' in the sense that they are no longer, for whatever reason, required as tools. In the case of scrapers, for example, it is apparent that they can be resharpened many times, a process which has been observed ethnographically and been required during experiment (Bienenfeld 1988, 225), and has been seen as a significant factor in the archaeological evidence (Dibble 1987). Not only does this throw some doubt on the utility of the typological sub-classification of Neolithic scrapers (Pollard 1999, 336), it makes it very uncertain whether any actual scraper from an archaeological deposit is exhausted, waiting to be resharpened, or still perfectly functional. This in turn will of course add complexity to any attempt to understand the presence of a scraper in a given context.

Also most archaeologists, including many lithic analysts, turn a blind eye to the question of hafts and hafting. It should have become routine to appreciate that most lithic implements were used in a hafted form (Stordeur 1987). The problem has of course been that these hafts and haft elements – of organic materials: wood, bone, antler, fibre, mastic, etc – do not survive in the conditions pertaining at most Neolithic sites. Even where the rare circumstance of waterlogging at causewayed enclosures has occurred, as at Etton, Cambridgeshire, only a single axe haft (minus axehead) was recovered (Taylor 1998). This problem is compounded in the case of small lithic tools, in that they rarely retain use-wear traces identifiable as the result of hafting, even where they have been used experimentally in hafted form (Unger-Hamilton *et al.* 1987, 282). However, since many if not most lithic implements at causewayed enclosures, if used on site at all, can be assumed to have been hafted, what happened to the hafts? Were they discarded with the lithic component, were the lithic components removed and discarded separately, and how would this affect incorporation into ditch or pit fills?

The raw materials used for flaked lithic artefacts at causewayed enclosures are generally local ones. Only axeheads and some arrowheads are often made from 'exotic' flints or cherts (Palmer 1970, 112–3; Smith 1971, 104–5), and even these raw materials may be locally unusual rather than necessarily long-distance imports. The absence of matching on-site cores and flakes does, however, indicate that it is the finished tools coming to the sites rather than the raw material as such.

It is furthermore the case that lithic artefacts from causewayed enclosures are normally in themselves rather unremarkable (Fig. 10.1). The types of artefact involved are the standard types of the early and middle Neolithic periods and can equally be found on all other site types of the period, as well as 'off-site'. The artefacts do not generally carry any clear signs of the way in which they have been used or how or why they have been deposited, and it is up to the excavator and analyst to determine, by such means as context, disposition, proximity, and condition, whether or not there may be relevances which assist inference on these issues.

However, the method of excavation at causewayed enclosures has rarely been such as to ensure high resolution in terms of artefact recovery. This is largely a consequence of scale, but also of attitude. Some enclosure excavations have been on a very large scale, commensurate with the size of the monuments being investigated, where logistics alone would preclude the kind of artefact recovery practised on, for example, a Mesolithic period site. Also, until recently, the attitude of enclosure excavators has tended to work against the recording, handling, and packaging of lithic artefacts in such as way as to maximise their potential for post-excavation analysis. There are obvious practical and historical reasons for this; pottery has tended to be the privileged artefact category during the excavation of Neolithic sites.

Moreover, some analysts have bemoaned the lack of publication of what lithic artefact evidence has been recovered in detail adequate to permit the requisite subsequent research (Bradley 1994, 152). Because causewayed enclosures are generally not too well preserved and because the lithic artefact evidence suffers from the problems already described, there is room for debate as to how much effort should go into high-definition studies of their lithic residues (Gowlett 1997). However, the point is that high-definition analysis and interpretation cannot be expected to emanate from what is normally, for whatever reason, relatively low-resolution artefact recovery.

There will always be the exception to this lack of resolution, and evidence of higher integrity is occasionally forthcoming. For example, during the excavation of the Stepleton enclosure ditches on Hambledon Hill, stratified clusters of lithic artefacts in ditch infills were found to represent the conjoining residues from specific knapping events (Saville 1990a). In this case the excavation evidence and the refitting analysis allowed a rare glimpse of the action of individuals in association with the enclosure to be reconstructed, insofar as nodule and core reduction sequences allow. This is perhaps the closest one can come to *chaîne opératoire* type analysis with material from causewayed enclosures, since it can only be applied fully at sites with localizable discard from complete sequences of activity, including tool use (Edmonds 1990; Grace 1997).

At the Stepleton enclosure, the formation process by which the deposit of artefacts arrived in the ditch fills remains obscure. Does it result, for example, from knapping in or into an open ditch, from discard from the ditch edge or bank, or from more formal deposition? This obscurity is generally the case, and it is rarely clear whether every so-called cache or concentration found in association with a causewayed enclosure really represents a single act of deposition, deliberate or otherwise. Such would apply, for example, to the 'cache' in ditch fill at Briar Hill, Northamptonshire (Bamford 1985, 78), the 'caches' from ditch fills at Windmill Hill (Whittle *et al.* 1999, 364), the 'cache' in buried soil at High Peak, Devon (Pollard 1966, 50–51), or the concentration in the ditch fill at Offham Hill, Sussex (Drewett 1977, plate 17, upper).

A different kind of higher integrity circumstance applied at Crickley Hill, Gloucestershire (Fig. 10.2). Here a remarkable density of leaf-shaped arrowheads, when plotted against the configuration of the final phase of the enclosure, could credibly be interpreted as the fossilized action of groups involved in defence and attack (Dixon 1988; and see below).

Such examples, where the recovery of higher-integrity lithic evidence points to actual events relating to the life of an enclosure, are rare. In all other situations it must be hoped that a broad-brush approach at a typological level, looking at overall assemblage composition, at considerations of presence/absence and percentage representations of types, at macro-distributions within sites, and at generalizing comparisons between site assemblages, will permit some sensible interpretations of the presence of lithic artefacts at the enclosures. This is the prospect I will explore in this paper, but before continuing it is necessary to consider the range of struck lithic artefacts and implements to be found at causewayed enclosures.

Flint manufacture seems always to have taken place at these sites – even if the nodules had to be brought to the site from the surrounding area (Healy 1998, 25) – so that discarded knapping debris of cores, core fragments, flaked lumps and chunks, as well as apparently unused flakes and spalls, is commonplace. Where primary knapping debris is more restricted, as at Briar Hill, Northamptonshire (Bamford 1985, 84–5), this is likely to reflect the paucity of local sources of appropriate raw material. There may be some debate over the degree to which the final stages of manufacture of tools took place and over the level of on-site use (Drewett 1977, 217), but all enclosures produce numerous implements. The basic tool inventory of axeheads, scrapers, leaf-shaped arrowheads, and 'knives' was outlined by Piggott (1954, 75–80), and further clarified by Smith (1965, 85–103). Smith showed that serrated flakes and 'utilized' flakes were the most significant types in the general category of cutting tool or 'knife', and that other knife forms, such as 'sickle-flints' and 'blunted-back knives' were numerically relatively unimportant. Following on from Clark *et al.* (1960, 223), Smith also itemized the 'laurel-leaf' type of bifacial pieces, which along with piercers and various minor categories such as 'fabricators', effectively complete the average lithic repertoire from a causewayed enclosure. The tool types are illustrated in Figure 1 by examples from Hambledon Hill.

CAUSEWAYED ENCLOSURE IMPLEMENTS

The excavations by Roger Mercer at Hambledon Hill, Dorset, investigated a hilltop enclosure complex within which were two causewayed enclosures (Mercer 1980; 1988). Nearly 90,000 struck lithic artefacts were recovered, from an enormous number of separate contexts, but with the advantage in terms of analysis that there seems to have been little or no pre-Neolithic activity on the hill, nor much sign from the lithic assemblage – in

the form of any distinctive types – for later Neolithic or Bronze Age discard. This contrasts with the one causewayed enclosure which has produced an even larger assemblage, Windmill Hill, Wiltshire (Pollard 1999, 333), where later Neolithic and Bronze Age flints bulk large (Smith 1965, 103–9).

Production took place on site at Hambledon Hill, in part at least exploiting the *in situ* flint resources exposed during earthwork construction, as is the case at other enclosures such as Maiden Castle, Dorset (Edmonds & Bellamy 1991, 216), and Offham, Sussex (Drewett 1977, 211). The Hambledon Hill assemblage overall is a 'balanced one', with cores, unretouched flakes, and retouched pieces present in the same kind of proportions encountered on most Neolithic sites. The specific implements are relatively few, and the tool inventory as a whole is dominated by scrapers and sharp-edge flake implements of various kinds. Piercing tools are the only other common type, with leaf-shaped arrowheads, 'laurel-leaf' bifacials, and polished axeheads all present but in small numbers.

This implement inventory for the most part reinforces expectations reached from considering other lithic assemblages from causewayed enclosures in England (Table 10.1). In looking at the bald figures in this table in this way, I am obviously ignoring numerous parameters, such as site size, extent and date of excavation, proximity to flint source, degree of later Neolithic and Bronze Age activity, and so on, and glossing over some of the problems of intercomparability of analysts' identifications and listings (Bradley 1994, 18). Nevertheless, these figures demonstrate, in particular, a clear dominance of scrapers and serrated-edge flakes and other edge-modified flakes, and the relative scarcity of leaf-shaped arrowheads, 'laurel-leaf' bifacial pieces, and axeheads. The assumption can be, and usually is, made that, irrespective of precise contextual information and just looking at presence/absence, these tools are reflecting activities which have taken place in some association with the causewayed enclosures from which they derive and hold a direct clue to their functions.

One of the most ambitious recent applications of this assumption has been with reference to the lithic assemblages from causewayed enclosures in Sussex (Drewett 1994; Drewett *et al.* 1988). Drewett divided lithic tools into functional groups or tool-kits.

> '... the heavy woodworking tools, essential for clearing land for agriculture, consist of flaked and polished flint axes, polished stone axes and chopping tools. Agricultural tools include heavy flint picks suitable for breaking up the ground and single-piece sickles or curved knives for cutting crops. ... Projectile points, probably used for hunting, were leaf-shaped flint arrowheads ... The laurel-leaf points may also have been used to kill animals. Trapped or domestic animals may have been killed using the flaked discoidal knives, and the carcasses and skins prepared using a variety of flint tools. These included the long- and short-end scrapers, side scrapers, flint choppers, backed and discoidal knives and serrated blades. For making fire ... 'fabricators' ... Craft

tools consisted of hammerstones for making flint tools and a variety of tools suitable for wood and bone working. Such tools include the end, side and hollow scrapers, notched flakes and awls'. (Drewett *et al.* 1988, 31)

These assumptions were then applied to the lithic assemblages from the Sussex sites, admittedly in combination with all the other data available at each site, to categorize the enclosures. Those with a wide range of tools and activities (Whitehawk and the Trundle) were seen as fortified settlement enclosures, those with a restricted range (Barkhale, Combe Hill, Offham, and Bury Hill) were unfortified ceremonial/ritual enclosures (Drewett *et al.* 1988, 40–43). While Drewett has subsequently modified this overall interpretation slightly, he has retained much the same diagnosis of the lithic material (Drewett 1994, 22).

The problem with Drewett's analysis is that it is *too* broad-brush and takes hypotheses about tool use and presence/absence beyond justifiable inference. It is worth remembering the general warning, expressed forcefully by Jensen (1994, 166) and others, that most flint tools in the Neolithic period relate to manufacturing and maintenance, not directly to subsistence. Flint tools are mostly used for making and mending utensils, implements, and equipment of other materials such as bone, wood, bark, reed, fibre, skin, hide, etc., rather than being used themselves for harvesting, gathering, hunting, fishing, butchery or other specifically subsistence purposes.

The quantity and range of implements present at most causewayed enclosures do immediately suggest 'domestic' activity, in contrast to the totally waste-dominated assemblages of industrial sites or the restricted assemblages from funerary monuments (Bradley 1994, 42; Holgate 1988, 50–51), but this is self-evident and hardly advances understanding. So can anything more incisive be said on the basis of the individual tool types represented?

Scrapers (Fig. 10.1: 14–17) are ubiquitous items from earlier and later prehistory at all types of site and their presence at causewayed enclosures is in a sense utterly predictable; they appear to be an essential part of everyday life in the Neolithic period (as indeed they are from the Middle Palaeolithic to the Bronze Age; cf. Lacaille 1947). The surprise would be if scrapers were not present at causewayed enclosures, which would imply something very out-of-the-ordinary.

It is often the case that an association between scrapers and hide-working can be assumed, deduced, or demonstrated (Moss 1983, 38), but use-wear studies confirm an association with wood-working as well (Andersen 1997, 62; Cantwell 1979; Jensen & Brinch Petersen 1985, 44). Hide and wood are also the two most commonly indicated raw materials from the ethnographic literature on the function of scrapers (e.g. Dunn 1931, 64–6), but the archaeological case has in addition been made for scraper use on antler (e.g. Ibáñez Estévez & González Urquijo 1996, 26) and bone (e.g. Dumont 1988, 66). Van Gijn (1998, 345) has raised the possibility of the

relationship between scraper type and function becoming looser during the Neolithic period in the Netherlands, from a concentration on hide-working to more multi-faceted use. Whether this might be so in Britain as well would require far more application of use-wear studies to Neolithic material than has hitherto been the case.

While the use-wear technique may be able to explain on which raw materials a tool like a scraper had predominantly been used, it will not explain what was being done with that raw material nor, of course, why it was being done. There is a multitude of ways in which 'hide' can be worked and to what purpose, and from different animal species (Hayden 1993), though the most probable stages of processing at which scrapers were used are dehairing and softening (Bienenfeld 1988, 224). If the assumption is made that scrapers have been discarded and recovered archaeologically from near their original place of use, then it is naturally of some interest that activities probably involving hide-working were taking place within or around causewayed enclosures. It would thus be of considerable interest if a use-wear study of scrapers from a causewayed enclosure in England were to be undertaken to explore any specificity about this, such as the type of animal involved, or indeed to quantify the degree of preference for scraper use on working hide as opposed to wood or any other raw material.

Until this is achieved, the presence of scrapers in large numbers does not have any particular implications for our vision of the enclosures, because they are 'essential' tools involved in a variety of manufacturing tasks on different raw materials.

Potentially more revealing among the tools which are prolific at causewayed enclosures are the serrated-edge flakes or microdenticulates (Fig. 10.1: 6–9; Bocquet 1980). Often these flakes have a band of edge-gloss in association with the serrations (Fig. 10.1: 7; Curwen 1930, 184). These are very common tools at most enclosures (Table 10.1), a situation long recognized since the early work at Whitehawk Camp, Sussex, where the *'small saw* [sic]' was *'... by far the commonest flint tool'* (Curwen 1937, 87), and at the Trundle, Sussex (Curwen 1937, 94; cf. Holgate 1988, 47). Serrated-edge flakes are also found in association with Neolithic enclosures across north-west Europe, at least from France (e.g. la Mercière, Charente: Burnez *et al.* 1999) to Denmark (e.g. Sarup, Fyn: Andersen 1997).

Use-wear studies of this tool-type appear to have shown conclusively that, despite earlier expectations (e.g. Bell 1977, 26), it was not used for cutting the stems of grasses and/or cereal crops (Jensen 1994, 50–68). This is because the predominant motion of use on serrated-edge flakes is not a sideways cutting, sawing, or slashing one, but a forwards one perpendicular to the serrated edge, as in whittling (Jensen 1988a, 235–9; *contra* Levi-Sala 1992, 246). A one-to-one link with any specific function has not been established, but those serrated-edge flakes with edge-gloss have probably been used on silicious plant material of some kind. Jensen (1988a,

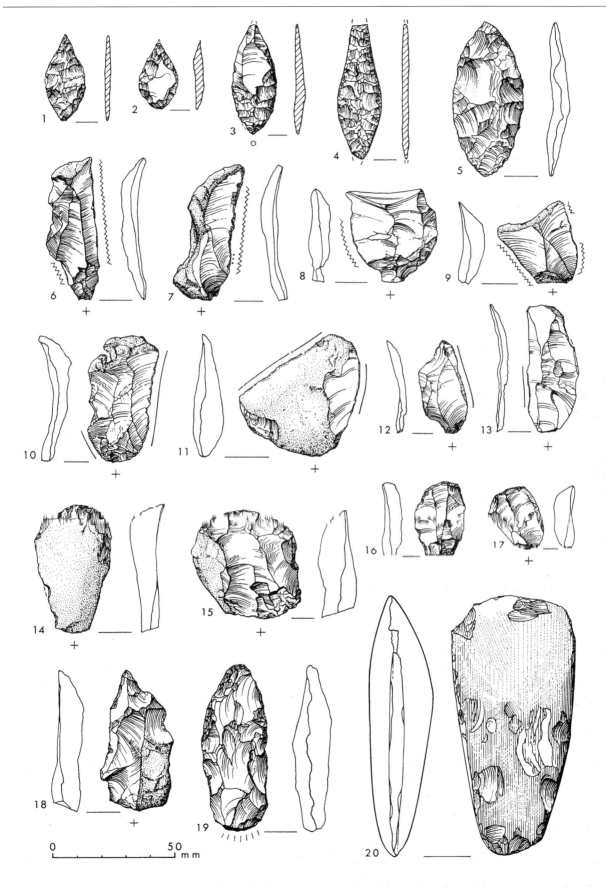

Fig. 10.1: Flint implements from Hambledon Hill, Dorset, as examples of the main tool types from causewayed enclosures. 1–4: leaf-shaped arrowheads; 5: 'laurel-leaf' bifacial; 6–9: serrated-edge flakes; 10–13: edge-trimmed flakes; 14–17 scrapers; 18: piercer; 19: 'fabricator'; 20: polished axehead. Scale 2:3. Redrawn by M O'Neil after originals by J Richards, courtesy of RJ Mercer and English Heritage.

248; 1988b, 135) has suggested working on vegetable fibres, perhaps as part of activities involving twine and rope or textiles, as a possibility; van Gijn (1998, 345) has mentioned fibre-making for clothing; and Barton (1992, 218) suggested scoring birch bark (though at least one microdenticulate from the Sarup enclosure in Denmark has been interpreted as used to cut meat (Andersen 1997, 62)). In her most recent discussion of the problems surrounding this implement type, Jensen (1994, 62–8) has stepped back from her previous suggestions involving work with fibres as too dogmatic. It is rather depressing to learn from the specialists that use-wear analysis will probably never discover any exact function of serrated-edge flakes (Jensen 1994, 68; Levi Sala 1996, 22).

As with scrapers, it is worth querying whether there really is any particular correlation between this tool type and causewayed enclosures. In fact it would appear that most substantial assemblages from the early/middle Neolithic period, irrespective of the type of site, have a serrated-edge flake component, sometimes substantial (e.g. Bishopstone, Sussex: Bell 1977, 19–39; Hurst Fen, Suffolk: Clark *et al.* 1960, 214). The most glaring exceptions in England, which might be used to argue a contrast with the causewayed enclosures, are the assemblages from Neolithic sites at Carn Brea, Cornwall (Mercer 1981) and Broome Heath, Norfolk (Wainwright 1972). The Carn Brea assemblage, which has only three serrated flakes, has been discussed from this perspective with the conclusion that the frequent edge-trimmed flakes, particularly those with edge-gloss, represent in this instance an equivalence (Saville 1981a, 144). However, the situation at Broome Heath is, at face value, altogether remarkable, since in an assemblage which includes 1,063 scrapers, there appear to have been only six serrated-edge flakes and virtually no other edge-trimmed or edge-retouched flakes which could be equivalents (Wainwright 1972, 67).

Perhaps the real question about serrated-edge flakes is why they become so prevalent in the early/middle Neolithic period, then decline markedly in Late Neolithic and Early Bronze Age assemblages (Healy 1993, 34), whereas axeheads, scrapers, piercers, arrowheads, and knives do not. Does this imply a particular technology or function from the earlier period was not continued into the later, or was an alternative tool, perhaps organic, adopted for the same purpose?

Edge-trimmed, edge-retouched, or edge-'utilized' flakes and blades are among the most common components of causewayed-enclosure assemblages (Fig. 10.1: 10–13; Table 10.1), but their relative presence is notoriously difficult to evaluate and compare because of the degree of subjectivity in definition of the type. To an extent they can simply be taken as a given, whether itemized or described in detail for any individual assemblage or not. The same is true to a lesser extent of piercers, which are always present (Table 10.1), but not always easy to identify unless of a fairly robust form and unbroken (Fig. 10.1: 18). In neither case have use-wear studies been especially revealing about the materials on which edge-trimmed flakes and piercers have been used, other than to indicate, as might be anticipated, that these are varied.

Possibly more informative components of the causewayed enclosure assemblages are some of the less well-represented tool categories. The reasons why some implement types are represented more than others can of course be complex and, apart from such parameters as ease of production, mode of use, and the frequency of specific tasks, there is potential influence from factors of style, status, and gender. However, scrapers, serrated-edge and other edge-trimmed flakes, and piercers are easy to produce, were probably in daily use, and were eminently expendable. Leaf-shaped arrowheads and polished axeheads, on the other hand, are more time-consuming to produce, may require 'exotic' raw material, and are highly curatable. Scrapers, serrated-edge flakes, and piercers are likely to be discarded whole once non-resharpenable, once the edges or points have been dulled or broken, or because they are covered with muck from use. Arrowheads and axeheads are unlikely to be discarded whole except by accident, though of course they can be deposited in other ways, for instance as grave-goods. In other words, arrowheads and axeheads are arguably rather different categories of tool within the hierarchy of lithic artefact production and use, and in terms of the variety of roles they may perform and any non-utilitarian values they may enshrine.

This is not to deny the inherent problems in the opposition between expediency and curation (Nash 1996; Odell 1996). These terms were coined for lithic studies in the context of mobile hunter-gatherer societies, with – to simplify the arguments involved – the fundamental contrast being drawn between those tools made, used, and discarded at a single site, and those carried from one site to another (though there are also overtones of contrast between personal and non-personal gear). It is by no means certain that these distinctions are always so clear-cut, nor that the situation will be the same for agricultural societies as for hunter-gatherers. In the final analysis it is down to the judgement of Occam's razor: arrowheads and axeheads can only function (as tools) when hafted as the tips of arrows and the blades of axes or adzes respectively, and the bow-and-arrow and the axe must in most imaginable circumstances be taken to their task rather than vice-versa.

Arrowheads are present at all enclosure sites, but generally in small numbers and generally fragmentary. There are now several instances from Britain of leaf-shaped arrowheads found embedded in human bones (Green 1984, 35), and it seems highly probable that the bow-and-arrow in the earlier Neolithic was a practical anti-personnel weapon, whether or not it was also used for hunting (for which there is no positive evidence) or functioned as an emblem of gender or age status. If it were assumed that causewayed enclosures were fortified sites, subject to defence and attack by opposed factions armed with bows-and-arrows, then one would expect leaf-shaped arrowheads to be rather more common finds than they are, because the arrowheads would become broken on site by use.

This assumption seems justified by the evidence from two sites, Carn Brea, Cornwall (Mercer 1981) and Crickley Hill, Gloucestershire (Dixon 1988). At Carn Brea, which was a defended hilltop settlement rather than a causewayed enclosure, the ratio of leaf-shaped arrowheads present, whatever criterion is used, is extraordinarily high. There were some 751 arrowheads in an assemblage of 26,000 pieces overall, among which there were only 131 scrapers and only 2065 retouched artefacts in total. Intra-site distributional information was limited at Carn Brea, but there was some evidence for clustering in the region of what was probably a main entrance (Saville 1981a, 146).

Similarly, at Crickley Hill the site had a high number of leaf-shaped arrowheads, and in its final phase as an entranced (rather than causewayed) enclosure displayed a remarkable clustering of arrowheads at entrance points through the ditches and along palisade lines (Fig. 10.2). As the excavator has described:

> '*The fate of this final enclosure was clearly shown by the thick spread of flint arrowheads, over 400 of which choked the eastern entrance passageways and fanned out along the roadways into the interior. The enclosure had quite obviously been defended against archery attack ...*' (Dixon 1988, 82).

These two sites set a standard whereby the absence of leaf-shaped arrowheads must be a decisive indicator that armed struggle has not played a hugely significant part in the history of an enclosure. Of the enclosure assemblages

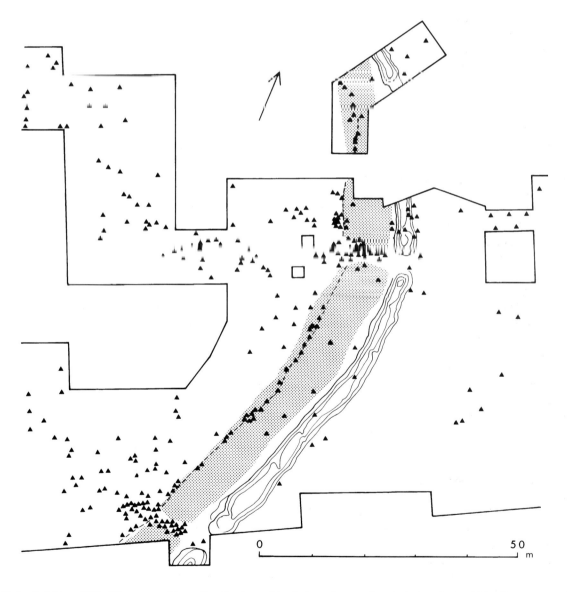

Fig 10.2: Crickley Hill, Gloucestershire: distribution of leaf-shaped arrowheads (triangles) within the excavated area straddling the bank (stippled) and ditch of the entranced enclosure. The dashed line represents the position of a palisade. Note the concentration of arrowheads in the two entrances and along the line of the palisade, and continuing within the enclosure (to the left) along probable roadways. Redrawn by M. O'Neil after Dixon (1988, fig. 4.5).

Table 10.1: Total numbers of selected flint implement types from various causewayed enclosures in England

Type	HH	Ste	Et	WH	BH	Sta	Ab	MC
Scrapers	351	240	253	1399	181	377	166	421
Edge-trimmed flakes	411	184	410	457	x	x	370	x
Serrated-edge flakes	343	146	219	627+	83	195+	272	188
Piercers	86	49	58	68	34	160	5	17
Leaf arrowheads	29	9	29	132	18	34	17	28
Axeheads, etc	19	15	18	90	3+	21	11	49
'Laurel-leaf' bifacials	3	3	5	25	1	66(?)	5	2
Knives	7	4	1	84+	11	104(?)	10	12
'Fabricators'/rods	7	6	9	2+	2	12	2	4

Key to enclosures:

HH	Hambledon Hill, Dorset, main enclosure	Sta	Staines, Surrey (Healey & Robertson-Mackay 1983 & 1987)
Ste	Hambledon Hill, Dorset, Stepleton enclosure		
Et	Etton, Cambridgeshire (Middleton 1998)	Ab	Abingdon, Oxfordshire (Avery 1982)
WH	Windmill Hill, Wiltshire (Smith 1965)	MC	Maiden Castle, Dorset (Edmonds & Bellamy 1991; Wheeler 1943)
BH	Briar Hill, Northamptonshire (Bamford 1985)		

listed in Table 10.1, only that from Windmill Hill has large numbers of leaf-shaped arrowheads. However, when considered in proportion to the whole collection from Windmill Hill, the presence of arrowheads is not actually prominent. In fact Hembury, Devon, is the only other enclosure, apart from Carn Brea and Crickley Hill, where arrowheads appear to have been a major feature within the assemblage, and even this is difficult to substantiate because of restricted documentation for the assemblage as a whole (Liddell 1935, 162).

Thus a general observation can be made, on the basis of lithic typology and assemblage analysis, that episodes of attack and defence were probably not the norm at causewayed enclosures. This is not to say that such episodes did not occur, since any find of a leaf-shaped arrowhead from an enclosure may testify to an incident of aggression. Such an incident may be indicated by the now well-known skeleton of a man from one of the ditch segments of the Stepleton enclosure at Hambledon Hill (Mercer 1980, figs 29–30; 1988, plate 5.IV.A; 1990, fig. 7). This has a broken, but unusually fine, elongated ogival arrowhead (Fig. 10.1: 4), contained, as the excavator put it, within the thoracic cavity of the body, and was ostensibly the cause of death (Mercer 1980, 51; 1988, 104; 1990, 41). Although this interpretation has caught the general imagination (Edmonds 1999, 135; Scarre 1998, 116) is not as clear-cut as one would wish, since the arrowhead is incomplete and the tip is not preserved in any of the bones of this skeleton. The arrowhead is also an exceptionally fancy one, both in general and in comparison to the others in this assemblage, and alternative explanations for its presence must be possible (e.g. retention for intended reworking).

Polished flint axeheads are not so specifically identifiable with a task or pattern of use, other than that they are most closely associated with wood-working. They are relatively rarely found intact at causewayed enclosure sites in Britain (Bradley 1994, table 5.3). Exceptions are cached finds: a group of three polished flint axeheads from the enclosure ditch at Combe Hill, Sussex (Drewett 1994, figs. 11–12); a group of three 'chipped and polished' flint axeheads, now lost, from an earlier excavation of the inner south cross-dyke ditch just outside the main enclosure at Hambledon Hill (Frances Healy pers. comm.); and a part-polished and an unpolished axehead found together in buried soil beneath an Iron Age bank at Maiden Castle (Wheeler 1943, fig. 39, 8–9). At Hambledon Hill there are otherwise only two intact flint axeheads from the recent excavations, one from a feature within the main enclosure (Fig. 10.1: 20), the other from an unstratified position by one of the outwork ditches, well away from the enclosures.

There are, of course, numerous fragmentary axeheads and flakes from polished axeheads at Hambledon Hill and other causewayed enclosures, but there are also several practical complications in the way of any simple assessment of the relative representation of axeheads. If a polished axehead breaks, it can be reworked or reground in a substantially similar form or a substantially altered form depending on the degree of breakage and the further use to which it is to be put. Reworking after breakage may not necessarily be obvious from the reworked axehead, but the archaeological record will receive the broken fragment and any flakes retaining a polished surface. If the flakes and fragments cannot be refitted, estimating the number of axeheads involved can be problematic. If an axehead breaks beyond repair, its segments can be exploited as cores or as blanks for smaller tools, and not all the products of this reworking will retain polished surfaces to make their origin apparent.

The evidence from Maiden Castle, Dorset, has been interpreted as indicating on-site manufacture of axeheads using flint obtained on the spot (Bradley & Edmonds 1993, 169). The same authors (1993, 50–51), following

Drewett (1977, 224), have also drawn attention to the fact that at other enclosures, the nature of the axehead evidence points towards actual use or 'consumption' of these implements, rather than their accumulation for exchange or other purposes.

That there are different pathways in how axeheads may be treated is obvious, since some are not reworked after breakage at all. It would also seem, to judge from the number of axehead fragments found burnt, that there can be some particular practice involving flint axeheads and fire, perhaps using what are intact rather than broken axeheads, which only become fragmentary as a result of burning. Some archaeologists have characterized this as negating or 'killing' an axehead by fire, and recent work in southern Sweden has indicated this sometimes took place on a grand scale in the Neolithic (Larsson 2000). Since at causewayed enclosures in England there are complete axeheads, reworked axeheads, small tools made on flakes from axeheads, and burnt axeheads (cf. Edmonds & Bellamy 1991, 227), it seems that different options were possible through time and space across the enclosures during their lifetime of use.

Of the other types of causewayed enclosure assemblage implements there is little which can usefully be said. 'Laurel-leaf' bifacial pieces (Fig. 10.1: 5) are of considerable interest in being time specific to the early/middle Neolithic. Their frequency of occurrence has, however, probably been exaggerated at some sites (particularly Staines: Healey & Robertson-Mackay 1987) because of insufficiently stringent typological definition. This is also the case with knives, which are flake tools with more regular and invasive retouch than the edge-trimmed category, but which are often very loosely defined.

So-called 'sickle-flints', which appear to be relatively common tools at some enclosures, in particular Windmill Hill, Wiltshire (Smith 1965, 97), are a 'rag bag' category in terms of morphology and probably have no coherence of function. The origins of the invasive surface glosses which are the main defining trait of 'sickle-flints' are unresolved. The suggestion that even the most classic type of curved bifacially flaked 'sickle' was more probably used to cut sods rather than cereals (van Gijn 1988) highlights the problem. That this kind of gloss could also form on implements used in pottery manufacture (Gassin & Garidel 1993) is potentially of considerable interest, as a question mark has usually remained over the on-site production of ceramics at causewayed enclosures. Furthermore, as Jensen (1988b, 138–41) has postulated, the apparent rareness of extensive invasive gloss directly attributable to use on cereals on early Neolithic tools, in this case in Denmark, might suggest that domesticated grain was only of minor importance until the middle Neolithic.

'Fabricators' (Fig. 10.1: 19) have been lumped together with rods in Table 10.1, since the published descriptions are often insufficiently precise (see Saville 1981b, 10–11, for definitions). The heavy wear, which is a definitive trait of 'fabricators' and may relate to fire-making (Stapert & Johansen 1999), suggests curation, and this is reinforced by the careful preliminary overall shaping they exhibit and their general robustness. It is difficult to imagine they would have ceased to be functional while they remained complete, so their presence in small numbers may reflect their longevity as tools and the infrequency with which they were lost or discarded, rather than their unimportance within the inventory.

One final point on individual implement types is whether in themselves they carry any significant information about gender that might inform understanding of the enclosures. As Gero (1991) has emphasized, there is no inherent reason why both sexes should not both produce and use flint tools. On the other hand, ethnographic data demonstrate that stone tool manufacture and use is normally gender-specific, albeit not necessarily in entirely predictable ways. Burial evidence, in the form of gender-recurrent grave-goods (Bradley 1999, 223), would be the most reliable archaeological indicator, but is not of course available given the nature of funerary practice in early to middle Neolithic Britain. The instance of one proven male flintknapper (Saville 1990b) does not dictate the norm. As usual, the archaeologist is forced to make generalizing assumptions, for example about the likelihood of axeheads and arrowheads belonging to the male domain and scrapers to the female. While these assumptions may be specious, it is probably reasonable to conclude that the broad range of tool-types present at causewayed enclosures does not indicate any over-arching gender restriction.

CONTEXTUAL AND DISTRIBUTIONAL DATA

Another aspect of broad brush analysis which can be applied to the causewayed enclosures involves contextual and distributional information. As already mentioned, rarely has detailed information about the precise positioning of artefacts within feature or ditch fills from causewayed enclosures been consistently recovered. Recent excavations at Etton, Cambridgeshire (Pryor 1998), have shown marked methodological advances in artefact recovery from both the interior and ditch of a causewayed enclosure, but Etton actually had relatively low artefact presence and its assemblage is compromised by serious problems of residuality and conflation, on a site whose early occupation was followed by Late Neolithic and Bronze Age activity. There was also very limited evidence for refitting (Middleton 1998, 220), which emphasizes the complexity of the formation processes involved.

Even so, at many enclosures there are overall contextual data which can be analysed. At the main enclosure on Hambledon Hill, excavation within the interior defined a total of 71 Neolithic pits which contained struck lithic artefacts, and the Stepleton causewayed enclosure had 93 pits with lithic artefacts. Most of these contained relatively few artefacts (Table 10.2), the maximum numbers per pit being 540 at the main enclosure and 376 at Stepleton.

Table 10.2: Quantification of lithic artefacts (including unclassified burnt pieces) from Neolithic pits within the main and Stepleton enclosures on Hambledon Hill, Dorset, expressed as ranges of total numbers per pit

	1–10 artefacts per pit	11–50 artefacts per pit	51–100 artefacts per pit	>101 artefacts per pit	Total number of pits
Main enclosure	18	29	14	10	71
Stepleton enclosure	48	31	5	9	93
Totals	66	60	19	19	164

Potential lithic content is obviously a factor of the size of each feature, and needs to be considered in relation to other finds – of pottery, animal bone, etc. – from each one. Searching for any kind of patterning among pits would of course be undermined by not knowing which, if any, of the features were strictly contemporary with each other. No conjoining lithic artefacts were noted between features at Hambledon Hill (there was one between features at Etton: Middleton 1998, 220; and ceramic conjoins were noted between pit and ditch infills at Hembury and Windmill Hill: Smith 1971, 96), but even if they had been this would not be a guarantee of contemporaneity. Otherwise one is left to examine patterning of the contents of individual features against the general background of the rest. Do the lithic contents of any one feature have any specificity either intrinsically, in relation to the features in which they occur, or in contrast to those from other features?

One of the larger collections of lithic artefacts from an individual feature within the Hambledon Hill main enclosure was examined in detail (Table 10.3). The artefacts included cores as well as flakes but there were no refits and the varied cortex on the secondary flakes and the cores indicated derivation from many different nodules. The flakes also had a range of discolouration effects which suggested they did not all arrive in the feature in a fresh condition or at the same time. Thus it was concluded that this collection represented mixed general knapping debris, and was certainly not the product of a nearby knapping event or the result of caching.

Small numbers of burnt flints occurring in most features alongside unburnt ones (Table 10.3) point both to the generalized spread of burnt material across the enclosure, and to the fact that the lithic contents of the features are unlikely to derive from a specific source, in which the flints might be expected to be either burnt or unburnt.

On the assumption that the pits with low numbers of lithic artefacts might be more likely to be the result of specific deposition or placement, the lithic composition of all pits with ten or fewer artefacts was examined. Of the 66 pits in question, 34 contained only unretouched flakes, one had a single scraper, while another had only an unclassified burnt fragment. The remaining pits had unretouched flakes in combination with one or more common waste artefact or implement type. The only pit in this group with a more 'elaborate' artefact, a

Table 10.3: Typology of lithic artefacts from the fill of pit N/ F7i within the main enclosure on Hambledon Hill, Dorset

Type	Number
Unretouched flakes, primary	10
Unretouched flakes, secondary	162
Unretouched flakes, tertiary	73
Unretouched flake, chert	1
Unretouched flakes, burnt	5
Cores	7
Core fragments	3
Flaked lumps	3
Serrated-edge flakes	11
Edge-trimmed flakes	7
Scrapers	3
Flake from polished flint axehead	1
Miscellaneous retouched piece	1
Unclassified burnt fragments	15
Total	302

fragmentary leaf-shaped arrowhead, also contained six unretouched flakes, one edge-trimmed flake, and one unclassified burnt fragment.

One collection of artefacts from a pit beneath the bank of the inner south cross-dyke, just outside the main Hambledon Hill enclosure (Mercer 1980, fig. 9) was by any measure remarkable, in that it included three leaf-shaped arrowheads of chert, and also three unretouched flakes of chert. The whole assemblage from the hilltop included only 39 artefacts of chert, and only six chert arrowheads. In other respects, however, the lithic contents of this pit cannot be said to be in any way exceptional (Table 10.4). The chert arrowheads themselves are all fragmentary, the three together weighing only 1.5 grams, while the three chert flakes are just chips, together weighing 0.7 of a gram. Without knowing how these particular pieces were located within the pit fill and what their spatial relations to each other and to the other artefacts were, it is difficult to interrogate this collection much further. There must be a significance to the 'concentration' of chert pieces in this pit, but this significance is in my judgement more likely to relate to action or actions in the immediate vicinity before the pit infilled, rather than betokening any 'special' nature for the pit or its fill.

There is bound to be subjectivity in these matters, but my conclusion is that the lithic artefact evidence from the enclosure features at Hambledon Hill does not

Table 10.4: Typology of lithic artefacts from the fill of pit P2/F14 in the area of the bank of the inner south cross-dyke, just south of the main causewayed enclosure on Hambledon Hill, Dorset

Type	Number
Unretouched flakes	431
Unretouched flakes, chert	3
Unretouched flakes, burnt	5
Cores	2
Flaked lump	1
Edge-trimmed flake	1
Scraper	1
Leaf-shaped arrowheads, fragmentary, chert	3
Flake from a polished flint axehead	1
Miscellaneous retouched piece	1
Unclassified burnt pieces	69
Total	518

indicate significant patterning nor support purposeful deposition, though I agree the latter can be a high probability at other enclosure sites in some instances. For example, the three axeheads from the ditch at Combe Hill, Sussex (Drewett 1994, fig. 11), or the two virtually complete axeheads side-by-side in a pit belonging to the Sarup II enclosure, Denmark (Andersen 1997, fig. 99), seem inescapably to be placed deposits, though perhaps cached rather than 'ritual'. Where only one 'special' implement is involved, as in the case of the single polished stone axehead from a pit within the Etton enclosure (Pryor 1998, fig. 108), then the question of placement must be rather more equivocal. The same applies perhaps to the pit within the main causewayed enclosure at Hambledon Hill with a complete stone axehead (Group XVI) together with a plain ceramic cup (Mercer 1980, fig. 12; 1988, plate 5.I.A), since in addition to other pottery in this pit, there were 66 struck flint artefacts (56 unretouched flakes; 1 burnt unretouched flake; 5 serrated-edge flakes; 3 edge-trimmed flakes; and 1 unclassified burnt fragment).

Of the less common implement types found in the features at Hambledon Hill, few are intact. The only examples whose condition might suggest special deposition are a well-preserved 'laurel-leaf' bifacial, a

rechipped axehead, and a polished axehead. But even the polished axehead (Fig 10.1: 20), though essentially complete, is not in pristine condition. It is damaged through use at the cutting edge and its morphology suggests it has already been reground at least once, so it might not, given its size, merit further regrinding (cf. the Etton stone axehead: Pryor 1998, 262; and perhaps those at Combe Hill: Drewett, fig. 12). Anyway, in each case at Hambledon Hill, these implements are accompanied in their feature fills by waste material of an entirely unremarkable nature of the kind found in every other excavated context. This to my mind argues against any special intentionality about the contents of each feature, which I would prefer to see on the whole as the result of chance.

Thus I would not agree with Andersen's criteria from Sarup for dividing pits into ritual examples on the basis of the contents including whole artefacts, especially whole pots, axeheads, or other special forms; nor in his distinction between secondary use of pits as for rubbish or tool caches, the latter being those pits with at least five stone tools and little waste, less than five pieces per tool; whereas waste disposal is defined by more than 12 pieces of waste to one tool in a pit (Andersen 1997, 321). The problem here is whether or not the lithic artefacts within the fill of a pit do or can have any direct bearing on the original or subsequent functions of that pit. In the few specific instances where placement can be determined (see above), then it is justifiable to identify pit usage for caching but in all other cases the relationship between the feature and its lithic artefact infill must remain ambiguous. This does not necessarily contradict the beliefs of those who would regard all such features associated with causewayed enclosures as the receptacles for deliberate structured deposits (Pryor 1998, 353–4; Thomas 1999, 64–74), it simply casts doubt on the relevance of the lithic artefact data to these kinds of interpretations.

On the other hand, there is perhaps some distinctiveness about the contents of features as a whole from the interiors of enclosures, when compared to the contents of the ditches. Put simply, this comes down to there being a slightly higher percentage of retouched pieces in the lithic collections from the features, or looked at in the opposite way, a higher percentage of primary knapping debris (cores and cortical flakes) in the ditches, at least at Hambledon Hill (Table 10.5). The simplest

Table 10.5: Lithic artefacts from pits and lower ditch fills of the main and Stepleton enclosures on Hambledon Hill, Dorset, expressed by number and percentage

Type	Main pits no.	Main pits %	Main ditch no.	Main ditch %	Stepleton pits no.	Stepleton pits %	Stepleton ditch no.	Stepleton ditch %
Unretouched flakes	2944	87	1722	93	2314	92	6643	97
Cores etc	34	1	53	3	27	1	161	2
All retouched	391	12	77	4	174	7	79	1
Totals	3369		1852		2515		6883	

explanation for this is that the industrial process of primary knapping was preferentially towards the edge of the enclosure, with discard in the ditches, and the use and discard of implements mainly within the enclosure.

This explanation can be argued for the evidence from Hambledon Hill and refined even further for the main Hambledon enclosure by considering the content of each ditch segment separately. It transpires that 70 per cent of the whole main enclosure ditch assemblage is from just four segments, one of which contains nearly 50 per cent of the total by itself. These four segments contain around 70 per cent of all the cores and waste flakes from the ditches, but only about 20 per cent of the implements. A very plausible explanation for this distribution is that, since these flint-rich segments traverse a pocket of clay-with-flints within the chalk, the knapping debris derives from the processing on the spot of nodules obtained from this pocket when the ditches were dug.

Common sense, supported by ethnographic observation (e.g. Clark 1991; Sillitoe 1988, 58), dictates that, other than on purely industrial sites, masses of sharp, freshly struck flints would not be left lying around where they would inconvenience, if not endanger, humans and animals. Freshly produced waste on a 'domestic' site would most probably be accumulated in obvious dumps and these might sensibly be situated towards or at the perimeter of the enclosure. The chances of finding such dumps on causewayed enclosures are remote after 5,000 years of subsequent land-use have smeared the picture (though there may have been traces at Windmill Hill: Whittle *et al.* 1999, 355), but the concentrations of waste in upper ditch fills may well reflect their former presence.

CONCLUDING REMARKS

At a time when we are enjoined to consider the individual biographies of artefacts and to take due cognizance of the way in which the function and value of an artefact can change during its lifetime of use, it is as well to remember that even the humble flint core need not be what it seems. We know from the burial of an individual within a chambered tomb at Hazleton, Gloucestershire (Saville 1990a, fig. 4; 1990b, fig. 234), dated to the mid-4th millennium BC, that a flint core can become an appropriate grave-good, thus reminding us that the notion of what might otherwise be considered a 'non-special' artefact is not so straightforward.

In fact, as we have seen, the assemblages from causewayed enclosures appear remarkably free of particularly 'special' implements, with inventories which match those from elsewhere. It would certainly not be possible, on the basis of the lithic artefact repertoire, to point to indications of specialized production or exceptional craft skill, which might suggest causewayed enclosures were in any sense centres of social power (Olausson 1997).

The significance and meaning of causewayed enclosures continue to be debated at length in fairly abstract terms (e.g. Bradley 1998; Edmonds 1993; 1999,

80–105; Harding 1998; Thomas 1999, 38–45). As would be expected, archaeologists publishing recent excavations at enclosures seek in their conclusions to encompass this debate and to relate their discoveries to it. In the case of both Etton, Cambridgeshire, and Windmill Hill, Wiltshire, the excavators suggest that deliberate, structured deposition of non-utilitarian character is the name of the game, for lithic artefacts as well as all the other material recovered (Pryor 1998, 253; Whittle *et al.* 1999, 364). This conviction is hard to share in a completely all-embracing fashion when the problem is approached from the perspective of the lithic artefacts themselves, and just such a conflict of opinion emerges clearly in the Etton report between analyst and excavator (Middleton 1998, 241; Pryor 1998, 251–55, 362).

This conflict finds a fascinating echo in an earlier version of the debate, when 'domestic' and 'ritual' were the rallying cries. In this case it was an excavator – of the Abingdon enclosure – who was adamant that '... *the flint industry seems to represent the residue of ordinary occupation*' (Avery 1982, 40), whereas his editors demurred (Case & Whittle 1982, 24–25) and his reviewer positively disagreed: '... *the material ... may have been accumulated and deposited with more formality than Avery supposed. In this respect it is entirely similar to the evidence from ... the main enclosure at Hambledon Hill, for which a ceremonial function is favoured*' (Bradley 1986, 186).

In the final analysis, and to the disappointment of many, lithic artefacts are in themselves usually quietly neutral on matters of context of production, use, and value. A flint implement cannot, in isolation, communicate to the archaeologist whether its role has been primarily domestic or ritual or both. To suppose that lithic artefact assemblages will have any simplistic bearing on such questions as the importance of animal husbandry as opposed to cereal cultivation to the communities building and using causewayed enclosures is wishful thinking. Like all material culture, lithic artefacts undoubtedly can and did have symbolic and social significance, but they can also be just so much backgound noise. Whilst one can make a case for the likelihood of the innovatory elements of material culture in the early/middle Neolithic, such as pottery (Thomas 1999, 89–125) and polished axeheads (Bradley & Edmonds 1993), having overarching symbolic associations which permeate their whole production and disposal cycle, it is much less easy to imagine this applying to those aspects of flintworking which had by then pertained for millennia.

Acknowledgements

Marion O'Neil prepared the illustrations for this paper and my colleagues in the National Museums of Scotland library provided their usual invaluable assistance. English Heritage funded my analyses of the Hambledon Hill assemblages and my continuing researches on lithic artefacts have been supported by the National Museums of Scotland. I am particularly indebted to Roger Mercer for allowing me to use data resulting from his excavations at Hambledon Hill in advance of definitive publication and for his continued encouragement of my work. Both Roger Mercer and Frances Healy kindly read this article in draft and offered helpful comments and criticism; they do not necessarily agree with my observations, for which I take sole responsibility.

BIBLIOGRAPHY

Andersen, N. H. 1997. *Sarup vol. 1: The Sarup Enclosures*. Moesgård. Jutland Archaeological Society.

Avery, M, 1982. The Neolithic causewayed enclosure, Abingdon. In H. J. Case & A. W. R. Whittle (eds), *Settlement patterns in the Oxford region: excavations at the Abingdon causewayed enclosure and other sites*. London. Council for British Archaeology Research Report 44. 10–50.

Bamford, H. M. 1985. *Briar Hill excavation 1974–1978*. Northampton. Northampton Development Corporation, Archaeological Monograph No. 3.

Barton, R. N. E. 1992. *Hengistbury Head, Dorset, Volume 2: the Late Upper Palaeolithic and Early Mesolithic sites*. Oxford. Oxford University Committee for Archaeology Monograph No. 34.

Bell, M. 1977. Excavations at Bishopstone, Sussex. *Sussex Archaeological Collections*, 115, 1–299.

Bienenfeld, P. 1988. Stone tool use and the organization of technology in the Dutch Neolithic. In S. Beyries (ed.), *Industries lithiques, tracéologie et technologie. Vol. 1: aspects archéologiques*. Oxford. British Archaeological Reports, International Series 411(i). 219–30.

Bocquet, A. 1980. Le microdenticulé, un outil mal connu: essai de typologie. *Bulletin de la Société Préhistorique Française*, 77(3), 76–85.

Bradley, P, 1994. *Assemblage variation and spatial patterning of artefacts in the earlier Neolithic of southern England, with special reference to causewayed enclosures*. Unpublished M.Phil. thesis. University of Sheffield.

Bradley, P. 1999. Worked flint. In A. Barclay, & C. Halpin, *Excavations at Barrow Hills, Radley, Oxfordshire. Vol.1. The Neolithic and Bronze Age monument complex*. Oxford. Oxford Archaeological Unit. 211–28.

Bradley, R. 1986. A reinterpretation of the Abingdon causewayed enclosure. *Oxoniensia*, 51, 183–7.

Bradley, R. 1998. Interpreting enclosures. In M. Edmonds & C. Richards (eds), *Understanding the Neolithic of north-western Europe*. Glasgow. Cruithne Press. 188–203.

Bradley, R. & Edmonds, M. 1993. *Interpreting the axe trade: production and exchange in Neolithic Britain*. Cambridge. Cambridge University Press.

Burnez, C. Braguier, S. Sicaud, F. & Tutard, J. 1999. Les enceintes du Néolithique récent et final de la Mercière à Jarnac-Champagne (Charente-Maritime). *Bulletin de la Société Préhistorique Française*, 96(3), 295–328.

Cantwell, A.-M. 1979. The functional analysis of scrapers: problems, new techniques and cautions. *Lithic Technology*, 8(1), 5–11.

Case, H. J. & Whittle, A. W. R. (eds). 1982. *Settlement patterns in the Oxford region: excavations at the Abingdon causewayed enclosure and other sites*. London. Council for British Archaeology Research Report 44.

Clark, J. E. 1991. Modern Lacandon lithic technology and blade workshops. In T. R. Hester & H. J. Shafer (eds), *Maya stone tools*, 251–65. Madison, Wisconsin. Prehistory Press (Monographs in World Archaeology No. 1).

Clark, J. G. D. Higgs, E. S. & Longworth, I. H. 1960. Excavations at the Neolithic site at Hurst Fen, Mildenhall, Suffolk (1954, 1957 and 1958). *Proceedings of the Prehistoric Society*, 26, 202–45.

Curwen, E. C. 1930. Prehistoric flint sickles. *Antiquity*, 4, 179–86.

Curwen, E. C. 1937. *The Archaeology of Sussex*. London. Methuen.

Dibble, H. 1987. The interpretation of Middle Palaeolithic scraper morphology. *American Antiquity*, 52, 109–17.

Dixon, P. 1988. The Neolithic settlements on Crickley Hill. In C. Burgess, P. Topping, C. Mordant, & M. Maddison (eds), *Enclosures and defences in the Neolithic of Western Europe*. Oxford. British Archaeological Reports, International Series 403(i). 75–87.

Drewett, P. 1977. The excavation of a Neolithic causewayed enclosure on Offham Hill, East Sussex, 1976. *Proceedings of the Prehistoric Society*, 43, 201–42.

Drewett, P. 1994. Dr V. Seton Williams' excavations at Combe Hill, 1962, and the role of Neolithic causewayed enclosures in Sussex. *Sussex Archaeological Collections*, 132, 7–24.

Drewett, P. Rudling, D, & Gardiner, M. 1988. *The South East to AD 1000*. Harlow. Longman.

Dumont, J. V. 1988. *A microwear analysis of selected artefact types from the Mesolithic sites of Star Carr and Mount Sandel*. Oxford. British Archaeological Reports, British Series 187(i).

Dunn, E. J. 1931. *The Bushman*. London. Griffin & Co.

Edmonds, M, 1990. Description, understanding and the *chaîne opératoire*. *Archaeological Review from Cambridge*, 9(1), 55–70.

Edmonds, M. 1993. Interpreting causewayed enclosures in the past and the present. In C. Tilley (ed.), *Interpretative archaeology*. Oxford. Berg. 99–142.

Edmonds, M. 1999. *Ancestral geographies of the Neolithic*. London. Routledge.

Edmonds, M. & Bellamy, P. 1991. The flaked stone. In N. M. Sharples, *Maiden Castle: excavations and field survey 1985–6*. London. English Heritage Archaeological Report No. 19. 214–29.

Gassin, B. & Garidel, Y. 1993. Des outils de silex pour la fabrication de la poterie. In P. C. Anderson, S. Beyries, M. Otte & H. Plisson (eds), *Traces et fonction: les gestes retrouvés, Vol. 1*. Liege (=ERAUL 50). 189–203.

Gero, J. M. 1991. Genderlithics: women's roles in stone tool production. In J. M. Gero & M. W. Conkey (eds), *Engendering archaeology: women and prehistory*. Oxford. Blackwell. 163–93.

van Gijn, A. 1988. The use of Bronze Age flint sickles in the Netherlands: a preliminary report. In S. Beyries (ed.), *Industries lithiques, tracéologie et technologie. Vol. 1: aspects archéologiques*. Oxford. British Archaeological Reports, International Series 411(i). 197–218.

van Gijn, A. 1998. Craft activities in the Dutch Neolithic: a lithic viewpoint. In M. Edmonds & C. Richards (eds), *Understanding the Neolithic of north-western Europe*. Glasgow. Cruithne Press. 328–50.

Gowlett, J. A. J. 1997. High definition archaeology: ideas and evaluation. *World Archaeology*, 29(2), 152–71.

Alan Saville

Grace, R. 1997. The 'chaîne opératoire' approach to lithic analysis. *Internet Archaeology*, 2 (http://intarch.ac.uk/journal/issue2/grace/index.html).

Green, H. S. 1984. Flint arrowheads: typology and interpretation. *Lithics*, 5, 19–39.

Harding, J. 1998. An architecture of meaning: the causewayed enclosures and henges of lowland England. In M. Edmonds & C. Richards (eds), *Understanding the Neolithic of northwestern Europe*. Glasgow. Cruithne Press. 204–30.

Healey, E. & Robertson-Mackay, R. 1983. The lithic industries from Staines causewayed enclosure and their relationship to other earlier Neolithic industries in southern Britain. *Lithics*, 4, 1–27.

Healey, E. & Robertson-Mackay, R. 1987. The flint industry. In R. Robertson-Mackay, The Neolithic causewayed enclosure at Staines, Surrey: excavations 1961–63. *Proceedings of the Prehistoric Society*, 53, 95–118.

Healy, F. 1993. Lithic material. In R. Bradley, P. Chowne, R. M. J Cleal, F. Healy & I. Kinnes, *Excavations on Redgate Hill, Hunstanton, Norfolk, and at Tattershall Thorpe, Lincolnshire*. Gressenhall. Norfolk Museums Service (East Anglian Archaeology No. 57). 28–39.

Healy, F. 1998. What do you mean by mobile? In A Woodward & J. Gardiner (eds), *Wessex before words: some new research directions for prehistoric Wessex*. Salisbury. Wessex Archaeology. 25–6.

Holgate, R. 1988. *Neolithic settlement of the Thames Basin*. Oxford. British Archaeological Reports, British Series 194.

Ibáñez Estévez, J. J. & González Urquijo, J. E. 1996. *From tool use to site function: use-wear analysis in some final Upper Palaeolithic sites in the Basque country*. Oxford. British Archaeological Reports, International Series 658.

Jensen, H. J. 1986. Unretouched blades in the late Mesolithic of South Scandinavia: a functional study. *Oxford Journal of Archaeology*, 5(1), 19–33.

Jensen, H. J. 1988a. Microdenticulates in the Danish Stone Age: a functional puzzle. In S. Beyries (ed.), *Industries lithiques, tracéologie et technologie. Volume 1: aspects archéologiques*. Oxford. British Archaeological Reports, International Series 411(i). 231–52.

Jensen, H. J. 1988b. Plant harvesting and processing with flint implements in the Danish Stone Age. *Acta Archaeologica*, 59, 131–42.

Jensen, H. J. 1994. *Flint tools and plant working*. Aarhus. Aarhus University Press.

Jensen, H. J. & Brinch Petersen, E. 1985. A functional study of lithics from Vaenget Nord, a Mesolithic site at Vedbaek, N. E. Sjaelland. *Journal of Danish Archaeology*, 4, 40–51.

Lacaille, A. D. 1947. The scraper in prehistoric culture. *Transactions of the Glasgow Archaeological Society*, 11, 38–93.

Larsson, L. 2000. The passage of axes: fire transformation of flint objects in the Neolithic of southern Sweden. *Antiquity*, 74, 602–10.

Levi-Sala, I. 1992. Functional analysis and post-depositional alterations of microdenticulates. In R. N. E. Barton, *Hengistbury Head, Dorset, Volume 2: the Late Upper Palaeolithic and Early Mesolithic sites*. Oxford. Oxford University Committee for Archaeology Monograph No. 34. 238–247.

Levi-Sala, I. 1996. *A Study of Microscopic Polish on Flint Implement*. Oxford. British Archaeological Reports, International Series 629.

Liddell, D. M. 1935. Report on the excavations at Hembury Fort, 4th and 5th seasons, 1934 and 1935. *Proceedings of the Devon Archaeological Exploration Society*, 2(3), 134–75.

Mercer, R. J. 1980. *Hambledon Hill: a Neolithic landscape*. Edinburgh. Edinburgh University Press.

Mercer, R. J. 1981. Excavations at Carn Brea, Illogan, Cornwall, 1970–73. *Cornish Archaeology*, 20, 1–204.

Mercer, R. J. 1988. Hambledon Hill, Dorset, England. In C. Burgess, P. Topping, C. Mordant & M. Maddison (eds), *Enclosures and defences in the Neolithic of Western Europe*. Oxford. British Archaeological Reports, International Series 403(i). 89–106.

Mercer, R. J. 1990. *Causewayed enclosures*. Princes Risborough. Shire.

Middleton, H. R. 1998. Flint and chert artefacts. In F. Pryor, *Etton: excavations at a Neolithic causewayed enclosure near Maxey, Cambridgeshire, 1982–7*. London. English Heritage Archaeological Report 18. 215–50.

Moss, E. H. 1983. *The functional analysis of flint implements. Pincevent and Pont d'Ambon: two case studies from the French final Palaeolithic*. Oxford. British Archaeological Reports, International Series 177.

Nash, S. E. 1996. Is curation a useful heuristic? In G. H. Odell (ed), *Stone tools: theoretical insights into human prehistory*. New York. Plenum. 81–99.

Odell, G. H. 1996. Economizing behavior and the concept of "curation". In G. H. Odell (ed.), *Stone tools: theoretical insights into human prehistory*. New York. Plenum. 51–80.

Olausson, D. 1997. Craft specialization as an agent of social power in the south Scandinavian Neolithic. In R. Schild & Z. Sulgostowska (eds), *Man and flint*. Warsaw. Institute of Archaeology and Ethnology, Polish Academy of Sciences. 269–77.

Palmer, R. 1976. Interrupted ditch enclosures in Britain: the use of aerial photography for comparative studies. *Proceedings of the Prehistoric Society*, 42, 161–86.

Palmer, S. 1970. The Stone Age industries of the Isle of Portland, Dorset, and the utilization of Portland chert as artifact material in southern England. *Proceedings of the Prehistoric Society*, 36, 82–115.

Piggott, S. 1954. *The Neolithic cultures of the British Isles*. Cambridge. Cambridge University Press.

Pollard, J. 1999. Flint. In A. Whittle, J. Pollard, & C. Grigson, *The harmony of symbols: the Windmill Hill causewayed enclosure, Wiltshire*. Oxford. Oxbow Books. 318–37.

Pollard, S. H. M. 1966. Neolithic and Dark Age settlements on High Peak, Sidmouth, Devon. *Proceedings of the Devon Archaeological Exploration Society*, 23, 35–59.

Pryor, F. 1998. *Etton: excavations at a Neolithic causewayed enclosure near Maxey, Cambridgeshire, 1982–7*. London. English Heritage Archaeological Report 18.

Saville, A. 1981a. The flint and chert artefacts. In R. J. Mercer, Excavations at Carn Brea, Illogan, Cornwall, 1970–73. *Cornish Archaeology*, 20, 101–52.

Saville, A. 1981b. *Grimes Graves, Norfolk, excavations 1971–72, Vol. 2: the flint assemblage*. London. Department of the Environment Archaeological Reports No.11.

Saville, A. 1990a. Recent research on flint assemblages from Hazleton, Gloucestershire and Hambledon Hill, Dorset, England. In M.-R. Séronie-Vivien & M. Lenoir (eds), *Le Silex de sa Genèse à l'Outil*. Paris. Centre National de la Recherche Scientifique, Cahiers du Quaternaire N°17. 365–72.

Saville, A. 1990b. *Hazleton North: the excavation of a Neolithic long cairn of the Cotswold-Severn group.* London. English Heritage Archaeological Report No. 13.

Scarre, C. 1998. Arenas of action? Enclosure entrances in Neolithic western France *c.*3500–2500 BC. *Proceedings of the Prehistoric Society,* 64, 115–37.

Sillitoe, P. 1988. *Made in Niugini: technology in the Highlands of Papua New Guinea.* London. British Museum Publications.

Smith, I. F. 1965. *Windmill Hill and Avebury: excavations by Alexander Keiller 1925–1939.* Oxford. Clarendon Press.

Smith, I. F. 1971. Causewayed enclosures. In D. D. A. Simpson (ed.), *Economy and settlement in Neolithic and Early Bronze Age Britain and Europe.* Leicester. Leicester University Press. 89–112.

Stapert, D. & Johansen, L. 1999. Flint and pyrite: making fire in the Stone Age. *Antiquity,* 73, 765–77.

Stordeur, D. 1987. Manches et emmanchments préhistoriques: quelques propositions préliminaires. In D. Stordeur (ed.), *La main et l'outil: manches et emmanchments préhistoriques.* Lyon. Travaux de la Maison de l'Orient N°15. 11–34.

Taylor, M. 1998. Wood and bark from the enclosure ditch. In F. Pryor, *Etton: excavations at a Neolithic causewayed enclosure near Maxey, Cambridgeshire, 1982–7.* London. English Heritage Archaeological Report 18. 115–59.

Thomas, J. 1999. *Understanding the Neolithic.* London. Routledge.

Unger-Hamilton, R. Grace, R. Miller, R. & Bergman, C. 1987. Drill bits from Abu Salabikh, Iraq. In D. Stordeur (ed.), *La main et l'outil: manches et emmanchments préhistoriques.* Lyon. Travaux de la Maison de l'Orient N°15. 269–85.

Wainwright, G. J. 1972. The excavation of a Neolithic settlement on Broome Heath, Ditchingham, Norfolk, England. *Proceedings of the Prehistoric Society,* 38, 1–97.

Wheeler, R. E. M. 1943. *Maiden Castle, Dorset.* Oxford. Reports of the Research Committee of the Society of Antiquaries of London No. 12.

Whittle, A., Pollard, J. & Grigson, C. 1999. *The harmony of symbols: the Windmill Hill causewayed enclosure.* Oxford. Oxbow Books.

11. A Causewayed Enclosure at Husbands Bosworth, Leicestershire

Adrian Butler, Patrick Clay and John Thomas

Causewayed enclosures are rarely associated with the East Midlands with very few examples recorded on the local Sites and Monuments Record despite considerable aerial photographic cover since the 1970's (e.g. Pickering and Hartley 1985; Pickering 1989). While three are known from Northamptonshire and four possible sites are known from Lincolnshire, none are known from Derbyshire and Nottinghamshire. The picture was the same for Leicestershire with no causewayed enclosures recorded other than a very dubious single ditched enclosure at Appleby Magna (Liddle 1982, 12; Clay 1999, 7). However, one has now been located at Husbands Bosworth, southwest of Market Harborough in the south of the county following fieldwork in 1998 and 1999 (Fig. 11.1; Thomas and Butler 1999; Clay 1999, 7).

No visible traces of the monument are present on the ground surface and when the area was allocated in the 1995 Leicestershire Local Plan for the extension of a gravel quarry the only known archaeological material from the area was an Anglo-Saxon brooch of very uncertain provenance. In view of the proposed quarry extension a fieldwalking survey was undertaken by Leicestershire Museums which located a scatter of lithics of Neolithic/ Early Bronze Age date, with some Mesolithic material, forming three possible *foci*. In the light of these results geophysical survey was undertaken by University of Leicester Archaeological Services (ULAS), directed by Adrian Butler. Scanning by fluxgate gradiometer at 20m intervals and follow-up detailed survey targeting the flint concentrations at 1m by 0.5 m resolution located two parallel series of curvilinear positive anomalies. Further geophysical survey at greater resolution and trial trenching confirmed the presence of a closely-grouped concentric circuit consisting of a double ring of interrupted ditches enclosing an ovoid area covering *c*.1.5 ha together with other features including circular and U-shaped enclosures (Fig. 11.2). In the light of the results the monument has now been excluded from the proposed quarry extension.

A limited programme of trial trenching undertaken by ULAS, directed by John Thomas, included sample excavation of an outer ditch segment. This revealed a surprising depth of survival with evidence for at least one recut after partial infilling. Finds of later Neolithic impressed wares, transverse flint arrowheads and a thumbnail scraper were located in the latest fills of the ditch. Earlier flint material including laurel leaf projectile points and serrated blades were found on the surface. No banks had survived as surface features although possible evidence for an internal bank may be inferred from a thick stony layer which had slumped into the ditch from the interior of the site. A small concentration of post holes between the two ditches may have served as timber revetment to a bank to ensure stability. Trial trenching to test anomalies outside the monument to the west located pits of Iron Age date.

The monument is located on a plateau of glacial sand and gravel, at 147m OD, overlooking a small stream to the northwest. The area forms a natural promontory with the land sloping away steeply to the north, west and south. Analysis of the results from the geophysical survey indicated that the spacing between the two ditches averaged nine metres falling into Palmer's 'narrow' category (Palmer 1976, Type 3). While interpretation from geophysical anomalies must be treated with caution a U- shaped 'annexe' to the southwest of the monument has some affinities with a Neolithic 'oval' barrow also associated with a causewayed enclosure at Abingdon, Oxfordshire (Bradley 1992). The monument itself is similar in form to other examples from Barholm in Lincolnshire and Briar Hill in Northamptonshire (Palmer 1976, p. 184 figs 14– 15; Bamford 1985). The nearest causewayed enclosures to the Husbands Bosworth example are from Northampton-shire at Dallington and Briar Hill, 25 km and 30 km to the southeast respectively and Southwick, 40 km to the east (S. Kidd pers. comm.) while to the north the nearest examples are from Uffington in Lincolnshire 55 km to the northeast and Alrewas in Staffordshire 58 km to the northwest (Fig. 11.1; Palmer 1976).

The Husbands Bosworth causewayed enclosure adds to the growing evidence for Neolithic occupation in this area of the East Midlands (Clay 1996; 1999). Located between the watersheds of the Rivers Avon, Soar, Well-and and Swift, all valleys where Neolithic material has been found previously, the monument may have served

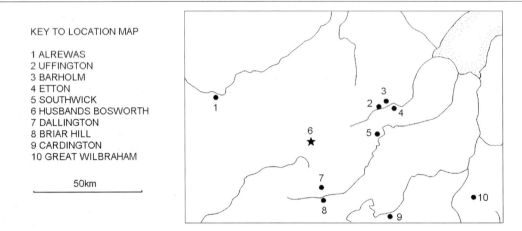

KEY TO LOCATION MAP

1 ALREWAS
2 UFFINGTON
3 BARHOLM
4 ETTON
5 SOUTHWICK
6 HUSBANDS BOSWORTH
7 DALLINGTON
8 BRIAR HILL
9 CARDINGTON
10 GREAT WILBRAHAM

50km

Fig. 11.1: Husbands Bosworth in relation to other causewayed enclosures in the region

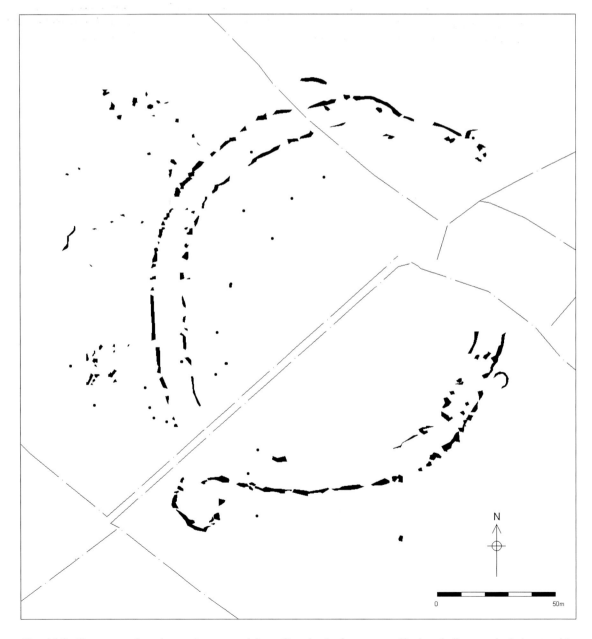

Fig. 11.2: Causewayed enclosure interpreted from Geophysical survey at Husbands Bosworth, Leicestershire

as a central meeting place at the interface of several different territories. The discovery highlights the problems of archaeological visibility in the East Midlands where the lack of earthwork and aerial photographic evidence may not necessarily mean the absence of important early prehistoric sites and monuments which may only be located following survey using a variety of different techniques.

(We would like to acknowledge the support of the archaeological sponsors Lafarge Redland Aggregates Ltd in the discovery of this site).

BIBLIOGRAPHY

Bamford, H. 1985. *Briar Hill, Northampton 1974–1978*. Northampton: Northampton Development Corporation Monograph 3.

Bradley, R. 1992. 'The excavation of an oval barrow beside the Abingdon causewayed enclosure, Oxfordshire'. *Proceedings of the Prehistoric Society* 58, 127–142.

Clay, P. 1996. *The exploitation of the East Midlands Claylands in later Prehistory. Aspects of settlement and land-use from the Mesolithic to the Iron Age.* University of Leicester unpublished Ph.D thesis.

Clay, P. 1999. 'The Neolithic and Bronze Age of Leicestershire and Rutland' *Transactions of the Leicestershire Archaeological and Historical Society* 73, 1–18.

Liddle, P. 1982. *Leicestershire Archaeology. The present state of knowledge. Part 1 to the end of the Roman Period* Leicester: Leicestershire Museums Art Galleries and Records Service Archaeological Report No. 4.

Palmer R. 1976. 'Interrupted Ditch Enclosures in Britain: the use of Aerial Photography for Comparative Studies'. *Proceedings of the Prehistoric Society* 46, 161–186.

Pickering, J. 1989. 'Discovering the Prehistoric Midlands'. In A. Gibson (ed.), *Midlands Prehistory*: 106–110. Oxford: British Archaeological Report (British Series) 204.

Pickering, J. and Hartley, R. F. 1985. *Past Worlds in a Landscape* Leicester: Leicestershire Museums, Art Galleries and Records Service.

Thomas, J. and Butler, A. 1999. 'Husbands Bosworth, Wheler Lodge Farm'. *Transactions of the Leicestershire Archaeological and Historical Society* 73, 100.

12. The Howe Robin Story: an unusual enclosure on Crosby Ravensworth Fell

Moraig Brown

INTRODUCTION

In June 1996 the former Royal Commission on the Historical Monuments of England (RCHME; now a part of English Heritage) surveyed the remains of an unusual enclosure at Howe Robin, near Penrith, Cumbria (NMR Number NY 61 SW 75). This survey was carried out as part of the '*Industry and Enclosure in the Neolithic*' Project, a national survey seeking to produce a corpus of analytical topographic surveys of Neolithic flint mines and enclosures in England.

Howe Robin is situated at NGR NY 624 105, 12km south-east of Penrith, Cumbria, on Crosby Ravensworth Fell among the northern foothills of the Howgill Fells (Fig. 12.1). The enclosure occupies a limestone pavement plateau 360m above OD, surrounded by open moorland which supports a dense cover of heather and provides views over several kilometres in all directions. The geology of the area comprises carboniferous limestone overlain by gley soils.

The site is not scheduled and was not recorded in the National Monuments Record prior to its survey. The Cumbrian SMR, contains a record dated 1992, describing the presence of the enclosure, *c*.3–4ha in area, utilising the limestone pavement and featuring traces of stone walling and a surrounding interrupted or segmented ditch (SMR Number 16761). The RCHME fieldwork is the first detailed survey of the enclosure to be undertaken.

ARCHAEOLOGICAL HISTORY

Little work appears to have been carried out in the immediate vicinity of Howe Robin until 15 or 20 years ago, when Cherry, Cherry and Ellwood began a program of fieldwalking of the limited arable land and collection of material from molehills on the rough pasture (Cherry *et al.* 1985). The enclosure at Howe Robin is only mentioned in passing by the team in the context of lithic artefacts found there; the enclosure is not described, nor is it mentioned in subsequent publications (ibid., 21).

The majority of the sites recorded by Cherry, Cherry and Ellwood (Fig. 12.2) are actually finds of lithic implements and flakes (mostly flint, but some chert and volcanic tuffs) which appear to occur in discrete concentrations, or at least within concentrations of molehills. Occasional sherds of pottery were also discovered (Nicholson in Cherry & Cherry 1992); a quantity of material was collected from within the enclosure itself. Most findspots were treated as occupation sites, though since the distribution is based primarily upon small mammal activity, this interpretation should be treated with caution. The lithic types suggest a broad date range spanning the Neolithic and Early Bronze Age, and this is supported by the pottery, which has been compared to Grimston, Peterborough, Grooved and Beaker wares. No Iron Age or Romano-British material has been found within 1.5km of Howe Robin, confirming the potential primacy of the Neolithic/Early Bronze Age chronological horizon suggested by this assemblage.

Subsequent to the original fieldwork programme, Ellwood has continued fieldwalking in the area, and his results broadly confirm the earlier findings, namely quantities of earlier prehistoric material. He also confirmed the significance of the enclosure at Howe Robin, and produced a sketch plan of it (Anthony Ellwood, pers comm).

Excavation and survey of numerous '*villages*' by Collingwood in the early years of the 20th century indicates that Crosby Ravensworth Fell was extensively settled during the Iron Age/Romano-British period. However it should be noted that the National Monuments Record has no record of activity of that date within a 1km radius of the enclosure at Howe Robin.

ARCHAEOLOGICAL DESCRIPTION AND INTERPRETATION

The summit of Howe Robin is topped by two outcrops of limestone pavement, with the main archaeological feature comprising an enclosure which incorporates the south-eastern pavement (Fig. 12.3). This pavement occupies a roughly heart-shaped area 250m north-south by 220m transversely; limestone outcrops along its south-eastern and south-western sides, dictating the overall shape of the enclosure.

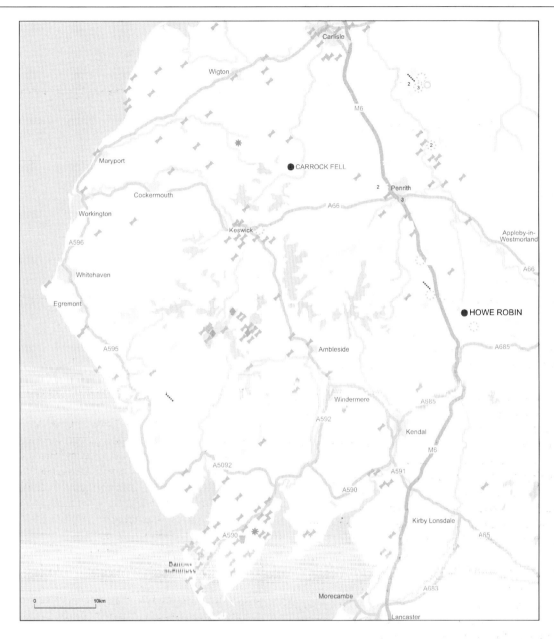

Fig. 12.1 The wider landscape of Howe Robin, showing the location of Neolithic and Bronze Age monuments and the distribution of Group VI (Langdale) and Group XXXIV (Carrock Fell) axes (distribution based upon the NMR and Clough & Cummins 1988)

The 4.55ha (11.24 acre) enclosure survives in the main as a discontinuous scarp, 0.8m to 1.5m high, linking outcrops of natural limestone escarpment; in places this is topped by a low earthen bank at best 2.2m wide and 0.3m high. Parts of the enclosure perimeter are clearly of artificial construction comprising an earthen bank and/or rubble scarp; in other places, the limestone pavement appears to have simply been roughly hewn to create the perimeter.

At the foot of the enclosure scarp, in places separated from it by a narrow berm, are a number of irregular shallow depressions cut into the limestone. The form of these depressions is extremely variable, ranging from clearly artificially constructed ditch segments with smooth sides and clean edges to what appear to be little

more than shallow scoops in the ground, roughly hewn out of the natural rock; the best example measures 8.0m by 2.9m by 0.3m deep. There appears to be a rough correlation between good sections of bank and well-defined ditch segments.

A short section of bank surmounted by at least four orthostatic rocks, describes a simple curve almost connecting the two limestone pavements (see Fig. 12.2). This bank, measuring 21.5m by 1.8m by 0.4m high, and although its original function is unclear, it may have defined the southern side of a small enclosure situated in the gully between the two limestone pavements, though it should be noted that no other evidence of such an enclosure survives.

Fig. 12.2 The local landscape at Howe Robin, showing the location of finds in the vicinity of the enclosure (© Crown Copyright. NMR)

DISCUSSION

Until the early 1980s, all discussion of Crosby Ravensworth Fell related to the Iron Age/Romano-British activity (Collingwood 1933), though neither Collingwood nor the National Monuments Record note any late prehistoric activity within 1km of Howe Robin. The recent work undertaken by Cherry, Cherry and Ellwood has highlighted evidence for Neolithic and Bronze Age activity around Howe Robin and beyond, though with no clear focus. No prehistoric monuments other than cairns are noted; they mention the enclosure at Howe Robin in passing, and may not have attributed much importance to it, though they do refer to it as an '*old enclosure*' (Cherry & Cherry 1992, 21). The impression from their fieldwalking is that the discoveries range over the later Neolithic to Early Bronze Age periods, though others view the assemblage with greater caution suggesting that little can be assigned to

anything other than a general prehistoric date (Martyn Barber, pers comm).

The enclosure could not be said to be a typical causewayed enclosure, but it does share some similarities with Neolithic or 'early prehistoric' enclosures in Cornwall, such as at Carn Brea (NMR Number SW 64 SE 5), Roughtor (SX 18 SW 38), Tregarrick Tor (SX 27 SW 105) and Helman Tor (SX 06 SE 33). Characteristics of these include a prominent location in the landscape, the utilisation or incorporation of rock outcrops, and the relative slightness of the earthen or stone-built perimeters. The bank construction at Howe Robin, however, differs from the Cornish sites, which are generally represented by boulder ramparts rather than of earth as found at the Cumbrian site. The reasons for this are not apparent, since the excavation of the ditches would surely have provided sufficient material for similar banks. Another dissimilarity between Howe Robin and the south-western sites is the seemingly deliberate cutting of the limestone to steepen the natural scarp, though this may have been less easy to achieve on the granite upon which the Cornish sites are located. Segmented ditches are also rare at the Neolithic enclosures in the south-west.

The suggestion, however, that sites such as Howe Robin may form part of a regional type of Neolithic enclosure should be treated with caution given the possible Neolithic earthen enclosure at Skelmore Heads (SD 27 NE 2) near Barrow-in-Furness (Brown 1996), and, more importantly, by the recent discovery of what appears to be a 'typical' causewayed enclosure at Green How (NY 23 NE 12), some 45km north-west of Howe Robin on Aughertree Fell (Horne *et al.* 2001). Neither of these is similar to Howe Robin.

The sky-line location of the enclosure was almost certainly important, and may have had significance in terms of visibility from and/or to the enclosure. This would have been particularly important in a Neolithic context bearing in mind that ritual sites such as the Shap

Avenue and various long cairns are situated in the vicinity and may have formed part of a dispersed, possibly ceremonial, landscape focussing upon the routeways leading into and out of the Eden Valley (see Fig. 12. 1). This network of routes linked the south-western parts of Cumbria with the tracks leading into central Lakeland and access to the axe 'factories', via ceremonial foci such as the Penrith henges (of broadly similar date to the collected artefacts at Howe Robin), all forming part of a holistic, structured landscape (Peter Topping, pers. comm.). If the Howe Robin enclosure truly lies in a Neolithic chronological context, then its location would comfortably fit within this pattern of discretely linked – but dispersed – sites stretching across the Cumbrian Fells.

It remains a possibility that the enclosure on Howe Robin may not be of Neolithic origin. The location of the enclosure on a site with no real natural defensive attributes, or effective man-made barriers, mitigates against an interpretation as some form of Iron Age fort, as does the apparent lack of any relevant material culture collected in the immediate vicinity of the site. Secondly,

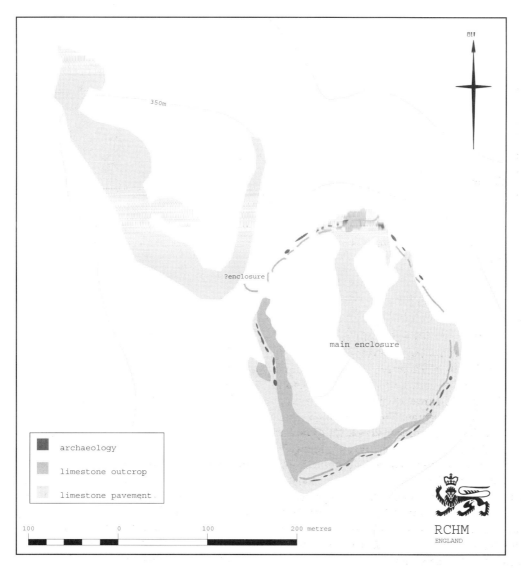

Fig. 12. 3: The enclosure at Howe Robin, demonstrating its relationship with the local geology (© Crown Copyright.NMR)

the lack of structural similarity between the Howe Robin enclosure and the Iron Age/Romano-British settlements further afield on Crosby Ravensworth Fell (cf. Collingwood 1933) suggests the possibility of a different chronological context. It may even be possible that Howe Robin was originally a Medieval stock enclosure, although the sheer size of the monument, and the total absence of artefactual material of that date renders this interpretation unlikely.

In summary, the artefact assemblage collected by fieldwalking from the area points to activity at or close to Howe Robin during the Neolithic and Early Bronze Age periods and the recovery of substantial amounts of worked flint from within the enclosure itself confirms its importance as a focal point during this period. The lack of any later material from the area, despite the presence of Iron Age/Romano British settlements further afield on Crosby Ravensworth Fell, supports the interpretation that the earlier material is not merely stray finds but potentially a true reflection of the chronological horizon of the activity – or occupation – at Howe Robin. The enclosure bears some similarity with Neolithic enclosures elsewhere in the country, particularly those in the uplands of the south-west. A defensive interpretation is unlikely given the size of the enclosure bank and its location on relatively level ground. The limestone pavement may well have had particular significance for the builders of the enclosure, though the reasons for choosing the southern rather than the northern outcrop is unclear.

Acknowledgements
The archaeological survey of Howe Robin was carried out by the author and Keith Blood, with assistance from Amy Lax and Trevor Pearson. The author would like to thank Martyn Barber for providing documentary sources and discussing various issues linked to the interpretation of the artefact assemblages, and Pete Topping for discussing this paper and providing additional information.

The site archive (NMR Number NY 61 SW 75) and a copy of the full site report have been deposited in the National Monuments Record Centre, Kemble Drive, Swindon SN2 2GZ, to where further enquiries should be directed.

© English Heritage

BIBLIOGRAPHY

Brown, M. 1996. Skelmore Heads, Urswick, Cumbria (unpublished RCHME archaeological survey report)

Cherry, J., Cherry, P. J. & Ellwood, C. A. 1984. Archaeological Survey of Crosby Ravensworth Fell: Occupational Evidence. *Transactions of the Cumberland and Westmorland Antiquarian and Archaeological Society*, 84, 19–30

Cherry, J., Cherry, P. J. & Ellwood, C. A. 1985. Archaeological Survey of the Howe Robin and Raven Gill Area – Orton: Occupational Evidence. *Transactions of the Cumberland and Westmorland Antiquarian and Archaeological Society*, 85, 19–34

Cherry, J. & Cherry, P. J. 1992. Further Research on the Prehistory of the Cumbrian Limestone Uplands: The Ceramic Evidence. *Transactions of the Cumberland and Westmorland Antiquarian and Archaeological Society*, 92, 13–22

Clough, T. H. McK. & Cummins, W. A. 1988. *Stone Axe Studies Volume 2: The petrology of prehistoric stone implements from the British Isles* CBA Research Report, 67 (Countil for British Archaeology)

Collingwood, R. G. 1933. Prehistoric settlements near Crosby Ravensworth. *Transactions of the Cumberland and Westmorland Antiquarian and Archaeological Society*, 33, 201–226

Ferguson, R. S. 1893 An Archaeological Survey of Cumberland and Westmorland. *Archaeologia*, 53

Horne, P., MacLeod, D. & Oswald, A. 2001. A probable Neolithic causewayed enclosure in northern England *Antiquity*, 75, 17–8

Ordnance Survey, nd. 1st Edition 25-inch Westmorland Sheets XXI.8 & XXI.12

Ordnance Survey, 1898. 2nd Edition 25-inch Westmorland Sheets XXI.8 & XXI.12

Ordnance Survey, 1977. 1:10,000 Plan NY 61 SW

Ordnance Survey, 1978. 1:10,000 Plan NY 60 NW

Saxton, C 1936 *An Atlas of England and Wales between 1574 and 1579* (London. British Museum)

13. The Seventieth Causwayed Enclosure in the British Isles?

Peter D. Horne, David MacLeod and Alastair Oswald

INTRODUCTION

A recent overview of causewayed enclosures in the British Isles reached a tally of sixty-nine certain and probable sites identified up to January 2000 (Oswald, Dyer & Barber 2001). Of these, all but a handful lay in central and southern England, with outlying examples in Northern Ireland, the Isle of Anglesey and the Isle of Man. In England, the northernmost causewayed enclosures identified with confidence were located in the Midlands at Mavesyn Ridware and at Alrewas, next to the River Trent; these two sites had marked the northerly limit of the distribution for more than twenty-five years (Palmer 1976). Not for the first time, the compilation of a 'comprehensive' inventory of sites was to be immediately overtaken by a new discovery.

On the evening of 16th June 2000, routine aerial reconnaissance by the English Heritage Aerial Survey team from York identified what is very probably the first Neolithic causewayed enclosure to be discovered in northern England (Fig. 13.1 and NMRa). In view of the potential importance of the monument, an analytical field survey was undertaken by English Heritage in the wake of the discovery.

THE LOCATION OF THE MONUMENT (Fig. 13.2)

The newly discovered probable causewayed enclosure occupies a prominent hill known as Green How, which lies towards the western end of Aughertree Fell in northern Cumbria (centred at National Grid Reference NY2574

Fig. 13.1: Green How from the northeast, 16th June 2000. (Photo © English Heritage. NMR 17468/10)

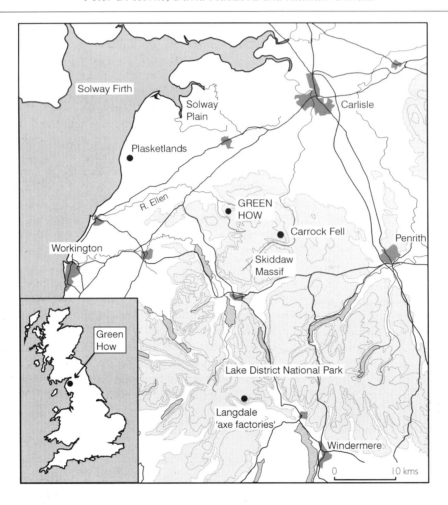

Fig. 13.2: Location of Green How in northwest England.

3746). Aughertree Fell forms part of an extensive tract of undulating limestone moorland between 250m and 450m above sea level (Swift 1998), lying to the north-west of the higher Skiddaw slate massif, on the north-western fringes of the Lake District National Park. Green How effectively forms the tip of a spur that projects north-westwards between the valley of the River Ellen on the south-west and the valley of a smaller tributary on the north. The summit of the hill reaches an altitude of 321m and commands panoramic views, with a particularly impressive prospect north-westwards towards the Solway Plain, an area with relatively abundant evidence for Mesolithic and earlier Neolithic settlement. Conversely, when seen from the low-lying plain, the hilltop is an eye-catching topographic feature against the background of the Skiddaw massif.

The villages of Uldale and Aughertree are situated near to Green How, but the area is otherwise very sparsely populated. The moorland currently supports unimproved pasture that is for the most part lightly grazed by sheep. As common land, the area has been subject to various forms of small-scale exploitation in the relatively recent past, including the quarrying of limestone, both as a building material and for the production of lime-based fertilisers. Land-use may have been somewhat more

intensive in the distant past: three supposed enclosed settlements, thought to be of late Iron Age or Romano-British date, lie *c*.700m to the north-east of Green How. These enclosures appear to be broadly contemporary with an extensive embanked field system in the environs of the hilltop, which is associated with a number of hollowed trackways and smaller enclosures (Bellhouse 1967; Higham 1978). Further settlements whose date remains uncertain lie to the south and south-west.

DESCRIPTION OF THE ENCLOSURE (see Figs 13.1 & 13.3)

The probable causewayed enclosure comprises a single circuit of discontinuous bank and ditch; there is no surface evidence for any contemporary features in the interior. In plan, the perimeter describes an elongated oval whose long axis corresponds more or less to the orientation of the natural topography of the spur. The interior has maximum dimensions of 132m long by 56m wide, and an area of 0.62ha (1.53 acres), which would make the enclosure typical of certain and probable causewayed enclosures elsewhere in the country. The circuit cannot strictly be said to occupy the summit of the hill, for while the eastern end does just encompass the highest point, the western end lies some 10m down the slope. This pronounced 'tilt' across the contours, which effectively orients the enclosure north-westwards towards the low-lying Solway Plain, is a trait common to almost every other causewayed enclosure in an upland location. In passing, it is perhaps worth commenting that it is a characteristic seldom found amongst Iron Age hillforts, especially those in topographic situations similar to the hilltop at Green How.

The circuit of the enclosure is essentially complete, but comprises segments of bank of irregular length, generally with corresponding causeways in the course of the ditch. Slight changes of alignment occur at several of the major causeways. This characteristic is typical of other known causewayed enclosures, but not of 'unfinished' hillforts of Iron Age date. In places, a narrow berm separates the base of the bank from the lip of the adjacent ditch, a characteristic which has been noted at several proven causewayed enclosures surviving as earthworks. On the most recent aerial photographs, it would appear that there are about seven major segments of bank, but field survey has identified more frequent minor interruptions. Even where the bank is best preserved, it has a smooth and regular appearance, with a maximum height of 0.3m.

the outer face is generally somewhat more prominent, especially towards the western end of the circuit, where the artificial scarp is accentuated by the steeper natural gradient. Similarly, even the most distinct ditch segments are no more than 0.2m deep with a smooth appearance, while long stretches which are fairly clear on the aerial photographs are either of minimal depth or do not survive at all as earthworks. Although it would be unwise to infer too much about the date of the earthworks from their condition, their appearance is consistent with other causewayed enclosures that survive as earthworks, and also contrasts strikingly with the sharply defined earthworks of the nearby late Iron Age or Romano-British enclosures.

Mid-way along the southern side of the circuit, there is a more pronounced off-set between the terminals of the adjacent segments, and the intervening causeway of intact ground is particularly broad. This causeway is interpreted as a principal, or perhaps the only, entrance into the enclosure. Possible parallels for this off-set design are to be found at various causewayed enclosures whose date has been established by excavation, such as those on Donegore Hill in County Antrim, Northern Ireland, and on Whitesheet Hill in Wiltshire.

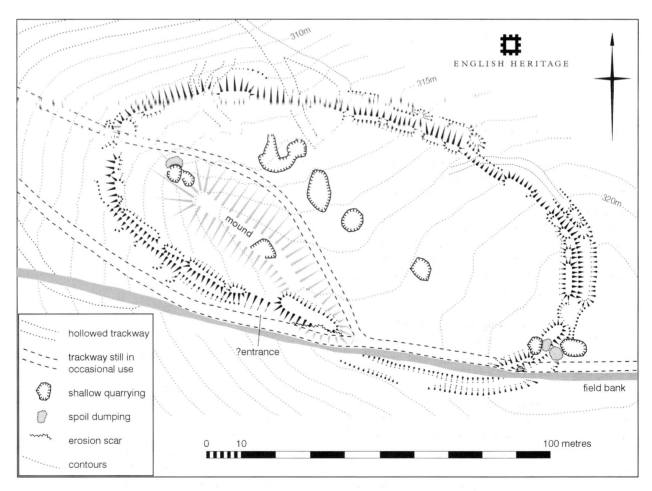

Fig. 13.3: Analytical field survey plan. (© English Heritage NMR)

The siting of the circuit also seems to take account of an elongated natural mound, located immediately to the west of the summit, which appears to be formed either by a glacial deposit or more probably by an outcrop of limestone modified by glacial action. The mound is approximately 22m wide at the base and 2m tall at its higher western end, tapering gradually towards its higher eastern end. The western end of the enclosure skirts around the base of the mound, while the southern side passes over its eastern end, as though deliberately designed to enclose the whole feature. The mound is unquestionably of natural origin, but bears a fairly strong resemblance in terms of its size, shape and position in the landscape to many earlier Neolithic long barrows. It is not impossible that the name Green How – 'how' being a local term for a burial mound – derives from the belief of more recent inhabitants of the area that the mound was a prehistoric funerary monument. Long barrows and long cairns are generally agreed to the oldest class of monuments still surviving as earthworks in the British Isles, the earliest having probably been built several centuries before the earliest causewayed enclosures. In the light of the apparently deliberate relationship of the enclosure to the mound, it is possible that the natural feature was misinterpreted as a long barrow by the builders of the enclosure. The link between causewayed enclosures and long barrows is well attested, and the two forms of monument are found in close proximity at a number of sites, including Hambledon Hill in Dorset, Abingdon in Oxfordshire and Haddenham in Cambridge-shire. The juxtaposition of a long cairn contributes circumstantial evidence to the suggestion that an enclosure at Howe Robin in Cumbria could be of Neolithic origin (Brown, this volume), but in that case the co-location may well be coincidental.

Various earthworks overlie or cut into the probable causewayed enclosure and are therefore demonstrably of later date. However, the field investigation was limited to the immediate environs of the enclosure, and a more extensive investigation would be necessary to ascertain the likely date of the later remains. On the northern side of the circuit, a series of hollowed trackways can be traced fairly clearly where they ascend the outer face of the earlier bank, generally making use of the pre-existing causeways to approach a series of shallow quarries in the interior of the enclosure. Beyond these more distinct sections, the trackways cannot be traced for more than a few metres either outside or within the circuit. The southern side of the enclosure is overlain by a field boundary bank, which also overlies a hollowed trackway to the south-west of the enclosure. The condition of the bank and the stratigraphic relationship with the hollowed trackway suggest that the boundary is unlikely to be earlier than medieval, although Higham (1978, Figure 16.6) depicts it as part of the late Iron Age or Romano-British field system. The bank appears to define the northern edge of an area where the surface has a smoothed appearance, suggestive of some form of land improvement or arable agriculture. The short stretch of the causewayed enclosure to the south of this boundary has evidently been affected by this cultivation, for it survives much less well and can only be traced as very degraded earthworks.

THE IMPLICATIONS OF THE DISCOVERY

The interpretation of the site as an earlier Neolithic causewayed enclosure relies on the morphology of the earthworks and the character of the location, without support from excavated evidence or stray finds in the vicinity. Nonetheless, the form and setting of the enclosure are so completely in keeping with certain and probable causewayed enclosures elsewhere in the British Isles that the interpretation is as secure as it can be without excavation. As such, the monument is clearly of importance in its own right: as only the seventieth causewayed enclosure known in the British Isles, and one of only fifteen that survive to any degree in earthwork form, the newly discovered site has great rarity value.

In a local context, the causewayed enclosure would appear to lie on the periphery of a more intensively exploited lowland area, the Solway Plain. As in many other cases, the monument appears to have been located on an eye-catching topographic feature, and sited deliberately so as to allow intervisibility between the enclosure and the lower ground. It is also worth remarking that the enclosure lies on the most direct route between the Solway Plain and the source of Group XXXIV axes in the Skiddaw massif (Fell & Davis 1988, 74), overlooking river valleys which may have acted as passages into the hinterland.

Perhaps more importantly, the discovery also has implications for the understanding of the earlier Neolithic in the British Isles as a whole (Fig. 13.4). The most northerly causewayed enclosures previously identified in England, at Alrewas and at Mavesyn Ridware, lie some 240kms (150 miles) to the south. Excavation of a small D-shaped enclosure at Plasketlands on the Solway Plain revealed earlier Neolithic pits in the vicinity, but recovered no indisputable dating evidence from the enclosure itself, nor any evidence that it was in any sense equivalent to a causewayed enclosure (Bewley 1993). The few possible causewayed enclosures identified in southern Scotland do exhibit the causewayed construction technique, but are not closely comparable in other aspects of their form (see Oswald *et al.* 2001). Perhaps the closest parallel in terms of morphology is an enclosure identified as a cropmark close to a *cursus* monument on Hasting Hill, Tyne and Wear (Newman 1976). However, the line of the ditch of the enclosure appears to respect a round barrow, which, taken at face value, must cast doubt on the assertion of an earlier Neolithic origin for the enclosure (Horne 1998).

On the other hand, it has been suggested that previous researchers, who have looked exclusively for enclosures with identical characteristics to those recognised on the chalk hills of southern England, may have overlooked regional variants in northern England and southern Scotland. Field survey has demonstrated that a rubble-

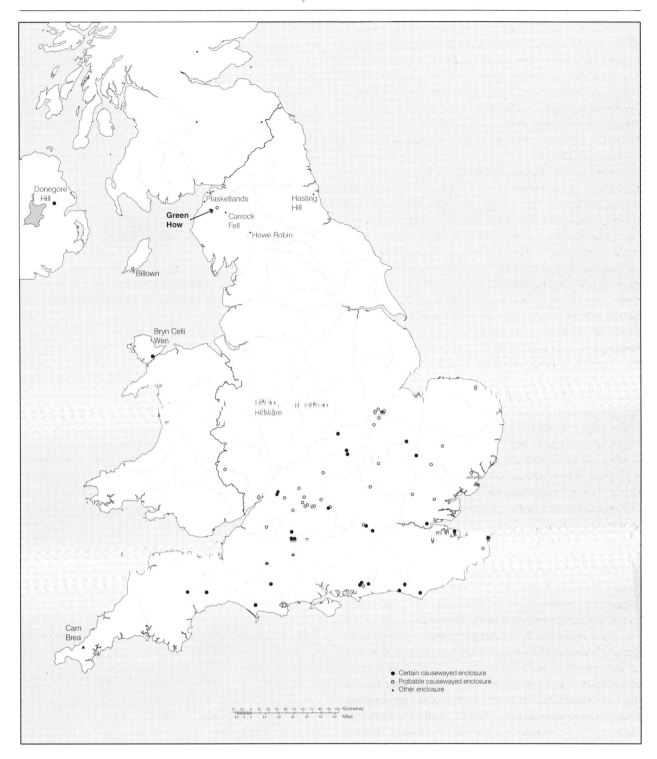

Fig 13.4: The distribution of causewayed enclosures and other enclosures of potentially Neolithic date in the north.

built enclosure with multiple entrances, at Gardom's Edge in the Derbyshire Peak District, is overlain by Bronze Age field systems and is therefore potentially of Neolithic origin (Ainsworth & Barnatt 1998). A number of other enclosures in northern England, including those nearer to Green How on Carrock Fell and at Howe Robin in Cumbria (see Pearson & Topping this volume; Brown, this volume), for long considered to be of Iron Age date, have since been put forward as possible Neolithic enclosures on much slighter evidence. The morphologies of the enclosures differ greatly from each other, but each is unusual in a regional context, and bears superficial comparison with the stone-built 'tor enclosures' of the South-West. In sharp contrast, the newly discovered enclosure on Green How, like that on Donegore Hill in Northern Ireland, has morphological characteristics entirely typical of causewayed enclosures in southern England. The existence of such 'conventional' causewayed enclosures suggests that it is premature to dilute the accepted definition of the class, based on the assumption that the sites would have been evenly distributed across the country. Rather, it may be more appropriate to accept that the distribution may have been genuinely sparse north of a line approximately between the Severn Estuary and The Wash. The newly discovered example overlooking the Solway Firth, together with those in Northern Ireland, on the Isle of Anglesey, and on the Isle of Man, may have been one of a number of isolated sites around the fringes of the Irish Sea (Higham 1986, 61). It is not intended by this to argue that earlier Neolithic enclosures other than causewayed enclosures did not exist; indeed, the excavation of the tor enclosure at Carn Brea (Mercer 1981) has already opened a Pandora's Box of such enclosures. Nor is it intended to imply that earlier Neolithic activity should be measured solely in terms of the distribution of causewayed enclosures. However, the discovery of a conventional causewayed enclosure so far north of the long-accepted distribution challenges the theory that 'regional variants' were widespread, but have as yet gone unrecognised.

Yet this begs the question as to why it has taken so long to discover the well-preserved and prominently located causewayed enclosure on Green How. It is perhaps understandable that, in spite of the long history of field survey by the Ordnance Survey and others, the existence of such slight earthworks has been overshadowed by more readily identifiable monuments, such as the impressive late Iron Age or Romano-British enclosures nearby. In addition, northern Cumbria as a whole has not seen extensive aerial reconnaissance, although work in the 1970s showed the potential of the area for identifying both cropmarks and earthworks from the air (Higham & Jones 1975). In August 1975 Barri Jones actually photographed the enclosure on Green How (NMRb) and should perhaps therefore be credited with its discovery, except that he apparently failed to interpret correctly what he had seen. The true morphology of the earthworks was missed again when more than half of the circuit of the enclosure was depicted as a field boundary in a plan of the late Iron Age or Romano-British enclosures and their associated field system, published by Nick Higham (1978). In both these instances, it is probably the expectations of the fliers themselves, rather than a lack of aerial reconnaissance *per se*, that accounts for the importance of the site being overlooked. In this sense, the history of non-discovery bears comparison with recent finds of complex rock art on prominent and often-visited outcrops in the Lake District (for example, Brown & Brown 1999). In a local context, there has been no tradition until now of discovering this type of monument.

BIBLIOGRAPHY

Bellhouse, R. L. 1967. 'The Aughertree Fell enclosures'. *Transactions of the Cumberland and Westmorland Antiquarian and Archaeological Society,* 67, 26–30.

Bewley, R. H. 1993. 'Survey and Excavation at a Crop-Mark enclosure, Plasketlands, Cumbria'. *Transactions of the Cumberland and Westmorland Antiquarian and Archaeological Society,* 93, 1–18.

Brown, P. & Brown, B. 1999. 'Previously unreported prehistoric rock carving at Copt Howe, Chapel Stile, Great Langdale, Cumbria'. *Archaeology North,* 16.

Fell, C. I. & Davis, R. V. 1988. 'The petrological identification of stone implements from Cumbria'. In T. H. McK. Clough & Cummins, W. A., (eds) *Stone Axe Studies, Volume 2.* London. Council for British Archaeology Research Report #67.

Higham, N. J. 1978. 'Early Field Survival in North Cumbria'. In H. C. Bowen & P. J. Fowler (eds) *Early land allotment.* Oxford. British Archaeological Reports, British Series 48. 119–25.

Higham, N. J. 1986. *The Northern Counties to AD 1000.* London. Longman.

Higham, N. J. & Jones, G. D. B. 1975. 'Frontiers, Forts and farmers: Cumbria Aerial Survey 1974–5'. *Archaeological Journal.* 132, 16–53.

Horne, P. D. 1998. 'A possible Neolithic enclosure and cursus monument at Hasting Hill, Sunderland, Tyne and Wear'. Unpublished RCHME report, available from the National Monuments Record Centre, Swindon.

NMRa. English Heritage aerial photographs held in the National Monuments Record ref: 17468, frame 10, 16-JUN-2000.

NMRb. Aerial photographs by Barri Jones, held in the National Monuments Record ref: NY2537, frames 1–3, AUG-1975.

Mercer, R. J., 1981. 'Excavations at Carn Brea, Illogan, Cornwall, 1970–3: a Neolithic fortified complex of the third millennium bc'. Cornish Archaeology.

Newman, M. 1976. 'A Crop-Mark Site at Hasting Hill, Tyne and Wear'. *Archaeologia Aeliana,* 5th Series, 4, 184–5.

Oswald, A. W. P, Dyer, C. & Barber, M. 2001. *The Creation of Monuments: Neolithic causewayed enclosures in the British Isles.* Swindon, English Heritage.

Palmer, R. 1976. Interrupted Ditch Enclosures in Britain: the use of Aerial Photography for Comparative Studies. *Proceedings of the Prehistoric Society,* 42, 161–86.

Swift, D. A. 1998. 'Origin and significance of a late Devensian meltwater channel system near Aughertree Fell, Northern Cumbria'. *Proceedings of the Cumberland Geological Society,* 6.2, 183–202.

14. Rethinking the Carrock Fell enclosure

Trevor Pearson and Peter Topping

INTRODUCTION

In June 1996 the former Royal Commission on the Historical Monuments of England (since merged with English Heritage in April 1999) undertook a 1:1000 scale detailed analytical earthwork survey of the hilltop enclosure upon Carrock Fell in the Skiddaw massif in the north-eastern Lake District (National Grid Reference NY3425 3364). The site had been surveyed previously, most notably by R. G. Collingwood in 1937, who concluded that the enclosure was an Early Iron Age hillfort that had been slighted by the Romans (Collingwood 1938, 32–41): subsequent accounts have generally followed Collingwood's interpretation of the site. However, more recently the identification of a stone axe source on the flanks of Carrock Fell at White Crag, combined with the unusual character of the enclosure, suggested that the site might be worthy of reconsideration. Consequently the enclosure was surveyed as part of the recent RCHME 'Industry and Enclosure in the Neolithic' Project to allow the traditional interpretation to be revisited and highlight the site as a possible focus for future research.

A full survey report including a detailed description of the site is available from the National Monuments Record Centre[1] (NMR Number: NY 33 SW 1). This paper presents a summary of the survey and explores the possibility of a Neolithic context for the monument.

DESCRIPTION

The roughly oval-shaped enclosure straddles the 650m high summit of Carrock Fell (Fig. 14.1) from where it commands extensive views north to the Solway Plain and east to the foothills of the Pennines. Some 3kms to the south the view is curtailed by the mass of Bowscale Fell and by the main range of the Caldbeck Fells the same distance to the west. Steep slopes below the southern and eastern sides of the enclosure fall some 400m to the valley of the River Caldew and, on the north side, to the lesser valley of the Carrock Beck. On the west there is a gentle descent to a saddle that extends across to the Caldbeck Fells.

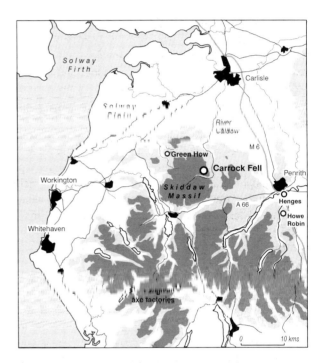

Fig. 14.1: Location of Carrock Fell in Cumbria, northwest England.

The enclosure (Fig. 14.2) is 220m long and orientated almost exactly east to west following the alignment of the hilltop and encloses the paired summits of the hill. It is 70m wide in the west broadening to a maximum width of 100m in the east. The perimeter is characterised by a discontinuous stone rubble bank that nowhere survives more than 1.6m in height and is mostly less than a metre. The enclosure comprises up to ten separate bank sections[2] enclosing an area of 1.94ha and has *nine* wide gaps or entrance breaks (Pearson 1996, 1). The scale of the Carrock Fell enclosure makes it significantly larger than any other 'hillfort' in Cumbria, contrasting noticeably with the much smaller internal areas of central Cumbrian hillforts which range from 0.06ha to 1.02ha[3] – all of which also have many fewer entrances (see Table 14.1 below).

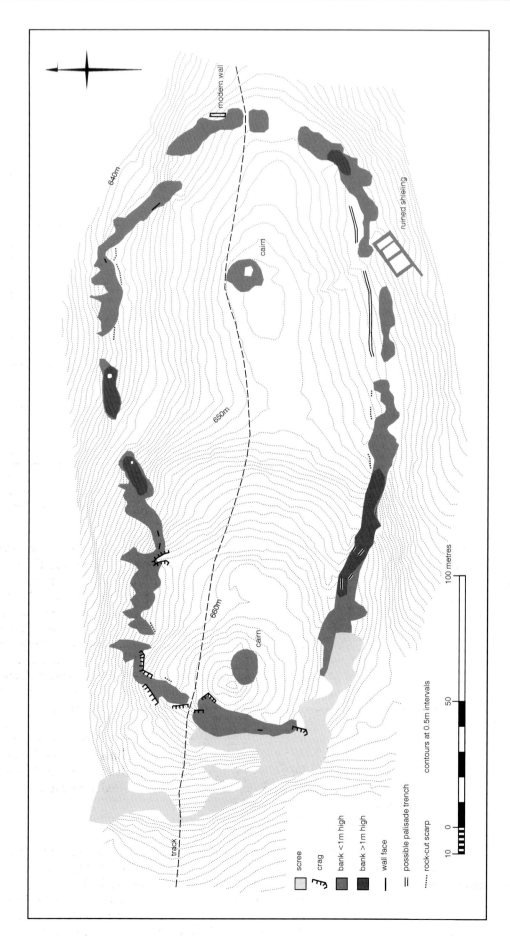

Fig. 14.2: The Carrock Fell enclosure. © Crown Copyright. NMR.

Table 14.1: Cumbrian hillfort data

Site name	Type	Entrances	Internal dimensions	Date
Allen Knott, Windermere [NY3414 5010]	Univallate	?1	135m x 76m [1.02ha]	Iron Age / Romano-British
Castle Crag, Borrowdale [NY3249 5159]	Univallate	?1	60m x 25m [0.14ha]	Iron Age / Romano-British
Castle Crags, Bampton [NY3469 5127]	?Univallate promontory	?2	46m x 22m [0.10ha]	Iron Age
Castle How, Wythop [NY3201 5308]	Multivallate	1	38.5m x 18m [0.06ha]	?Iron Age
Castlesteads, Natland [SD3530 4887]	Multivallate	?1	39m x 25m [0.09ha]	Iron Age
Castlesteads, Yanwath & Eamont Bridge [NY3518 5251]	Multivallate	2	53m x 53m [0.28ha]	Iron Age
Dunmallard, Dacre [NY3467 5246]	Multivallate	1	92m x 39m [0.35ha]	Iron Age
Maiden Castle, Mattdale [NY3451 5243]	Univallate	?1	45m x 65m [0.21ha]	Iron Age
Shoulthwaite Gill, Thirlmere [NY3299 5188]	Multivallate promontory	1	15m x 15m [0.02ha] 45m x 15m [0.06ha]	?Iron Age – Early Medieval
Carrock Fell, Caldbeck [NY3425 3364]	Univallate	?9	220m x >100m [1.94ha]	?

The loosely piled stones of the enclosure bank include short lengths of crude walling, suggesting that it was constructed with both external and internal faces. On the south side, the distance between these outer and inner wall faces varies between 2m and 6m, indicating that at least on this side of the enclosure the outer face may have been tiered, giving the bank a stepped profile. A rock-cut scarp is visible at the rear of the bank at several points on both the north and south sides but it is too close to the rear of the bank to have been a quarry trench. Instead the scarp could be the back of an artificial terrace cut into the hillside to make a level base for the construction of the bank. Most of the stone used for construction probably came from the extensive scree slopes surrounding the hilltop since there is no sign of any quarrying in the vicinity of the enclosure and there was no external ditch cut to provide the material.

There is slight evidence for the existence of a palisaded enclosure on the hilltop pre-dating the construction of the stone bank. A shallow, rock-cut trench up to 0.3m deep and 0.8m wide survives for a distance of 60m behind the bank on the south-east side of the enclosure. The trench is not obviously connected with the construction of the bank, which here is several metres further downslope, and it seems unlikely to be a 'marking out' trench

for the enclosure, given the effort needed to excavate such a feature into solid rock. A more attractive alternative is that it was a palisade trench, which raises the possibility that there might have been an earlier timber phase prior to the construction of the stone bank. However there is no visible evidence that the trench actually underlies the bank to help confirm their relative date.

Apart from the enclosure, the only other remains on the hilltop are the ruins of a three-roomed shieling of probable late medieval or post-medieval date outside the south-eastern angle of the monument and two cairns, one on each summit of the hill. Superficially, neither of the cairns appears to be convincing prehistoric burial mounds. A footpath crosses the enclosure from east to west and several small shelters on the enclosure bank have probably been constructed in recent times.

DISCUSSION

Carrock Fell is an unusual enclosure and is strictly undated. It is prominently located upon an east-facing spur of the Caldbeck Fells overlooking the major routeway into the central Lakes (now followed by the A66) with extensive panoramic views. Such a high degree of intervisibility is not necessarily extraordinary if the site were considered simply from a defensive perspective, its location creating a highly visible presence in the landscape. However, the ground plan and structure of the Carrock Fell enclosure suggests that this may not necessarily have been the case.

Traditionally the Carrock Fell enclosure has often been uncritically assumed to be a late prehistoric hillfort from the evidence of its location and the strength of its perimeter bank. However the defensive qualities of the site, and therefore its very interpretation as a hillfort, are somewhat compromised by the existence of the nine wide breaks in the perimeter. Although one of the breaks in the south may be the result of stone robbing for the adjacent shieling, and one on the east to accommodate the modern track, the complete lack of field walls or other structures in the vicinity suggest that later disturbance is unlikely to explain the other gaps in the bank. Even less attractive is the possibility that the gaps result from the deliberate slighting of the enclosure as suggested by Collingwood. Unlike Burnswark in eastern Dumfriesshire which is surrounded by two Roman camps (Jobey 1978; RCAHMS 1997, 179–182), none such appear near Carrock Fell (the nearest being at Troutbeck some 7kms to the south-south-east; cf. Welfare & Swan 1995) nor does the archaeological record seem to contain evidence of ballista balls or other siege artefacts from the site as evidenced at Burnswark. If slighting had

occurred at Carrock Fell, the perimeter could have been rendered indefensible by merely collapsing and levelling the bank without the enormous extra effort involved in casting the stones aside to create the wide gaps we see today. Indeed, contrary evidence can be put forward that suggests that the gaps may be an original part of the layout of the enclosure: there are no obvious residual footings lying across any of these gaps as might be anticipated if the bank had originally stretched across them, and there are no dumps of displaced stones.

The size of the breaks in the rampart are similar in scale to those at Maiden Castle in Dorset (Sharples 1991, Fig. 29 f. 38). However, unlike Maiden Castle where there are only 3 entrances, the multiple gaps in the Carrock Fell enclosure may not have been easily defensible – or easily characterised as hillfort-like. The presence of these gaps implies that access was more important than exclusion or defence. It is even possible that the gaps may have fossilised significant alignments when viewed from the interior, perhaps to landscape features or celestial events, or both. On the east side, between banks E and F, sunrise over the Pennines would have been visible, while sunset over Bowscale Fell could have been witnessed from one of the breaks in the southern perimeter. Other alignments may have been possible.

It is therefore unsafe to assume that the breaks in the perimeter are the result of later damage or erosion. It

Fig. 14.3: The Carrock Fell enclosure viewed from the west, 16th June 2000 (Photo: © English Heritage. NMR 17457/26)

could be argued that the perimeter was never completed, the site therefore being an unfinished hillfort, but this is contradicted by another piece of evidence. It is noticeable that on the N side of the enclosure, where the perimeter is best preserved, the terminals of two of the bank segments appear to have been deliberately rounded. This would not have occurred if the bank was merely unfinished, and suggests that the breaks were in fact integral to the original plan of the enclosure, which again contradicts the traditional interpretation. Moreover, the rock-cut trench, which it has been suggested may represent an earlier timber palisade,[4] ends on the west at the same point as a segment of the enclosure bank. This may be purely coincidental or it may indicate that the gaps in the stone wall fossilised those from a preceding timber enclosure. Although the survey evidence discussed above casts doubt over the defensive capabilities of the site, it offers no obvious clear alternative interpretation. The existence of a putative palisaded enclosure may offer a clue. Palisaded works are not uncommon precursors of later stone-built enclosures in the uplands of northern England and southern Scotland. However, at Carrock Fell the site must have lain some distance above the tree line and therefore logistically may not necessarily have been a natural choice for a timber enclosure. Even in the Neolithic, before widespread forest clearance had begun, the tree line is estimated to have only reached a height of *c.*500m above OD from palaeobotanical research at the Langdale axe factories (Claris and Quatermaine 1989, 6). If this were the case at Carrock Fell this would have brought woodland to within 350m of the hilltop. The effort involved in erecting a timber palisade on a hilltop of this height and then in placing it by a stone bank with no defensive purpose suggests that the act of enclosing the hilltop transcended purely practical considerations.

The unusual structure of the Carrock Fell enclosure could be seen as part of a rare upland tradition of monument building that encompassed a series of sites that exhibit extraordinary features and/or do not happily fit traditional typologies. Although it can never be claimed that an unusual ground plan is a guide to an early chronological context – and few of these enclosures are securely dated – some do have circumstantial evidence that suggests at least the possibility of an early context. At Howe Robin, some 19km to the south-east of Carrock Fell, a sub-rectangular enclosure has been constructed around a shelving limestone pavement, it has a discontinuous perimeter, and fieldwalking has produced a restricted range of artefacts from a Neolithic to Early Bronze Age horizon – nothing later (RCHME 1996, and Brown this volume). At Gardom's Edge in the Peak District, a massive stone-built enclosure over 600m long abuts a gritstone escarpment. A panel of prehistoric rock art has been found close to the enclosure, and the adjacent moor is littered with what appears to be a phase of ritual monuments comprising cairns and a standing stone which were supplanted by later Bronze Age field systems and settlements (RCHME 1987; Ainsworth &

Barnatt 1998). Although proximity is no assurance of context, the presence of early activity on these Derbyshire moors does open the possibility of a pre-Bronze Age date for this large D-shaped cliff-edge enclosure.

One new Cumbrian discovery of relevance is an enclosure on Green How on nearby Aughertree Fell (cf. Oswald this volume). This enclosure – although at present strictly undated – does display the structural characteristics of a causewayed enclosure and opens the possibility that such sites did indeed exist in the northern uplands. If this contextualisation is correct, then the question arises was Green How perhaps contemporary with others of less diagnostic plan such as Carrock Fell and Howe Robin? Only excavation might now answer this question.

The topographic setting of the Carrock Fell enclosure demonstrates that it has been carefully positioned. The enclosure perimeter surrounds the twin summits of Carrock Fell in a similar way to the major hillfort on Yeavering Bell in Northumberland, which also enclosed paired summits (*however*, it should be noted that there are significant structural differences between these two enclosures[5], cf. Pearson 1998). At Carrock Fell a putative prehistoric cairn sits atop both summits. However, it is the morphology of the natural topography that may have created a very loaded metaphor. This conjunction of topography and cairns may have led to the construction of the enclosure, an act that not only threw a barrier around the twin summits drawing attention to the terrain, but also created a psychological boundary that clearly demarcated it as a significant area within the cultural landscape.

Both ethnography and other archaeological contexts reveal the importance of landscape – and especially mountains – as cultural symbols and referents. Mountains can be used to centre elements of belief systems and sediment group identities within the landscape (e.g. Morphy 1995). Many mountains are considered to have mythical origins and spiritual powers that can influence the worldview of local communities. They become the physical and spiritual interface between the land and the living and the sky and its deities. Some mountains were revered as the residence of deities or significant ancestors. The latter could explain the presence of the summit cairns on Carrock Fell as evidence of local communities prominently centering their ancestors within the cultural landscape (cf. Buikstra & Charles 1999). Such positioning of the ancestral remains may have created or reinforced a role as intermediary for the ancestors, sanctioning them to communicate between the world of the living and that of the spirits. Clear similarities exist for this in North America, for example, where the historic and modern Hopi use the supernatural beings known as Katsinas (who coincidentally have a mountain home) to communicate prayers between the people and their gods, all co-ordinated by the relevant Katsina cult.

Mountains can also have less obvious roles to some cultures. In North America, the shamen of the Diné (Navajo) make regular pilgrimages to their sacred mountains to collect soil for earth bundles as part of renewal ceremonies (McPherson 1992, 17). At another level, the Diné are not alone in their belief that the land was created by the gods for the benefit of man, and that some landforms (both individually and in combination) are parts of mythological beings (McPherson 1992; Kelley & Francis 1995). Considering that many cultures revere the earth as a female entity, the potential breast-like symbolism of the Carrock Fell topography is unmistakable.

Circumstantial evidence from the hinterland of Carrock Fell opens further possibilities. One of the most significant recent discoveries has been the identification of a source of white, green-speckled leucogabbro rock at White Crag on the south flank of Carrock Fell, the origin of Group XXXIV stone axes (Fell and Davis 1988, 74). Although at present a direct association with the enclosure cannot be demonstrated, the juxtaposition of the axe source and the site on the same hill offer interesting possibilities, especially considering the proximity of the east to west routeway from the central Lakes to the Eden Valley and thence onward to north and south. At the eastern end of this route lay what may have been a traditional focus or meeting place near the junction of these two routeways, commemorated in the later Neolithic by the construction of the Penrith henge complex at Eamont Bridge. The importance of these routes is confirmed by the discovery of a Lakeland stone axe at the Penrith henges[6] (amongst several others locally), demonstrating one of the distribution routes of these artefacts (Fell & Davis 1988).

This group of henges or hengiform structures is of especial interest because of the structural disunity of the group and the inclusion of the novel Mayburgh henge, embanked and apparently *ditchless*, whose clearest parallels lie not in the UK but in Ireland[7] (Topping 1992, 262–3). Such structural non-conformity – if not innovation – amongst this group of sites demonstrates that at least by the later Neolithic period there was a local tradition of deliberate modification of traditional monument forms. The stimulus for such developments may have been a desire by local groups or communities to differentiate themselves from adjacent areas by creating their own regional versions of monuments. Consequently, since the archaeological record demonstrates clearly that unusual sites were being built in eastern Cumbria during the later Neolithic, the question arises as to whether this was part of a continuum which originated from an earlier tradition into which timeframe Carrock Fell might have fallen. Again, as with so much in this paper, speculation can only take the evidence so far, excavation may now be the only way to place the Carrock Fell enclosure into its correct chronological context.

Acknowledgements

The authors would like to thank John Hodgson and the LDNPA for facilitating the original RCHME 1996 survey and their encouragement with the research presented in this paper. In addition the authors would like to acknowledge the assistance of the Cumbria SMR in supplying details of the hillforts in the county. The survey was undertaken with the assistance of Keith Blood, Moraig Brown and Amy Lax. Other colleagues from the RCHME Neolithic Project team have either directly or indirectly input into the work presented here, namely: Martyn Barber, Carolyn Dyer, Dave Field, Dave McOmish, Al Oswald and Paul Pattison: to all go our thanks and appreciation. Dave McOmish also read and commented upon a draft of this paper. As ever, any misrepresentations or errors in this work are the responsibility of the authors.

NOTES

1. NMRC, Kemble Drive, Swindon, Wiltshire, SN2 2GZ.
2. Banks D and E in the east may have been separated by the ?modern footpath.
3. Interestingly, there is a contrasting tradition of larger forts in the adjacent parts of Lancashire and West Yorkshire.
4. Without excavation it is difficult to be certain of the identification of this feature. It may be possible that it represents the construction trench of a timer-laced rampart.
5. Yeavering has only 2 entrances, Carrock Fell ?9; Yeavering Bell has evidence of at least 125 hut circles, Carrock Fell 0.
6. cf: *Transactions of the Cumberland and Westmorland Antiquarian and Archaeological Society*, 1st Series, 3 (1876–77), xvi.
7. The presence of the 'Irish-type' Mayburgh henge may further illustrate the close contacts across the Irish Sea demonstrated by the discovery of numbers of Group VI Langdale stone axes in Ireland (cf. Cooney & Mandal 1998).

BIBLIOGRAPHY

Ainsworth, S. & Barnatt, J. 1998. A scarp-edge enclosure at Gardom's Edge, Baslow, Derbyshire. *Derbyshire Archaeological Journal*, 118, 5–23.

Buikstra, J. E. & Charles, D. K. 1999. Centering the Ancestors: Cemeteries, Mounds, and Sacred Landscapes of the Ancient North American Midcontinent. In W. Ashmore & A. B. Knapp (eds), *Archaeologies of Landscape*. Oxford. Blackwell. 201–228.

Claris, P. & Quatermaine, J. 1989. The Neolithic quarries and axe-factory sites of Great Langdale and Scafell Pike: a new field survey. *Proceedings of the Prehistoric Society* 55, 1–26.

Collingwood, R. G. 1938. The hillfort on Carrock Fell. *Transactions of the Cumberland and Westmorland Antiquarian and Archaeological Society* 38, 32–41.

Cooney, G. & Mandal, S. 1998. *Irish Stone Axe Project Monograph I*. Dublin. Wordwell.

Fell, C. I. & Davis, R. V. 1988. The petrological identification of stone implements from Cumbria. In T. H. M. cK. Clough and W. A. Cummins (eds) *Stone Axe Studies, Volume 2*. London. Council for British Archaeology, Research Report #67, 71–77, 270, 287.

Jobey, G. 1978. Burnswark Hill. *Transactions of the Dumfriesshire and Galloway Natural History and Antiquarian Society*, 3rd Series, 53 (1977–8), 57–104.

Kelley, K. B. & Francis, H. 1994. *Navajo Sacred Places*. Bloomington. Indiana University Press.

Morphy, H. 1995. Landscape and the Reproduction of the Ancestral Past. In E. Hirsch & M. O'Hanlon (eds) *The Anthropology of Landscape: Perspectives on Place and Space*. Oxford. Clarendon Press.

McPherson, R. S. 1992. *Sacred Land, Sacred View: Navajo perceptions of the Four Corners Region*. Salt Lake City. Brigham Young University (Charles Redd Monographs in Western History #19).

RCAHMS 1997. *Eastern Dunfriesshire: an archaeological landscape*. Edinburgh. The Stationery Office.

RCHME 1987. *Gardom's Edge, South Derbyshire*. Swindon. National Monuments Record (SK 27 SE 29).

RCHME 1996. *Howe Robin, Crosby Ravensworth, Cumbria*. Swindon. National Monuments Record (NY 61 SW 75).

Sharples, N. M. 1991. Maiden Castle: Excavations and field survey 1985–6. London. English Heritage (Archaeological Report # 19).

Topping, P. 1992. The Penrith henges: a survey by the Royal Commission on the Historical Monuments of England. *Proceedings of the Prehistoric Society*, 58, 249–264.

Welfare, H. & Swan, V. 1995. *Roman Camps in England: The Field Archaeology*. London. HMSO.